Cultures of Habitat

ON NATURE, CULTURE, AND STORY

Gary Paul Nabhan

COUNTERPOINT

WASHINGTON, D.C.

"Children in Touch, Creatures in Story" and "Finding the Wild
Thread" originally appeared in *The Geography of Childhood*, Gary Paul
Nabhan and Stephen Trimble (Beacon Press, Boston) ©1994;
"Cultural Parallax: The Wilderness Concept in Crisis" in an earlier
version in *Reinventing Nature*, Gary Paul Nabhan (Island Press,
Washington, D.C.) ©1995: "Let Us Now Praise Native Crops" in an
earlier version in *From Chiles to Chocolate,* Nelson Foster and Linda S.
Cordell, eds. (University of Arizona Press, Tucson, Arizona) ©1994;
and "Harvest Time" in *Enduring Seeds*, Gary Paul Nabhan (North
Point Press/Farrar, Straus & Giroux, Inc., San Francisco) ©1993.

Library of Congress Cataloging-in-Publication Data
Nabhan, Gary Paul.
Cultures of Habitat: on nature, culture, and story / Gary Paul Nabhan.
Includes bibliographical references.
1. Nature—Effect of human beings on. 2. Biological diversity.
3. Biotic communities. 4. Endangered ecosystems. I. Title.
GF75.N33   1997
304.2—dc21   97-30793
ISBN 1-887178-47-3 (clothbound) (alk. paper)

FIRST PRINTING

Book and jacket design by Amy Evans McClure

Printed in the United States of America on acid-free paper that
meets the American National Standards Institute Z39-48 Standard

COUNTERPOINT
P.O. Box 65793
Washington, D.C. 20035-5793

Distributed by Publishers Group West

1 3 5 7 9 10 8 6 4 2

Contents

Acknowledgments

I cannot take credit for divining the meaning of the patterns that I present in these essays. I have been helped along the way by friends and colleagues such as David Hancocks, Nancy Laney, Richard Nelson, Marta Turok, Robert Bye, Kay Fowler, Dave Harmon, Jim Hills, Janice Rosenburg, Richard Felger, Ofelia Zepeda, Kim Stafford, Delores Lewis, Ernesto Molina, Adolfo Burgos, Vic Cherikoff, Richard Kimber, Janette Brand, Barney Burns, Aggie Haury, Anne Fitzgerald, Lorraine Eiler, Luisa Maffi, Mary Beck Moser, Wendy Laird, Carlos Nagel, Luther Propst, Amadeo Rea, Mark Plotkin, Al Gentry, Ana Guadalupe Valenzuela, Jim Donovan, Robert Pyle, Sara St. Antoine, Stephen Trimble, Stephen Buchmann, Mrill Ingram, Alison Deming, Jack Turner, Naomi Shihab Nye, Felipe Molina, Enrique Salmon, Humberto Suzan, Josh Tewksbury, Kat Anderson, Tom Sheridan, Bill Broyles, Curt Meine, David Abram, Jacquie Kahn, John Tuxill, and Don Norman. Thanks to these and many other fellow travelers. Special thanks are due to Jack Shoemaker and Trish Hoard for developmental editing and critical guidance, and to Victoria Shoemaker, my agent and confidante.

My fieldwork and efforts toward conservation have received generous assistance over the years from the MacArthur Foundation, Agnese Haury, the Pew Memorial Trust, the Wallace Global Fund, the Wallace Genetics Foundation, the W. Alton Jones Foundation, the National Science Foundation, the C. S. Fund, the Hewlett Foundation, the Ford Foundation, the Ruth Mott Fund, David Lennette, John Hay, the De Grazia Foundation, the Arizona Humanities Council, the Lannan Foundation, and the Ethnobiology and Conservation Team. Thanks to the donors and staffs of these sources of support for having faith in the team of people with whom I work and in the range of concerns we share.

I am also indebted to editors who helped improve individual essays in earlier forms: Nelson Foster, Chris Szuter, Deanne Urmy, Chip Blake, Barbara Dean, Thomas Christensen, John Davis, Steve Cox, William R. Jordan III, David Burks, Kurt Brown, Reed Noss, Michael Soulé, Gary Lease, Nancy Harmon Jenkins, John Bancroft, Carolyn Servid, Thom Lyon, Judy Rice, Stephen Corey, Mary Troychak, Gary Avey, Melody Allen, Stephen Kellert, Mark Cheater, Lee Fleming, James Trulove, Joe Wilder, Doug Biggers, and Kevin Dahl. I am especially grateful to Thomas Christensen and Nancy Palmer Jones for re-editing the entire manuscript for cohesion and tone. Finally, I must add that many voices—human and otherwise—have found their way into these pages; they underscore how rich the diversity around us truly is.

Cultures of Habitat

*I see him more as one of those spare men of the desert, who
travel from oasis to oasis, trading legends as if it is the
exchange of seeds, consuming everything without
suspicion, piecing together a mirage.*
MICHAEL ONDAATJE, *The English Patient*

Poets, seed trackers, and biogeographers all have a penchant for pattern recognition. Once they perceive a pattern, however, they may spend hours trying to figure out whether it is as fleeting as a mirage or as steadfast as the earth itself.

"Take a look at these two maps I've torn out of different *Atlantic Monthly* issues," David Hancocks said as I came into his office at the Arizona-Sonora Desert Museum. David, then the executive director of the museum, is always profoundly curious about the world around him. As director of science at the museum, I was in the office across the hall from his, and frequently one of us would call the other over when we'd discovered something peculiar, absurd, or thought-provoking.

He had two maps laid out atop his desk, one entitled "Staying Put," the other "The Geography of Endangerment." Both were maps of the continental United States displaying color-coded data county by county. Without offering any interpretation or comparison, David asked me to look at one, then the other. "Staying Put" displayed the relative duration of residency within each county. "The Geography of Endangerment" documented which counties had the most threatened or endangered species on the federal government's lists.

Suddenly, I went goggle-eyed: the fit was not perfect, but the correlation between the two patterns was undeniable. Where human populations had stayed in the same place for the greatest duration, fewer plants and animals had become endangered species; in parts of the country where massive in-migrations and exoduses were taking place, more had become endangered. In places such as southern California, Florida, southern Nevada, and Hawaii, urbanization and invasion by exotic species have created "hot spots" of endangered native species.

"Could it be, David, that the more stable a community is...the better it can buffer native plants and animals from otherwise pervasive threats?" I asked.

"You're the conservation biologist," David offered casually. "You tell me."

The mosaic of essays in this book developed from David's juxtaposition of those maps. For the past three years, I have tackled riddles regarding relationships among cultural diversity, community stability, and the conservation of biological diversity in natural habitats. Why are naturally diverse regions also culturally diverse? What allows certain communities to resist harmful economic and social change? Do these communities retain more intact habitats in their homeland because of this resistance? Why do such similar forces seem to undercut both biological and cultural diversity, and what can we do to control these forces? For that matter, what "good" is diversity? And do most people (not just natural scientists) have some visceral sense of its value?

These questions have unhinged some doors that had long ago swung shut in my own world. I began to wonder why I preferred to work on conservation issues in cross-cultural settings, settings that made many biologists uneasy. Could my upbringing within a clan of Lebanese immigrants have contributed to my receptivity to the "other"?

Who actually believes that everyone of Eurasian descent in North America was predisposed to acting less sensitively to the land than Native Americans? As Wes Jackson has asked, what will it take to make us all (or our descendants five centuries from now) native to this place? Are the Amish and the Mennonites already native to their Midwestern homelands? Have urban Sioux in Minneapolis-St. Paul relinquished their status as native to the humid land of their ancient origins in the Southeast or to the plains to which they later moved? Does lumping together all minorities living in North America as "people of color" obscure significant differences in their allegiance to place or their depth of knowledge of local biodiversity?

Ecologist Ray Dasmann once used the term *ecosystem peoples* to contrast indigenous communities having long tenure in one habitat complex with their more cosmopolitan neighbors:

> I have attempted to describe the differences between people who live in one place and are dependent on the local ecosystem for support and those who do not. If one is totally dependent, or largely so, on the animals and plants of a particular area, one must learn some reasonable balance…. It follows that people who have lived for centuries or longer in the same places, without major sources of supply from the outside, must develop some working relationship with the species surrounding them. I have called these people *ecosystem people*, because they occupy one, or a few, local ecosystems.

But how do we decide who exemplifies the ways of ecosystem people? Can we reasonably dismiss the Scots-Irish, the Kickapoo, or the Quichua who have expanded their domain beyond their pre-Columbian region of origin, restricting the use of the term to place-specific cultures such as the Hopi, the Cucupa, the Mandan, or Ojibway? Do Mennonites, Lapps, Basques, and Bedouins qualify as "traditional peoples," "ecosystem peoples," or "indigenes" as much as "Native Americans" do?

This book arises from my interest in human communities that have a long history of interaction with one particular kind of terrain and its wildlife. Dasmann would call them "ecosystem peoples," but I prefer to speak of "cultures of habitat." The term *ecosystem* comes from the scientific tradition of identifying discrete but somewhat arbitrary units of the natural world as though each functioned like an organic machine. In contrast, the term *habitat* is etymologically related to *habit*, *inhabit*, and *habitable*; it suggests a place worth dwelling in, one that has *abiding* qualities. I could not make a machinelike *ecosystem* my abode for long, but I could comfortably nestle down within a *habitat*.

The term *culture* may likewise be preferable to the value-neutral *people*; *culture* implies that we learn from our elders and neighbors a way of living in a place that is more refined or better adapted than our genes alone can offer. I am attempting to blur the traditional distinction between *nature* and *nurture*. As I show in my discussion of diets and diabetes among Native Americans, we are only beginning to understand how gene-environment interactions shape human lives (as Darwinians believe they have shaped the lives of all other species). A stable human community may have both genetic and orally transmitted cultural adaptations to place that often escape the eye; whether these adaptations offer a greater capacity for conserving the biodiversity around them, I do not yet know. For many conservationists, the notion of *cultural stewards* of *wildlands habitats* is a contradiction in terms, if not a heresy—we should leave wild nature "alone." For deconstructionists, on the other hand, "wild nature" is a cultural construct, and they claim it does not exist outside the mind of those indoctrinated by Western civilization. A vast terrain lies between the poles set up by conventional conservationists and deconstructionists, a terrain more fertile than that in which either pole actually sits.

This is the terrain I will chart, not so much with parameters and statistics, but through story. Many of these stories will be tales from "the Far Outside," that realm in which diverse natural habitats and indigenous cultures coexist without one overwhelming the other. It harbors homes and habitats quite unlike the homogenized landscapes now dominating what we see on our television screens. It is a refreshing contrast to the manmade world described in the "urban dysfunctional literature" written by solipsists who refer to novels set in this vast realm as "nature literature." It is the terrain in which relatively few people now live, although it has been the evolutionary ground where our bodies, minds, and hearts have taken shape throughout most of human history.

Simply put, the Far Outside is the seedbed for our souls. I hope these stories will grow like sprouted gourd seeds, vining out and twining high into the surrounding space. Perhaps they will come to be cross-fertilized with your own stories, brought from the places of your ancestors, to produce fruits sweeter and tastier—and more diverse—than those cloned from a single source.

ONE

The Shape and Scope of Diversity

Natural diversity and cultural diversity share
many of the same patterns of distribution across
the face of the earth, and enrich our lives
in many of the same ways.

Finding Ourselves in the Far Outside

The world in which the kestrel moves, the world that it sees, is,
and will always be, entirely beyond us. That there are such
worlds all around us is an essential feature of our world.
MARY MIDGLEY, *Beast and Man*

When I heard it, I was in a small meeting room in Alaska, and that was part of the trouble. I was supposed to be paying attention to what was being said in the room, where I was taking part in a symposium about the meaning of the natural world. But from my seat I could hear ravens coming in to roost in the spruce trees above us, and I wondered how their calls were different from those of the Chihuahuan ravens down where I live. I could look out the windows and see bald eagles swooping over the waters of the sound. More distracting still, I already had the stain and smell of salmonberries on my hands and had been perplexed all morning as to why the ripe berries on two adjacent bushes were entirely different colors.

And that's when I heard it. A familiar warble came out of the well-educated, widely read humanist sitting a few chairs away from me. She asserted a truism I had been hearing in one form or another for nearly thirty years: "Each of us has to go *inside* before we can go *outside*! How can we give any meaning to the natural world until each individual finds out who he or she is as a human being, until each of us finds our own internal source of peace?"

I immediately felt nauseated. Something had stuck in my craw. I had to leave the room. Our moderator followed me out to the porch, where I gasped for air.

"Are you *okay?*" she asked earnestly. "You looked *green* all of a sudden."

"I dunno." I breathed deeply and looked up at the crisp blue sky. "I must be...uh...under the weather a little. If you don't mind, I had better go for a walk and get some fresh air."

As I ambled along a trail lined with totem poles, taking a loop through the coastal rain forest, I tried to spiral in on what had disoriented me. I realized I was uncomfortable with the notion of humans giving the natural world its "meaning." The plants and animals I have observed over twenty years as a field biologist hardly seem to be waiting for *me* to give *them* meaning.

But most of the folks at the symposium wanted to feel that *we* are meaningful, and so we project *our* meanings onto the rest of the world. We read meaning into other species' behavior, but with few exceptions, they are unlikely to do the same toward us.

Humans may be rare even among primates in the attention we give to the tracks, calls, and movements of a wide range of other species. To paraphrase one prominent primatologist: "If their inattention to their neighbors other than predators is any indication, most monkeys are extremely poor naturalists." The same can be said of many other wild animals that live in sight of, and in spite of, human habitations.

While it may somehow be good for *us* to think, watch, sing, or write about the astonishing diversity of plants and animals within our surroundings, are we sure that this does any good for *them?* I am reminded of the realization John Daniel came to while hopping through a snake-laden boulder field: the snakes were not fazed by his thoughts, fears, or needs. Daniel writes in *The Trail Home*: "The rattlesnakes beneath the boulders instructed me, in a way no book could have, that the natural world did not exist entirely for my comfort and pleasure; indeed, that it did not particularly care whether my small human life continued to exist at all."

Walking along, my restlessness increased as I considered the premise put forth in the meeting room: that the shortest road to wisdom and peace with the world is the one that turns inward, away from direct sensory contact with other creatures. I will not assert that meditation, psychotherapy, and philosophical introspection are unproductive, but I simply can't accept that inward is the only or best way for everyone to turn. The more disciplined practitioners of contemplative traditions can turn inward and still get beyond the self, but many others simply become swamped by self-indulgence. There are far too many people living in our society who forget daily that other creatures—five kingdoms' worth of them—are cohabiting the planet with us.

Over half a century ago, Robinson Jeffers suggested that it may be just as valid to turn outward: "The whole human race spends too much emotion on itself. The happiest and freest man is the scientist investigating nature or the artist admiring it, the person who is interested in things that are not human. Or if he is interested in human beings, let him regard them objectively as a small part of the great music."

I finished my walk on the forest's edge, where the great music of crashing waves flooded into the tide pools, where wind ruffled devil's club leaves, and hermit thrushes sang. I reminded myself that the wisest, most inspired people I knew had all taken this second path, heading for what I call the Far Outside. It is the path found when one falls into "the naturalist's trance," the hunter's pursuit of wild game, the *curandera*'s search for hidden roots, the fisherman's casting of the net into the current, the water witcher's trust of the forked willow branch, the rock climber's fixation on the slightest details of a cliff face. Why is it that when we are hanging from the cliff—beyond the reach of civilization's safety net, rather than in it—we are most likely to gain the deepest sense of what it is to be alive? Arctic writer-ethnographer Hugh Brody has brooded over this question while working in the most remote human communities and wildest places he can find. There, he admits, "at the periphery is where I can come to understand the central issues of living."

Unlike more monotonous conditions within the metropolitan grid, the Far Outside still offers comic juxtapositions worthy of a Gary Larson cartoon. The flood suddenly looms large before Noah can get the diversity of the human family onto the ark full of animals. The bugs in the test tube have the last say about the experiment. That experiment is the one in which you and I participate, whether we are at home, in a laboratory, or in the wilderness. It is the Great Improvisation—the diversification of life on earth—which has led to golden as well as reddish-purple salmonberries, Sitka as well as blue spruce, and northwestern as well as Chihuahuan ravens.

When I returned home from the rain forest to the Stinkin' Hot Desert in Arizona, I decided to see how an elder among my O'odham neighbors might view this apparent dichotomy between inward and outward paths—or for that matter, the dichotomy between culture and nature. I drove a hundred miles across the desert to visit a seventy-four-year-old O'odham farmer who had worked all his life "outdoors": tending native crops, chopping wood, driving teams of horses, gathering cactus fruit, hunting, and building ceremonial houses for his tribe's rain-bringing rites. He was consistently wise in ways that my brief bouts with Jungian analysis, meditation practice, and Franciscan prayer had not enabled me to be. And I knew that because he'd had a brush with death in the last year, he had been made sedentary and was forced to be alone in his home for a longer time than ever before. I found him sitting outside on an old wooden bench, a crutch on either side of him, looking out at a small field that he would not be able to plant this year. I asked him what he had been working over in his mind the last few months.

"I'd like to make a trip," he said, nonchalantly for a man who had only traveled once beyond the limits of the desert—all the way to Gallup—and who at the end of his life lived less than thirty miles from where he was born.

"Yes, before I die, I'd like to go over there to the ocean," he nodded to the southwest, where the Sea of Cortez lay a hundred miles away. It was a sacred place for the desert O'odham, where they used to go as pilgrims for ocean power, for salt, and for songs. My elderly friend paused, then continued.

"Yes, I would like to hear the birds there in the sea. I would like to hear those ocean birds sing in my native language."

"In *O'odham ha-neoki?*" I asked. I must have looked surprised that he felt the birds spoke *his* language, for he then offered to explain his comment as if it had been scribbled in a shorthand indecipherable to me.

"Whenever my people used to walk over there to the ocean for salt, they would stand on the edge and listen to those birds sing. And the birds are in many of the songs we still sing today, even though we haven't walked or ridden horses there since the hoof-and-mouth quarantines in the forties. In the old days, they didn't start to sing those songs while they were still at the ocean. No, the people would go back home, and then some night, those ocean birds would begin singing in their dreams. That's where our songs come from. They would come to our medicine men, from the ocean, in their dreams. Maybe the ones who play the violin would hear them in their sleep, and their voices would turn up in their fiddle tunes. Maybe the *pascola* dancers would hear the way they flew, and it would end up in the way they sounded when they danced with their rattles. Those birds have ended up in our songs, and I want to hear them at the ocean before I die."

I was moved by my friend's desire to hear those birds for himself at the edge of the ocean. For a lifelong dweller in a riverless desert, the ocean must be a landscape wilder than the imagination, truly unfathomable. In the end, he sought to juxtapose his culture's aural imagery of ocean birds with what the birds themselves were saying. He desired to experience nature directly, as a measure of the cultural symbols and sounds he had carried with him most of his life.

My friend's songs and stories reflect the larger, other-than-human landscape, one intrinsic to his culture's literature, music, or ways of healing. When I arrived at his home once, years ago, I saw him carrying into the kitchen a mockingbird he had captured in a seed trap, killed, and carefully butchered, in order to cook the meat and feed it to his grandson. Mockingbirds are not simply good mimics, they are irrepressibly loquacious; his grandson was not. The boy was nearly three years old and had not spoken a word. My friend recalled the sympathetic ritual of his people for curing such difficulties: feed the mute one the flesh of a mocker or a thrasher. He will have the best chance of being able to express himself if he ingests the wild world around him.

This is where "inner" and "outer" become not a duality but a dynamic—like every breath we take. We are *inspired* by what surrounds us; we take it into our bodies, and we respond with *expression*. What we have inside us is, ultimately, always of the larger, wilder world. Nature is not just "out there," beyond the individual. The

O'odham boy now has seed, bird, and O'odham history in his very muscles, in the cells of his tongue, in his reverberating voice box. Today, the boy speaks aloud to the entire world.

Lynn Margulis has pointed out that there are myriad other lives inside each human "individual." For every cell of our own genetic background there are a thousand times more cells of other species within and upon each of our bodies. It would be more fitting to imagine each human corpus as a diverse wildlife habitat than to persist in the illusion of the individual *self*.

Or better, each of us may truly be a living corpus of *stories*: bacteria having the final word within our own mouths; fungi breeding between our toes; other microbes collaborating to digest the world within our intestines; archetypal images from our evolutionary past roaming among nerve synapses, pitting our groin muscles against our brain tissues.

If I could distill what I have learned during a thousand and one nights working as a field biologist, waiting around campfires while mist-netting bats, running lines of live traps, or pressing plants, it would be this: each plant or animal has a story of some unique way of living in this world. By tracking their stories down to the finest detail, our own lives may be informed and enriched.

It is easy for such a notion to be obfuscated by high-tech science. The zoologist who radio-collars a mountain lion may call his research a "range utilization analysis," but he is simply tracking that critter's odyssey. An ecologist interested in the nutcracker's dispersal of pine seeds is slowly learning the language of the forest, and the birds are her newly found verbs.

Perhaps because of what Paul Ehrlich calls "physics envy," many biologists feel inclined to mask their recording of stories behind numbers, jargon, and theory. We find their remarkable insights buried beneath technobabble about life histories, optimal foraging tests, or paleoecological reconstructions. Most of them, however, are merely tracing the trajectory of another life as it demonstrates ways to survive in the Far Outside.

In *Writing Natural History*, two-time Pulitzer Prize–winner E. O. Wilson describes the struggle scientists have simply to be storytellers: "Scientists live and die by their ability to depart from the tribe and go out into an unknown terrain and bring back, like a carcass newly speared, some new discovery or new fact or theoretical insight and lay it in front of the tribe; and then they all gather and dance around it. Symposia are held in the National Academy of Sciences and prizes are given. There is fundamentally no difference from a Paleolithic campsite celebration." Yet, even with these campsite celebrations, we have only the crudest of character sketches of most of the floral and faunal members of our community. As Wilson reminds us,

> Even though some 1.4 million species of organisms have been discovered (in the minimal sense of having specimens collected and formal scientific names attached), the total number alive on the earth is somewhere between 10 and 100 million…. Of the species given scientific names, fewer than 10 percent have been studied at a level deeper than gross anatomy. [Intensively studied species make up]…a still smaller fraction, including colon bacteria, corn, fruit flies, Norway rats, rhesus monkeys, and human beings, altogether comprising no more than a hundred species.

Try to imagine the still-untold stories, the sudden flowerings, the cataclysmic extinctions, the episodic turnovers in dominance, the failed attempts at mutualistic relationships, and the climaxes that took hundreds of years to achieve. In every biotic community, there are story lines that fiction writers would give their eyeteeth for: Desert tortoises with allegiances to place that have lasted upward of 40,000 years, dwarfing any dynasty in China. Fidelities between hummingbird and montane penstemon that make the fidelities in Wendell Berry's Port William, Kentucky, seem like puppy love. Dormancies of lotus seeds that outdistance Rip Van Winkle's longest nap. Promiscuities among neighboring oak trees that would make even Nabokov and his Lolita blush. Or all-female lizard species with reproductive habits more radical than anything in lesbian literature.

Still, with the myriad stories around and within us, how many of them do we recognize as touching our lives in some way? Most natural history essays are so limited in their range of plot, character development, and emotive currents that Joyce Carol Oates has come to an erroneous, near-fatal assumption about nature itself. In her essay "Against Nature," Oates claims that nature "inspires a painfully limited set of responses in 'nature writers'...*reverence, awe, piety, mystical oneness.*"

Most environmental journalists offer an even more limited set of "news" stories: either (1) that someone has momentarily succeeded in disrupting the plans of the bastards who are ruining the world; or (2) that the bastards are still ruining the world. Most newspaper and magazine journalists who ostensibly cover biological diversity tell the same doom-and-gloom story over and over, while they include virtually nothing substantial about the nonhuman lives embedded in that diversity. One week, *Paradise Lost* is told with the yew tree as the victim in the temperate rain forest; the next, the scene has shifted to peyote in the Chihuahuan desert—but the plot is still the same.

Our existence is being degraded by ignorance of these diverse stories. In stark contrast to the wide range of creatures that my O'odham friend has encountered in his dreams, fewer and fewer creatures are inhabiting the dreams of those in mainstream society. I know another elderly man who lives in the midst of metropolitan Phoenix. Although he is a few years younger than my friend the Indian farmer, he seems far closer to death; I can feel it every time I visit him. He too was formerly an outdoorsman and farmer, skilled with horses, hunting, building, and wood carving. But now he has emphysema and cannot even go outside and sit, the contaminated air of Phoenix is so vile. Yet that is not all that is killing him. Confined to a hermetically sealed tract house, he sits in front of a television all day long and hears just three stories repeated ad nauseam: (1) Saddam Hussein and other foreign despots are out to get us; (2) substance-abusing street gangs are out to get us; and (3) mutant microbes are out to get us. He seems drained of all resilience, a man without hope. He feels as though he has lost all contact with the wildlife, the Far Outside, that had been his source of renewal most of his life.

Harkening back to William Carlos Williams, we might say that society pays little attention to these myriad lives, but people die for lack of contact with them every day. By the end of this decade, 25,000 species—25,000 distinctive stories, ways of living in this world—are likely to be lost unless we begin to learn of these beings in ways that move us to halt our destructive behavior.

Scientists cannot do the work by themselves. Now, more urgently than ever before, we all need to come face to face with other lives in the Far Outside—with the Bali mynah, and the Furbish lousewort, and the microbes within our guts. We need to hear the stories of these creatures revered by other cultures, from Inuit whale hunters in the arctic circle, to O'odham singers of sacred datura songs in the deserts, to Mayan beekeepers in the rain forests of the Yucatán peninsula. What might happen if some of those who now turn inward, apprenticing themselves to all kinds of gurus, therapists, and Webmasters, would turn outward as apprentices to other species: Komodo dragons, marbled murrelets, desert pupfish, beer-making yeasts, Texas wild rice, or flower-loving flies.

I can't help but wonder if the dilemma of our society is not unlike that of the mute child who needs to eat the songbird in order to speak. Unless we come to incorporate the songs from the Far Outside, we will be left dumb before an increasingly frightening world. But this incorporation is just the first step. Once we have begun to express in our own ways the stories inspired by those other lives, we need to keep seeking out those lives in order to compare constantly the images we have conjured up with the beings themselves.

It is time to go Outside, farther than we have ever gone together before. It is time to hear the seabirds singing at the edge of the world and to bring them back, freshly, into our cultural stories, into our dreams.

Pledging Allegiance to All Sorts of Diversity

*If...we wish to recall what it is like to feel fully a part of
this wild earth—if, that is, we wish to reclaim our place
as plain members of the biotic community—then we
shall have to start speaking somewhat differently.*
DAVID ABRAM, "Returning to Our Animal Senses," *Wild Earth*

It happened again on the Day of the Dead—*El Día de los Muertos*, as
we call it back in the salsa-soaked hinterlands of North America. Once
again my body was attending a conference but my mind was wandering. I was in the nation's capital, sitting with other so-called environmentalists in a big, sterile room, trying to fathom what we could
collectively do to save the Endangered Species Act.

Despite the urgency of the task, I was having trouble grasping anything in that conference room. There was not a tree trunk to hold
onto or even to see, not a house finch or starling within earshot. Worse
yet, the activists, bureaucrats, and media consultants in the room had
been repeating the same two phrases over and over—*endangered species*
and *loss of biodiversity*—until these terms had become paltry abstrac-
tions. The lectures we were hearing were as slick as the linoleum floors
and Formica tables before us. There was no roughness, nothing to get
a purchase on.

My mind drifted away. The night before, I had walked the streets
of the Adams-Morgan district in Washington to celebrate the Day
of the Dead. I had eaten with some of my dearest friends at the

Tamarindo, a Central American restaurant featuring fruits, vegetables, tubers, and spices from the tropics. In the midst of a cosmopolitan city such as Washington, it is now common to encounter a wide range of ethnic restaurants, but I had been charmed last night by more than ethnicity. Behind a window display of *calaveras*—skeletons happily feasting on their favorite dishes—I sat rapt in conversation, enjoying camaraderie and Latin cuisine, grateful to be alive in a world filled with such unaccountable riches. The tastes, the smells, the textures of fresh, playfully prepared food in my mouth, the voices and laughter of lovers, *compadres*, and *comadres*, the music of fiestas—what more could one ask for?

I heard someone cough. Again I was with forty sober people in the huge conference room; we listened to the litany of ill-fated legislative actions and international policy initiatives, efforts desperately needed to keep species in addition to our own alive and thriving on this planet. It felt as if we were doing autopsies on failed patients for whom we had been responsible: we had been ineffective in overcoming the 1994 efforts to gut the Endangered Species Act; ineffective in correcting misguided U.S. leaders at the 1992 Earth Summit in Rio de Janeiro; ineffective in responding to subsequent critiques of U.S. environmental policy that ignores the Biodiversity Convention.

Those of us scattered around the spacious conference room that cold November day in 1994 were being told in so many words that we were doing a piss-poor job of making others care as much about the conservation of flora and fauna as we ourselves did. We were informed that the environment was the single most important voting issue for only 3 percent of Americans. When asked if protecting jobs was more important than protecting species, most Americans opted for jobs; jobs can feed you, but a spotted owl atop a bed of Douglas fir needles can't.

Pollsters barraged us with statistics to convince us of our failings. The rapid rate of plant and animal extinctions ranked only eighth among environmental issues in importance. The loss of biodiversity, they reminded us, had *never* ranked as a major environmental problem in any poll. In fact, less than one in five Americans had even heard of this phrase, the *loss of biodiversity*. Worse yet, there was little agreement about what the term meant. While nearly half of those polled by Beldon and Rusonello equated this term with either the loss or the "blending" of species, others assumed that it referred to the destruction of habitats, ecosystems, gene pools, or cells. Seventeen percent had heard the term *biodiversity* but admitted that they'd flunk the test if they had to say what it meant.

Everyone seemed depressed by this news. A few still hoped that a wider range of Americans could get excited about biodiversity. Some had experience in this realm—they could get ranchers, riparian conservationists, and federal lands managers together in the same room to talk and could get back out again before they all killed each other. Others had worked with farmers and gardeners to rescue imperiled seed stocks of hard-to-come-by vegetables, such as okra, rutabagas, and Jerusalem artichokes. Still others had initiated public awareness campaigns in order to save endangered slugs, flies, wombats, and swamps.

When each person told about his or her work back home with the local wildlife, peoples, and habitats, it was hard to fathom why we were doing autopsies instead of sending our patients out of the recovery room waving their crutches over their heads. Yet as each project was summarized in a few short words on the flip chart before us, I realized that each friend's lifework was being boiled down to tasteless sludge. It was as if I were watching that Latin American restaurant from the night before—with all its friendliness and fragrances—being turned into a fast-food drive-in where faceless people lined up for fries and burgers.

And perhaps that was the trouble: we had been letting the stories of the remarkable lives around us get dumbed down into sound bites. Whatever we had been doing for the past few years to promote biodiversity through the media had hardly been enough to move people to take radically responsible action.

Look at what happened when the biodiversity dilemma was reduced to being simply a "species extinction problem." Thirty-nine percent of Americans responding to a Harris Poll were frantic or despondent, claiming that they were "very concerned" about each species being lost. Unfortunately, some of those who claimed to be most concerned thought that the mention of impending "mass extinctions" actually referred to dinosaur extinctions, as though charismatic megafauna were going extinct this week and would not be on TV next week. As the American Museum of Natural History staff conceded from their review of the 1994 Harris Poll they commissioned, most Americans "are clearly unaware of some of the most fundamental facts about the diversity of life."

I got up from the conference room table, went to the door, and scanned the neighborhood for Irish pubs or Mexican cantinas. Slugging down a Guinness Stout or a Tequila Sunrise for the Day of the Dead was my way of conceding that many of my fellow Americans are clueless about one basic fact of life: biodiversity is vital to us all.

During the years since that November 1994 meeting, I have thought back over the innumerable polls, focus group results, and opinion surveys presented to us that day. I now realize that I was far too tough on those who admit they can't get excited over *biological diversity*. Biodiversity—and its rate of loss—*is* hard to grasp. Like the elephant before the blind men, it is hard to tell which way it is facing, let alone determine its mass.

Critics of the Endangered Species Act have had a field day attacking conservation biologists for appearing inarticulate as they try to define biodiversity. The Paul Ehrlichs, Peter Ravens, and Norman Myers have been chided for their imprecision in estimating current rates of biodiversity loss; sometimes, these doomsayers have even contradicted their own earlier prognostications. If the "experts" cannot agree on a definition of biodiversity and on reliable estimates for the rate of species loss, why should any governmental policy be based on their projections?

Such critics wrongly take the loss of biodiversity to be a matter of counting how many species are already on their way out the door. For Kent Redford of the Nature Conservancy (TNC), biologists have too frequently let journalists and politicians equate the term *biodiversity loss* with "diminishing numbers of species":

> "Biodiversity" often has been interpreted as "species richness"—that is, the number of species in a given area. But a species-focused approach to biodiversity has proved limiting for a number of reasons.... [The] use of just species as a measure of biodiversity resulted in conservation efforts focusing on relatively few ecosystems while other highly

threatened ones were ignored. Species do not exist in a vacuum, and any [valid] definition of biodiversity must include the ecological complexes in which organisms naturally occur and the ways in which they interact with one another and their surroundings.

Nature Conservancy projects now run through an inventory of *levels* of biodiversity—genetic diversity, species diversity, community diversity, and so on—whenever they assess a region's value. But such an inventory does not *define* biodiversity any more than a parts list defines a car. In fact, TNC's Redford is clear that biodiversity should not be regarded as merely a mass of *things*—it is also a complex of interactions. And that notion—to which most ecologists subscribe, I believe—no doubt sends Endangered Species Act lobbyists and media consultants up the wall. How can they ask the American public to vote for the candidates most likely to protect "a complex of ecological interactions" that biological soothsayers deem somehow critical to the future of life on this planet? This notion may indeed make pollsters and lobbyists nervous, but it is exactly what Australian ecologist D. M. S. J. Bowman has emphasized in his lavishly literary explanation of biological diversity:

> So what is biodiversity? My belief is that the variety of life on the planet is like an extra-ordinarily complex, unfinished, and incomplete manuscript with a hugely varied alphabet, an ever-expanding lexicon, and a poorly understood grammar. Nonetheless, some scholars (for example, Charles Darwin) have been able to translate enough of the text to apprehend that it speaks of profound matters concerning our origins and our destiny. Ripping the manuscript to pieces because we want to use the paper makes little sense, especially if the manuscript says that "to survive you shall not destroy what you don't understand." Our mission as ecologists must be to *interpret* the meaning of biodiversity. The urgent need for this mission, and our current ecological ignorance, must be forcefully communicated to the public.

The analogy between biodiversity and language complexity is apt, for both are wellsprings of information. Both percolate with time-tried wisdom of ways to live well in this world, ways that are now being sucked out of existence. In fact, some of the very same forces are destroying habitats, extinguishing species, and forcing languages out of use. While biologists have been writing epitaphs for species, linguists have been doing the same for the indigenous languages left on the planet. While botanists have been assessing how many plant species survive with less than 500 individuals in their breeding pools and will soon be *inviable*, linguists have determined that more than a quarter of all languages still spoken on earth already have fewer than one thousand speakers and will soon be *moribund*. Of course, these linguists recognize that the health of a language cannot be determined solely by counting speakers or counting the number of words they use; syntax, grammar, cadence—those more elusive interactions between sound and sound or word and word—give any tongue its vitality.

While biologists liken the destruction of biodiversity to a manuscript—or a language—being ripped to shreds, languages are indeed being ripped to shreds, and the last chance to transcribe their oral literature is being lost. Soon, whatever we can read about biodiversity will be written in less than 5 percent of the languages that have existed since Gutenberg's print revolution. Other cultures' ways of speaking and singing about the richness of plants and animals around them will have been lost, even if the local biota itself is not lost by that time.

But such grim statistics and fuzzy definitions did not disturb me, on that gloomy day in the conference room, as much as my colleagues' responses to them. One mortician kept urging that we retreat to the simplest possible message, for the American public obviously could never get the drift of a notion as complex as biodiversity. I tried to scribble down her entire reductionist manifesto, but my pencil broke somewhere during her soliloquy, perhaps because I was exerting so much pressure:

"Just tell them it [biodiversity] means endangered species," she argued. "Or better yet, drop the term *biodiversity* altogether, and tell them that every time we lose a unique plant or animal we may be losing a cure for cancer or for AIDS. That's what they worry about."

But do the majority of Americans worry about what disease will ultimately kill them, forsaking concern for the other-than-human world? Ethnobiologists Willett Kempton and James Boster have put such a question to both Earth First!ers and to truck drivers for urban dry-cleaning firms. They reported the results in *Environmental Values in American Culture*, a book that grants mainstream America much more savvy than most environmental pollsters do. An astonishing 53 percent of the truckers *sided with* 90 percent of the Earth First!ers, the group that affirmed they would "rather see a few fellow humans suffer or even die than see an entire species go extinct."

However, if you asked both groups whether they would attempt to save their mother's life if an endangered bear chased after her, nearly everyone (except one or two of the most die-hard Earth First!ers) would gallantly try to rescue Momma. In short, most Americans still have some common sense, some compassion for their next of kin, and even for distant kin like snail darters and flower-loving flies. Other lives besides their own still matter. Kempton and Boster maintain that most Americans share deep-seated values about the environment that can be called on to support biodiversity. Despite Americans' being globally criticized for placing everything in which they believe on the front of their T-shirts—and changing their values as often as they change those shirts—they do ascribe to a lasting value with regard to the spiritual, aesthetic, and practical worth of the natural world, a value they share with their forefathers and foremothers.

Many Americans do not restrict their notion of conservation to the rescue of individual imperiled species. They are drawn to such concepts as "the balance of nature" and "the integrity of habitats." They may not be able to list all the species on the hill behind their home, but almost all want to leave that habitat intact as a legacy for future generations. Some of my colleagues, however, insist that mainstream America can only focus on a single organism at a time. So they choose to highlight the plight of one flagship species, a card-carrying member of the charismatic megafauna—a canary in the coal mine—as a surrogate for an entire biotic community. "If schoolchildren tell us that they feel the most threatening environmental problem is the extinction of tigers, then let's help them organize a Save the Tigers Campaign," these colleagues might say. "That's an image they see on TV, so they feel compassion for tigers. Instead of explaining biodiversity to them, just tell them that tigers need a safe place to live. If we end up with some tiger habitat saved, you and I know that a lot of biodiversity will be saved with it."

Unfortunately, placing tigers or leopards in the spotlight has not necessarily protected the other organisms in "cat habitat." This is because most support for big-cat conservation goes to zoos rather than to the management of wildlands where hundreds of other species could continue to coexist with the felines. Katherine Jope of the National Park Service has tried to steer conservation educators away from this approach: "While zoos may conserve a species' genetic resources, at least for a time, they fall short of conserving the interrelationships and emergent properties of an ecosystem.... For too long we have accepted without question [a paradigm of species-based conservation that is now] proving a hindrance to our ability to conserve the biodiversity of the earth."

How can we respect the integrity and complexity associated with biodiversity if all our public utterances reduce it to its lowest common denominator? We are convincing our children that it is enough to care only for the charming animals that frequent our cartoons and cereal boxes. This assumes that Americans will never again have attention spans longer than the average commercial. Worse, it arrogantly assumes that only those conversant with the scientific jargon summed up in the term *biodiversity* care about the variety of life on earth.

As I left Washington and headed south onto the coastal plains of Virginia, I was struck by the sight of men and women, *ordinary people*, out in the hardwood forests, down in little swales where wetland vegetation emerges, rustling about in gardens, walking through woodlots on farmsteads, watching migratory waterfowl, gathering brightly colored leaves, and bringing pumpkins in from fields. Many people do care deeply about biodiversity and certainly understand that their lives are enabled and enriched by it.

Still, while people appreciate biodiversity, they may not consider the biological world separate from the culture in which they live. And they are right to integrate these concepts. At his home in Mexico, my friend Bob Bye likes to show his guests the many shapes and sizes of maize or maguey to remind us of the wealth of folk knowledge that allowed these ancient crops to diversify into so many forms, tastes, textures. "When you talk about biodiversity, it's not just the genetic information in plants and animals. It's the cultural information that goes along with them as well," he says.

It is a bit ironic that we've surgically removed most discussions of biodiversity from the cultures within which the diversity is nested, for these cultures may well be where it is best protected. It is even more ironic that most media and lobbying consultants to endangered species activists have ignored these rich cultural connections to biodiversity, since they may be the easiest ways for the layperson to relate to the issue.

If I had to choose five ambassadors for biodiversity, I would not select scientists; I would choose a singer, an herbalist, a photographer/gardener, a gastronomist, and a crafts promoter. These individuals might not have the global statistics that E. O. Wilson, Paul Ehrlich, Donella Meadows, and Norman Myers have at their disposal. But they certainly share their passion. And they also have a knack for celebrating the ways in which contact with a wide range of the earth's floral and faunal riches can bless our daily lives.

Take the case of an unusual couple—he the singer, she the herbalist—who have resided all their lives along the coast of the Sea of Cortez in Mexico. Adolfo Burgos is a Seri Indian fisherman who also happens to know dozens of songs about marine and terrestrial animals. Amalia Astorga regularly harvests a wide variety of medicinal plants from the desert without depleting their populations; she is also a deer dancer and singer. Her father, José Astorga, founded the ironwood-carving tradition among the Seri, but Amalia draws and paints as much as she carves animal figurines. As "professors" of Seri folklife, Adolfo and Amalia have visited Europe and the United States, including several of the Native American communities in the U.S. Southwest, for cultural exchanges. But what they offer to the world is not just of interest to cultural geographers and ethnologists; they have detailed biological knowledge of a wide range of fish, turtles, lizards, mammals, birds, and plants on which their community depends. When they teach biological "facts" to younger Seri people, they often teach ethical considerations as well.

Consider what Adolfo told Seri children who went with him to visit the only known population of the rare boojum tree on mainland Mexico: "*Before*, the boojums were people—people called *Cotootaj*. They were once people who were trying to climb high up to the tops of those hills when it happened. They were climbing because they were terrified of the tide that was rising. In that time, tidal waves came to terminate the world. This tide was rising up toward the top of the world, to finish off the world. The *Cotootaj* were so scared that they were trying to escape. They were people then, but they were changed as the rising sea reached their feet.

"Today, if you try to break off a branch or pull the plant up, a fierce wind will come. A fierce wind will strike anyone who even grabs a branch. It's very dangerous to do such a thing.... Because of all that, we need to respect this plant."

What Adolfo and Amalia do with stories, songs, dances, and herbal remedies, David Cavagnaro does with gardens, orchards, and photographs. There is hardly a garden, food, or natural history magazine in the United States that has not already used one of David's luscious montages of heirloom vegetables and fruits on its cover. But what those who admire his work may not realize is that David grows most of what he photographs. As garden manager for the Seed Savers' Exchange, David would typically plant 300 to 1,200 kinds of vegetables in a single season. In addition to his work at the Seed Savers' Heritage Farm, David and his family grow an astonishing variety of fruit trees, spices, flowers, and vegetables at home. Many of David's "vegetable profiles" come freshly picked from his gardens, sliced or sorted in ways that remind us of how truly compelling nature's own designs can be.

I once spent a morning a few yards away from David in the garden, both of us down on our bellies in the midst of row after row of flowers. David was ostensibly teaching me about close-up photography, but more importantly he was teaching me how to see the world intimately. His photos of pumpkin diversity and sweet pea blossoms remind us that the most direct ways to a human heart are through the stomach and through the eyes. No one who has walked in David's garden or eaten at his table will ever again dismiss cultivated plant diversity as trivial or boring. As a former field entomologist who is just as interested in insects as in plants, he has captured the intimacies of pollinating and nectaring as well as any photographer I know. No life exists in a vacuum before David's sharp and compassionate eyes.

Vic Cherikoff is another scientist turned food promoter. His foodstuffs do not come from cultivated plants; they are "bush tuckers" from the wild outback of Australia. Although he had done casual foraging bush walking through national parks as a student at the New South Wales Institute of Technology, Vic developed his knowledge of Aboriginal uses of native foods from the bush country after he graduated. In the early 1980s, Vic joined world-renowned wild plants nutritionist Janette Brand Miller at the University of Sydney, where she was conducting a survey of some 500 different bush foods for their vitamin, mineral, dietary fiber, oil, and protein contents. Vic not only collected and prepared many of the samples himself, but he personally analyzed many of the foods. He then reported the results of eight Brand-and-Cherikoff technical studies to Aboriginal communities all across Australia. During this time, it became painfully clear that many of the ancient wild foods of Australia were falling out of use, even though they were prolific, nutritious, and tasty when produced under outback conditions.

Cherikoff soon began to field requests from chefs and gastronomists for some of the "winners" from the nutritional analyses. The Kakadu or billy-goat plum appears to be one of the richest sources of vitamin C of any fruit in the world. Wattle seeds and certain tubers may be effective in controlling blood-sugar levels for sufferers of diabetes. Cherikoff realized that commercial foraging could offer remote Aboriginal communities a needed source of income. He contracted with one community to collect more than five metric tons of a wild bush tomato during a year of good rains. Cherikoff's avocation gradually led him to form the Bush Tucker Supply Ltd., Australia's leading marketer of wild foods to restaurants, health food enthusiasts, and bush walkers. He also played a key role in the formation of the Wattle Seed, a delicatessen that features the wild foods collectively called "bush tuckers" on its menu. As an educator, writer, and promoter, he has coauthored two books on bush tuckers that have found their way into the hands of thousands of Aussies seeking to affirm their unique identity and the distinctive richness of outback habitats.

Cherikoff, in his *Bush Food Handbook* written with Jennifer Isaacs, has observed that "many foods available from the bush are instantly appealing to all palates.... Other bush delicacies may challenge description, being entirely new in flavor and fragrance. [But] in the last few years, Australian interest in bush foods has grown prodigiously. Once macadamia nuts were the solitary and exclusive Australian native contribution to world foods. Now, the number of restaurants utilizing wild plums, nuts, seeds and meats has grown from one to more than twenty establishments, including restaurants, catering firms and hotels."

Vic once treated me to a clambake, with sea urchins, wild fruits, and wattle-seed pastries on the side. As we sat around a campfire and played a didgeridoo under the stars, I felt grateful that the legacy of Aboriginal Australia had not been completely forgotten; Vic and his many Aboriginal coworkers in the outback are ensuring that the tastes and sounds of the bush retain a place in the modern world.

Marta Turok is the Mexican equivalent of the Smithsonian's Center for Folklife Programs wrapped into one petite, good-humored, colorfully dressed, and vastly talented woman. She has worked as an anthropologist, a weaver, a national director of government folk arts programs, and a human rights activist in Chiapas. But the threads that weave her life together are her skill at promoting handmade crafts derived from native plants and animals, her care for how these "raw materials" are harvested from wild habitats, and her concern that indigenous artisans receive adequate recognition and compensation for their work. Because she realized that Mexico's indigenous communities needed help maintaining all three threads in their own lives and work, she founded her own organization in 1989, called AMACUP: la Asociación Mexicana de Arte y Cultura Popular, A. C. As she recently told me, "I love to see what artisans can really do when they feel that someone is finally taking care of their interests and marketing their products respectfully. And personally, I love to take traditional designs and native materials shaped by indigenous artisans and reach new markets with them."

Geographically, her work has included collaborations with the highland Mayan textile-weaving guilds in Chiapas; with the Mixteca of Oaxaca and Nahua of Michoacán, who make a unique dye from a shellfish, *purpura pansa*, that was being imperiled by coastal developers and Japanese competitors along the Pacific seaboard; and with Seri Indian crafts cooperatives in Sonora, assisting them in obtaining collective trademarks to protect their traditional basketry, carvings, necklaces, and dolls. She has also promoted the conservation of indigenous *amate* parchment paper-making traditions, production of natural brown *coyuchi* cottons, and expansion of the weaving of *ayate* washcloths and scrubbers made from agave fibers. The goal of her latest project, a national inventory of natural materials used in the indigenous crafts of Mexico, is to determine which plants and animals can be harvested to help generate local income *without* leading to overexploitation and depletion of resources. In describing the AMACUP initiative that she has nicknamed *Amate*—short for "Artisans, Environment, and Technology"—Marta is obviously setting her sights higher than the development of a few new markets for traditionally made natural products: "I'm trying to create a space for dialogue and exchange among artisans, researchers, and organizations concerned with the management and use of natural resources for crafts production. At the same time, I'm hoping that sustainable management of diverse natural resources used in crafts can help us maintain an equilibrium among economic development, ecological conservation, and cultural revitalization."

These may seem like lofty, hard-to-achieve goals, until you see handiwork that Marta wears and showcases in her household: dozens of colorful fibers and dyes dazzle your eyes with a warmth and richness deeply rooted in an ancient world. She has a knack for making the unacquainted feel that this diversity of tints, textures, and designs should not be relegated to the past but should enrich our contemporary lives as well. By encouraging the rediversification of Mexican crafts markets, she is giving rural communities incentives for taking better care of their plants and animals.

Each of these individuals has come upon a unique way of celebrating the diversity of lives around us rather than letting these lives slip out of sight, out of mind, and out of existence. The challenge for the rest of us is to reinstill in our own communities the sense that a variety of life-forms and a heterogeneity of habitats can keep our lives from being as boring as that linoleum-lined conference room in Washington. Metaphorically nesting biological diversity within cultural expressions that inspire and delight us can be an easier way to encourage its protection than through a Save the Tiger or Preserve the Periwinkle media blitz, or through a Someone Will Die of Leukemia guilt trip. We must begin to explore metaphors and images that appeal to basket weavers, butterfly farmers, fishermen, and furniture makers in ways that terms like *ecosystem services*, *germ-plasm resources*, *nontimber forest products*, and even *biodiversity* cannot.

Unless we can engage people from all walks of life in the celebration and stewardship of all kinds of life-forms, our epitaph may well read: "They died of a peculiar strain of reductionism, complicated by a sudden attack of elitism, even though there were ready natural cures close at hand."

Missing the Boat

Why Cultural Diversity Didn't Make It onto the Ark

{We're describing as new to science} a large, locally common tree well known to local people. Indeed, we even ate our meals while sitting on sections of a trunk of this species. . . . {But} by the time this document is published, much of the forest that we saw during our travels though western Ecuador will have been destroyed.

AL GENTRY, Rapid Assessment Project
Team report to Conservation International

My career as a biologist might have been different had I not missed the boat. Or more precisely, I might not have become an "ethno"-biologist had my ship come in, on time, as expected. If the *Cristobal Carrier* had whisked me and my fellow students off to the Galápagos as soon as we had landed in Ecuador, we might have become evolutionary biologists as "pure" as we presumed Darwin himself to be.

But with this, as with most rites of passage that have been scheduled for me, something went awry. I did not become a "pure" anything. Instead of spending the summer engaged with the beak of a finch or the cactus-eating habits of the giant tortoises in Darwin's island laboratories, I fell under the spell of a dazzling diversity of tropical South American fruits. I succumbed to the guavas, papayas, bananas, and custard apples cultivated by indigenous farming communities—and to the indigenous folk themselves. Lured by their handiwork, I became as consumed by the "cultural selection" of fruits and seeds as Darwin's disciples are by the "natural selection" of bones and beaks.

But let me back up a bit and brush more paint onto the canvas. It was the summer of 1973, the year the tropical rain forest was first proclaimed "a nonrenewable resource" in the pages of *Science*. The seventies would be the most productive decade that island biogeography has witnessed since the era of Darwin and Wallace. It was also around the time that "Lonesome George" was found—the last surviving individual of a Galápago tortoise subspecies that had been presumed extinct for decades. My status was far less noteworthy; I was just one of two dozen college students recruited for the first ill-fated course of the Charles Darwin Research Institute. Given scholarships for a summer of traveling around the Galápagos on a well-equipped oceanographic vessel, many of us were hoping to walk, wade, or swim in Darwin's footsteps. We gathered in a moldy hotel in Guayaquil, Ecuador, our duffels full of snorkels, fins, field guides, and cameras. We were ready to ride the waves, convinced we were to have the wildest summer of our lives.

Such hopes were dashed—or at least detoured—when we belatedly learned that the institute was not financially solvent. Within a week of congregating in front of the rotting docks on the Rio Guayas, we learned that a check from the institute had bounced, and the oceanographic vessel would not be arriving in port. If we were to get out to the Galápagos at all, it would be as second-class passengers on a rusty diesel-fueled freighter, the *Cristóbal Carrier*.

The freighter was not immediately scheduled for a trip to the archipelago, so we decided to spend the next couple of weeks exploring the biological and cultural wealth of mainland Ecuador. We headed inland, riding atop overstuffed buses into the Andean highlands. This sudden turn of events radically shifted my trajectory as a field scientist. Instead of spending an entire summer captivated by marine iguanas, giant prickly pears, and flightless cormorants, my eyes and nose delighted in marketplaces laden with hundreds of varieties of weird and wonderful fruits and herbs, dozens of multicolored "messenger" beans, and oodles of potatoes and other tubers. I haggled with Otavaleño Indian salesmen over the price of gold necklaces and hand-woven weavings. With my traveling buddy, Steve Trimble, I hiked along the Inca Trail to outposts where Quechuan runners had once relayed messages from hundreds of miles away. We visited Santa Domingo de los Colorados where all the villagers treated their hair with bright red dyes of *achiote* derived from the tropical plant *annatto*. People coloring their lives with local plants? The metaphor struck me as fitting.

We did eventually make it out to the Galápagos, but my mind kept wandering away from the evolutionary processes made manifest by the island life. Just a first few steps after landing on San Cristobal Island, I duly directed my field note-taking toward Darwin's ground finches, the ubiquitous yellow warblers, and an endemic grapsid crab. But once I left the shore of Wreck Bay behind me, my notes veered into the realm of "bananas, oranges, datura-like *campanas*, morning glories, and bougainvilleas ornamenting every yard." As we made our way through the islands, I gradually grew impatient with the reve-lations of scientists who stayed in the archipelago only long enough to "use" the insular creatures there to prove some theory. I was more inclined to spend time with local residents, my journal recalls: "the people who have adopted the islands as their home, who have given their existence over to the archipelago."

One such encounter was with Miguel Castro, the first Ecuadorean conservation officer for the islands. Born and raised in the Galápagos, Castro had the knack of making sense to Ecuadorean fishermen and foreign scientists alike. He loved diving with marine iguanas and Galápagos penguins but was not averse to the dirty work of conser-vation; he spent many days clambering over "clinkers" (lava cobbles), shooting at the feral cats, dogs, and goats that were decimating the eggs and the young of the islands' most imperiled native fauna.

From Wreck Bay, I journeyed up to the humid highlands of Pro-greso, where I recorded the names of crops, weeds, and orchard trees grown by Ecuadorean immigrants. The first human settlement in the Galápagos had been a penal colony established on Floreana in 1832, but since then there had been a constant introduction of exotic plants and animals to the archipelago, with much damage done to the local biota. There was something "unsettling" about highland villages in the Galápagos compared to those in the Andes, where human history ran so deeply. Humankind with all its weedy and ratty hitchhikers had somehow tainted the islands' atmosphere.

The squish and stench of rotting avocados showed that domesticated plants had not been fully integrated within the biotic communities. At Progreso, Steve Trimble and I asked a family of farmers how much ten avocados would cost. They replied that they would sell us ten avocados from their dooryard garden for a dollar. Surprised by the low price, Steve thought that we should go ahead and bargain for thirty avocados, enough for us to make guacamole for our entire crew.

"What's the cost of thirty avocados?" I asked in my rudimentary Spanish.

The family discussed the question for a moment, then quoted the same price for thirty as they had for ten.

"*¿El mismo precio?*" we repeated, dumbfounded.

"Well, we have so many overripe avocados, we can't give them away. The birds hardly touch them, the rats seem not to care. Take this paper bag, and collect all you want."

Back on the South American continent, I began tracking down every treatise and unpublished thesis I could find on local uses of the native flora. This literature opened up my mind to different questions than those classic evolutionary riddles that every student of Darwin is sent to master. Yet, as I later realized, some of those questions were just the sort that Darwin himself attempted to tackle in *The Variation of Animals and Plants Under Domestication*, written sixteen years after *The Origin of Species*. No purist, Darwin never restricted his inquiries to the wild, as many of his followers have, but was stimulated by the diversity of flowers, fruits, and beasts of burden within cultural landscapes as well.

My questions ranged from the origin of individual fruit varieties to the shaping of entire landscapes. Which fruits in those Ecuadorean marketplaces were truly wild, and which had been domesticated through the handiwork of native horticulturists? How did the Andean highlands look before prehistoric peoples worked their slopes into terraces and planted each terrace rim with agave-like *Furcraeas*? Why was it that most of Ecuador's fourteen indigenous cultures remained in the rain forests of the Amazon and not in the once-fertile valleys between the Andean cordilleras? Was Ecuador's cultural diversity "good" in some way, just as some ecologists believed that plant diversity was "good" for stabilizing soils, maintaining yields, and speeding up revegetation after a disaster? Were place-based ethnic communities stewards of biological diversity, or did they deplete the natural world around them? Why did Ecuador seem richer in both biota and cultural history than places I'd been to of comparable size, like Nevada or Colorado?

I did not know then what even armchair geographers know today: Ecuador is one of the world's "hot spots" of biodiversity. It is home to some 1,100 kinds of butterflies and nearly 300 species of birds, mammals, reptiles, and amphibians. It harbors more plants in its 110,000 square miles than you can find in the entire United States— some 20,000 species. Its indigenous cultures name more than 900 kinds of trees and woody vines, and they use most of them for fiber, fuel, food, or medicine. In fact, hundreds of native plants are intentionally sown, grown from cuttings, or otherwise encouraged in ways that blur the line between natural and cultural. You cannot go too far in the Ecuadorean highlands or in their Amazonian drainages without feeling the presence of ancient indigenous cultures.

Yet mainland Ecuador had many hungry people, and every fruit, every piece of meat produced, seemed to make it to some human mouth. Because of rapid population growth, there was intense economic pressure bearing down on nearly every square mile of Ecuadorean forest. Over the past half century, 54 percent of all of its remaining forests have been cut, with more than 90 percent of its Pacific lowland and foothill forest plowed into plantations of oil palms and other exotic crops. Perhaps as many as 3,200 native species of plants have been doomed to extinction in the process. The biotic diversity that developed over hundreds of thousands of years and coexisted with indigenous cultures for several thousand has been imperiled in less than fifty. Ecuador, I recently realized, is not merely one of the world's biological and cultural wonders, it also contains some of the world's most rapidly changing landscapes.

As the Ecuadorean forests came down to the ground this past half century, many conservationists around the world wondered what they could do to slow the unprecedented loss of species. Through a program to swap Ecuador's national debt for the establishment of new conservation projects, they encouraged the government to establish protected areas such as the Sumaco-Naco Galeras National Park and the Yasuni National Park, both east of the Andes in the Ecuadorean Amazon. Several environmental organizations and agencies have begun to manage such protected areas in Ecuador since my first visit two decades ago. Such organizations have known full well that indigenous peoples were farming or foraging in these areas. If they had any empathy for indigenous foragers at all, they assumed that formal land conservation would incidentally buffer these people from assaults by oil, mining, and logging operations.

Unfortunately, few biologists involved in Ecuador's conservation programs fully comprehended that the establishment of parks could be potentially threatening to certain indigenous groups. Even though Huaorani, Tukaho, and Zapara peoples had hunted, fished, foraged, and tended garden plots in the Yasuni vicinity for centuries, none of them had title to their lands when the government decreed Yasuni National Park in 1979. It was later designated a UNESCO biosphere reserve as well, an honorary status acknowledging that indigenous stewardship of the forest was related to how much of its habitat remained intact. Nevertheless, the indigenous inhabitants of the region feared that the very presence of the park implied the usurpation of their own land rights.

In 1981, the Confederation of Indigenous Nations of Ecuadorial Amazon (CONFENIAE) began to defend the traditional territory of the Huaorani against other claims. By 1990, CONFENIAE was claiming title to 2,160,000 acres on behalf of the Huaorani, but the Ecuadorean legal system has yet to acknowledge these rights. The government still maintains at least nominal control over the park, but it continues to grant concessions to oil companies, logging operations, and non-Huaorani ecotourist guides, all of whom compete with indigenous inhabitants in not-so-subtle ways.

Jason Clay, the founder of the nonprofit group Rights to Resources, has spent years fighting for cultural survival; he has not been surprised by such conflicts:

During the past decade, conservationists have come to realize that most "pristine" areas of Latin America are occupied by indigenous peoples. In fact, for the region as a whole, indigenous people have legal communal claims to areas that are easily ten times the size of all conservation units combined—parks, biological reserves.... Unfortunately, it has not been easy to convert overlapping areas of interest into effective conservation strategies involving both indigenous peoples and conservationists. While most conservationists realize that indigenous peoples are not their enemy, it has been difficult to figure out how to include [them].

As anthropologist Natalia Wray and her Ecuadorean colleague Jorge Alvarado found at Sumaco National Park, "the state declared areas as protected based more on ecological criteria than on social or cultural considerations. The direct management by the indigenous people of protected territory was not considered."

Not far away, in the Yasuni area on the Rio Napo, conservation officials have considered comanaging natural resources with the indigenous residents of the biosphere reserve. Still, the very presence of the reserve and the ecotourism it attracts have aggravated age-old conflicts between the Huaorani and their Quechuan-speaking neighbors. Quechuan-speaking guides working in conjunction with non-Indian tour operators have intruded on Huaorani hunting and fishing grounds, bringing outsiders with them on sports outings. This has raised the wrath of some Huaorani, who claim that the Quechua would not be so bold if the land were simply a Huaorani reserve and not a biosphere reserve.

The Yasuni biosphere reserve formally provides protection for 34 percent of all mammal species and 43 percent of all bird species in Ecuador, but it has failed to protect the traditional land and water rights necessary for cultural survival. Worse, tourism has created a more attenuated competition for economic resources among members of various local indigenous groups as well as between these groups and non-Indians. As a result of the increased cash flow into the Rio Napo watershed, Jason Clay notes, indigenous communities "do not want to live exactly as their ancestors [did]. They [now] have wants and needs that will only be met through the cash economy."

Most environmentalists working in the area find indigenous people's current interest in purchasing guns, axes, or boom boxes both destructive and repulsive. Natalia Wray has wryly written that "for most conservationists, indigenous people's needs are secondary.... [At best] the people are seen merely as useful guardians of the protected areas.... Thus it is common to hear conservationists express frustration when the indigenous people's lifestyle changes, because such changes threaten resource conservation. But the processes of change are not studied in depth to find the causes of change and possible alternatives."

Conservationists have again and again tried to build "an ark for biodiversity." Like Noah, they have been willing to usher along every kind of plant and animal as long as no other *peoples* are given a place aboard the ark, forgetting that until the very moment of crisis, a diversity of cultures served to safeguard that biodiversity. The Huaorani, Tukano, and Zapara have not been offered berths to ensure their own survival. Conservationists have given them little place in their plans except as bystanders, allowed to watch as all the animals go two by two up to higher ground.

It is ironic how many conservationists have presumed that biodiversity can survive where indigenous cultures have been displaced or at least disrupted from practicing their traditional land-management strategies. Ironic because most biodiversity remaining on earth today occurs in areas where cultural diversity also persists. Of the nine countries in which 60 percent of the world's remaining 6,500 languages are spoken, six of them are also centers of megadiversity for flora and fauna: Mexico, Brazil, Indonesia, India, Zaire, and Australia. Geographer David Harmon has made lists of the twenty-five countries harboring the greatest number of endemic wildlife species within their boundaries and of the twenty-five countries where the greatest number of endemic languages are spoken. Those two lists have sixteen countries in common. It is fair to say that wherever many cultures have coexisted within the same region, biodiversity has also survived.

Let me state this principle as a negative correlation, like a scratchboard etching: wherever empires have spread to suppress other cultures' languages and land-tenure traditions, the loss of biodiversity has been dramatic. Civilizations that conquer other cultures and force them to adopt extensive grain agriculture or livestock grazing are particularly taxing on regionally restricted floras and faunas. With colonists at the helm, arks inevitably sink.

David Harmon has wondered why, despite these significant correlations between the distributions of biodiversity hot spots and linguistically rich cultural areas, some conservation biologists still don't see the survival of cultural diversity as related to their own concerns. If such biologists are typically attracted to E. O. Wilson's "biophilia hypothesis"—that humans have an intrinsic need for meaningful contact with other life-forms—then why, he asks, do they not necessarily assume that we have a hard-wired predilection for *cross-cultural* contact: "I suppose that we are waiting for a cultural analog of the biophilia hypothesis, one which does not merely claim that cultural diversity is 'interesting' but one which explains why contact with cultural diversity makes us fully human."

While we grope for a cogent argument to convince biologists that cultural diversity "functions" on behalf of biodiversity, mainland Ecuador is being cut to pieces by chain saws. Its rate of forest loss is the second highest in South America and the ninth highest in the world. Because Ecuador's annual increase in human population density is also the highest in all of Latin America, some biologists simply say that the problem is *people*—not too many people, not recently immigrated people without traditions in the forest but *all people*, period. They dismiss cultural survival concerns by claiming that future population booms among indigenous people will be just as bad for the land as the current population boom of non-Indian immigrants to the rain forests. They do not realize that Ecuador's growing population is decreasing cultural diversity at the same time that it is depleting biodiversity.

Frightened by how population growth and land conversion leave few species alive in their wake, conservationists have desperately tried to erect fences around remaining biological riches. But fencing native peoples out of their homelands is bound to fail to achieve the ultimate goal. As Latin American ethnobiologist Bob Bye warns, "we can't just put all biodiversity in a museum and expect it to survive. Biological diversity depends on human diversity."

———

If any biologist had independently come to appreciate the richness of both the biota and the cultural knowledge nested within Ecuadorean landscapes, it was Alwyn Gentry. Gentry first went to South America in 1974, the same year I first visited there. South America has called me back only once since then; it called Gentry back on more than thirty additional trips. Over the course of those trips, he collected more specimens of tropical plants than any other living botanist. In addition to pressing more than 50,000 specimens during his own field excursions in the rain forests of Ecuador and adjacent countries, he maintained a database on another 50,000 specimens of neotropical plants that he personally examined while visiting more than one hundred herbaria around the world.

On August 3, 1993, he and four others died when their small airplane crashed into an isolated mountain ridge hidden in the mists not far from Guayaquil, Ecuador. In between his first trip through the region in 1974 and his untimely death nineteen years later, Gentry undoubtedly learned more about Ecuador's floristic diversity and ethnobotany than any Western scientist had before him. Medicinal plant explorer Mark Plotkin recalls how thoroughly Gentry had assimilated the lessons of indigenous botanists:

> When I gave my first presentation at the Missouri Botanical Garden in 1983, I showed some slides of medicine men and said that these people can identify every species in the forest without looking at the fruit or flowers and that no university-trained botanist could ever hope to do that. Almost before I was even finished, this skinny guy had come racing up to the podium, shook my hand, said I'm Al Gentry and I could do that. So I handed him a pile of these miserable sterile specimens that the Indians had given me: a piece of bark here, a piece of leaf there, and within minutes, Al had identified everything to species.

His knowledge of Ecuadorean plants did not stop with his ability to identify and classify them; he also learned their distributions, their indigenous names, and their uses. In one forest on the Pacific coast of Ecuador, he determined that one out of every five plants he encountered along his transects existed nowhere else in the world. He personally recorded more than 800 indigenous names for trees from northwestern South America and wrote a dozen papers on medicinal and other nontimber forest uses of tropical species. Some of these "uses" Al knew from personal experience. When we roomed together once at a meeting in Panama, he confided that tropical aphrodisiacs really do "work." Relaxing after a long flight from Ecuador, his muddy boots, plant press, and backpack spread out on the floor in front of the hotel bed, Al hilariously recounted incidents when members of his field crew had unexpectedly come under the spell of plants that locals later confirmed to be aphrodisiacs.

Sometimes I wonder whether I was the only person who ever saw Al Gentry resting; what sticks in the minds of most of his friends is how he would press plants long into the night after a full day of sloshing across streams, crossing mountainsides, or climbing trees. His Missouri Botanical Garden colleague Jim Miller sensed "that tirelessness was a reflection of Gentry's belief in the fundamental importance, even urgency, of understanding tropical forests. How could one rest when there were so many marvels to be uncovered, so many undescribed species, so many vanishing before they could ever be described?"

Al once persisted at inventorying the vegetation at one end of his diversity transect while a bulldozer slashed a roadway through the other end, huge trees crashing down all around him. With his Rapid Assessment Project (RAP) Team colleagues in southwestern Ecuador, he reported that "studies of the fauna were made difficult by the constant whine of chain saws." With orchid expert Calloway Dodson, he reported trends in "biological extinction in western Ecuador" in 1991. With his student Oliver Phillips he assessed "increasing turnover through time in tropical rain forests" for the readers of *Science*. Finally, in 1996, three years after his death, his review of evidence regarding "species extirpations and extinction rates" was published by Oxford University Press in a book called *Biodiversity in Managed Landscapes*.

Despite his many technical publications, Al once told me that he was proudest of the way information from his studies of tropical *Ceibas* (kapok trees) had found their way into a children's book by illustrator Lynn Cherry, *The Great Kapok Tree*. In 1988, he had coauthored a paper entitled "Where have all the *Ceibas* gone? A case of mismanagement of a tropical resource." That paper's richness of information was passed on from mouth to mouth until it was transformed into

Cherry's fine treatment of indigenous uses and modern abuses of the kapok tree. Her illustrations highlighted in a somber but colorful way young peoples' concerns about the alarming loss of tropical resources. *The Great Kapok Tree* has now been read by over a million children around the world.

As we hiked together during a rendezvous of Pew Conservation Scholars the year before he died, Al surprised me with his delight at how Lynn's book could communicate to people the beauty and the ecological and ethnobotanical value of kapok trees in a way that his own technical papers could not. He was thrilled that his pioneering studies of *Ceiba* ethnobotany had served as a catalyst for helping so many children learn to love kapoks.

There was something childlike in the purity of Al's motivations. When he was two years old, he started collecting bugs in jars; by three he became fascinated with collecting butterflies, and by age four, he'd begun his own pinned collection of them. At the ripe old age of twenty-one, he wrote an essay in which he proclaimed, "I need to be out of doors as much as possible, just to be close to the sheer beauty of the natural world...to feel the mysterious perfection of the organisms, the how and the why...I feel a very strong desire to be more than just a scientist.... [If I become] a teacher I want to stimulate others to question why they are students and consider their debt to society."

By the end of his life, Al recognized that *society* was not some uniform monolith. He taught Colombian, Ecuadorean, Brazilian, and Peruvian students as often as he did North Americans. He attended conferences and instructed field workshops with leaders and healers from tribes throughout Latin America, and their knowledge of plants is liberally sprinkled through his writings. Once, on a mountaintop thought to be remote from any settlement, Al stumbled on a group of indigenous people who threatened him with sharpened sticks for entering their territory unannounced. As quickly as he had made his way into trouble, he made his way back out, humbled by the knowledge that he was not the first human to wander in those parts.

Some 160 years after Darwin visited South America on his way out to the nearly uninhabited Galápagos, Al Gentry had fine-tuned a way of looking at the world: as patterns of diversity, shaped by soil, climate, evolutionary history, and cultural modes of land management. In Darwin's day, cultural diversity was still quite prone to miss the boat; by the time Gentry and three friends crashed into a dimly visible mountainside, cultural diversity could no longer be dismissed as an extraneous part of the story. It should never again be left out when conservation options are being considered—especially not in a country such as Ecuador.

If I were twenty-two again and given the choice of being the umpteenth naturalist to visit the Galápagos since Darwin or of following in Gentry's mud-caked footsteps into a rain forest where indigenous people still lay claim to luscious fruits and powerful medicines, I know which path I would choose. This time I would miss the boat on purpose, knowing that somewhere ahead of me a load of tropical aphrodisiacs might lie waiting, a host of cultural stories surrounding them like protective bracts around a flower bud.

Sierra Madre Upshot

Ecological and Agricultural Health

*Mountain people, in their vertical archipelagoes of human
and natural variety, have become the guardians of
irreplaceable global assets.*
DEREK DENNISTON, *High Priorities: Conserving
Mountain Ecosystems and Cultures*

"We must be coming up to the Great Divide," I yelled over the engine
noise of the old Dodge van. It was chugging in low gear over the six-
teenth ridge in a row, this one covered with pines, the others below
it with junipers and oaks; below that, we had begun our day in the
cactus-studded warmth of the Sonoran Desert near Tucson. Now we
were some 200 miles southeast, in the northernmost thrust of the
Sierra Madre Occidental, the Mother Mountains.

"How can you tell we're close to the divide?" Anne wondered. It
was her first time in the Sierra, and she was trying to take it all in.

"There to the west of us, look, the washes all seem to be draining
away to the southwest. That's the Rio Bavispe watershed. They'll coa-
lesce with other arroyos draining the western slopes of the Sierra,
become the Rio Yaqui, and spill into the Sea of Cortez. I'm not sure
about these to the east of us—right now they're heading northeast,
maybe to tributaries of the Rio Grande.... Aggie, can you see them
on the map?"

Aggie Haury, our septuagenarian navigator, sat in the seat behind Anne and me, maps on her lap, eyes scanning the horizons. "We must be in Chihuahua already," she surmised, "and if we're east of the Animas Mountains, which should be in New Mexico to the north of us, they either dump into playas or into the Rio Grande."

A last scent of the pines wafted in as I rolled up my window. It was getting cold, for although the light was still flooding the ridge in front of us with a brilliant golden wash, we were within a half hour of sunset and more than six thousand feet above sea level.

We inched up over the ridge and began our descent onto the high, tree-stippled plateau of far western Chihuahua. This was a relief, for I was feeling nauseated from lurching around so many turns, swerving and plunging to follow so many switchbacks. If I had not been hanging onto the steering wheel, I would surely have lost my lunch by now.

There was another reason for my near-nausea. Compared to my traveling companions, I had burdened myself with an almost impossible goal for our weeklong journey in the Sierra. Anne Fitzgerald had come here to document the history of the Americas according to the tortilla, the Mesoamerican bread of life, in all its varied cultural manifestations. Aggie Haury had come to learn more of the cultural connections between the U.S. Southwest and Mesoamerica as manifested in Casas Grandes, a prehistoric trade center between the two regions.

And I had come to search for the ghost of Aldo Leopold, who sixty years before had heard the song of the Rio Gavilán clear as a mountain stream in these Sierra. He had come here late in his career, and it was perhaps the first and the last large tract of healthy landscape he would see before he died. Toward the end of his life, he admitted that it was in the Sierra Madre that he "first clearly realized that the land is an organism, that in all my life I had seen only sick land, whereas here was a biota still in perfect aboriginal health."

In the two weeks of his first trip here, he saw no overgrazing, but ample signs of wolves and mountain lions. He saw no fire suppression, but scant brush and ample spacing of pines where wildfires regularly moved through the forests. The guacamaya, or thick-billed parrot, nearly extirpated from the adjacent United States, gave the forest's music its cadence.

Perhaps most telling of all indicators was Leopold's sense that the watershed of the Rio Gavilán was intact, "a picture of ecological health," with slow, clear-running streams of water suitable for drinking. Yet he noticed something curious about the watercourses draining into the Gavilán: they were all punctuated with check dams of dry masonry put in place by prehistoric Native Americans. Although Leopold was not aware of recent Indian affairs—the last Apache raid in the Rio Gavilán had been only the year before he first visited the watershed—he felt a strong affinity with its earlier indigenous inhabitants:

> There once were men capable of inhabiting a river without disrupting the harmony of its life. They must have lived in thousands on the Rio Gavilán, for their works are everywhere. Ascend any draw debouching on any canyon and you find yourself climbing little rock terraces or check dams, the crest of one level with the base of the next. Behind each dam is a little plot of soil that was once a field or garden, subirrigated by the showers which fell on the steep adjoining slopes …the deer love to lie on these little terraces. They afford a level bed, free of rocks, upholstered with oak leaves, curtained by shrubs. One bound over the dam and the deer is out of sight of an intruder.

In nine days, Leopold and his friends saw more than 180 deer among those terraced slopes; a year later, visiting with his brother and son, he saw another 250 deer in sixteen days. Though he ostensibly took both trips for sports hunting, Leopold himself did not shoot a single deer during his brief immersion in the Sierra Madre. Instead, he wrote notes that eventually wove their way into two of the most sonorous essays within *A Sand County Almanac*: "Song of the Gavilán" and "Guacamaya." In these essays he goes furthest toward defining ecological health in tangible terms.

"The Sierra Madre," he mused, "offers us the chance to describe, in actual ecological measurements, the lineaments and physiology of an unspoiled mountain landscape." But there is a nuance missed by most of Leopold's philosophical disciples over the four decades since the Sand County and Round River essays did much to forge the developing ethics of the so-called environmental movement. Like other montane ecosystems, which collectively cover one-fifth of the world's land, the Sierra had not only been heavily peopled at one time but their inhabitants had also managed them in a way that did not deplete their diversity. Leopold suggested that indigenous people must instead have contributed to its ecological health and stability. The obvious human manipulations of the watershed did not keep Leopold from calling it "unspoiled." For him, the term "unspoiled wilderness" took on new meaning, one that could include the appropriate presence of cultural features set in place by any inhabitants, not only "Indians." This entire notion remains a contradiction in terms for most wilderness advocates today, who cannot imagine any appropriate cultural presence in "the wild."

Although we would be traveling to the north, south, and east of the Gavilán watershed where Leopold had hunted for ecological health, I was still hoping to catch an earful of that same music. What was the benchmark of health that Leopold had found, more precious than the fountain of youth sought by Ponce de Léon centuries before? Could I still hear, as Leopold apparently had, how human voices might blend with that larger harmony rather than transforming the concert into cacophony?

At this point in my life, perhaps more than any other, I needed such a benchmark of health. I had begun to come out of the malaise of a three-year bout with chronic fatigue; at the same time, my marriage was suffering from innumerable pressures, and my work conserving the native seeds of the Sierra Madre was suffering as well. I needed to remember why wildness had mattered to me to begin with: mountains and rivers, compadres and partners, Native American traditions and natural forests, wild chiles and ancient beans, breathtaking barrancas and prehistoric terraces where century plants were formerly cultivated. I needed to be wooed again by the sheer diversity of life found in one pocket of this continent, to be grateful again about having glimpsed the mountains that mothered much of this diversity. And I knew it was a diversity facing pressures of unprecedented scale. As Derek Dennisten has warned, "there is a dangerous disproportion between the great importance of mountain ecosystems and their cultures and the attention they receive from national governments and international organizations—a disparity that increases the risks that now confront both the mountains themselves and all those who rely on them."

Just after dawn one cool December morning, Aggie, Anne, and I walked out onto a precipice overlooking la Cascada de Basaseachic, watching water fall for close to a thousand feet, atomizing into mist before it hit a large plunge pool on the canyon floor. We shivered as we stood on a huge boulder of volcanic tuff, a mix of conifers above us, wind whisking through their needles. Apache pine. Chihuahua pine. Ponderosa. And my favorite, with its downturned needles forming a crown of frowns: *pino triste*. We were less than fifty miles from the continental divide, perched at seven thousand feet above sea level, wrapped in multiple layers of clothes. Still, the wind whipped through these layers, chilling our skin into goose-bump-pocked hides.

As I scanned the cliff face across from us—now partially veiled in mist, fog, and wood smoke—I remembered a previous visit I made to Basaseachic, during early fall. With a Tohono O'odham linguist and a Portuguese-American zoologist, I had climbed down a near-vertical set of rotting log steps to see the cascade from below. I was struck by the presence of so many plants other than pines, positioned in "window boxes" along the cliffs where they would be relatively protected from freezes. I recognized five kinds of century plants, including the *mescalito* the Indians call *taiehcholi*, which is restricted to middle elevations of the northern cordillera and found nowhere beyond it. And three little grayish-blue succulents in the crassula family clung to rock faces even though I associate them more with the foggy coasts of Baja California. Then there was a strange species of sotol nearby, akin to those of the Durango highlands. Lower down, I believe I spotted a handful of bromeliad species, relatives of pineapples and Spanish moss, life-forms with an orientation toward the tropics.

As we looked down on the barranca from pine-topped plateau to deeply carved canyon bottom, I realized that we were facing a microcosm of the entire Sierra. Its steep elevational gradients allowed strange juxtapositions of tropical and subalpine life within a matter of miles; palms and pines, columnar cacti and junipers grew together in some canyons. Balconies and window boxes along canyon walls maintained refugia of plants and animals hundreds of miles from their core distributions. Rich Spellenberg, Toutcha Lebgue, and Rafael Corral, who have compiled records of plants collected at Basaseachic over the decades, have tallied up 825 species inhabiting an area of less than twenty square miles. That is perhaps one-fifth of all the kinds of plants now identified from the northern Sierra Madre.

Yet what humbled me in the face of this barranca was not merely its depth, its size, its precipitousness. It was how little we actually fathom of life in the Sierra. When botanists Richard Felger and Robert Bye helped me nominate the Sierra Madre Occidental to the World Conservation Union and World Wildlife Fund as one of the few centers of megadiversity for plants anywhere in North America, we had to concede that botanists have probably identified as yet only five out of every eight plants that may grow in the region. My Desert Museum coworker Tom Van Devender is discovering two or three new species there every year, even though he is not primarily a plant taxonomist. When all the region's plants have been catalogued and identified— if that mythic moment ever occurs—it is likely that four thousand kinds of plants will be tallied from the northern reaches of the Sierra Madre. In an area less than a quarter of the size of Texas, these mountains mother about the same number of plant species as the whole state does. Japan, too, harbors roughly the same number of plants, but its islands cover twice the area of the northern Sierra. The Sierra that stretched before me clear up to the spot where Leopold camped in the Rio Gavilán harbor the northernmost blending of Mexico's two richest floras—and Mexico ranks among the top three centers of biodiversity in the world.

The current preoccupation with assessing the plant diversity of various regions was not in vogue when Aldo Leopold entered the Sierra. Diversity in and of itself did not factor into his definition of ecological health. But he knew when an area's richness of plant life had been depleted by cows, sheep, or goats grazing at unsupportable densities; he knew when their cropping of understory vegetation resulted in fire suppression and diminished heterogeneity among forest patches. Leopold probably didn't know that Apaches, who had kept the forests of the Gavilán burning until just the year before his first trip there, had made raids that kept ranchers from overstocking the watershed, as other ranchers had overstocked the ranges just north of the Chihuahuan border.

Leopold's forays into the Sierra were as short as my own, a couple of weeks at a time at most. That's not enough time to grasp the full richness of its flora and fauna. I could identify by sight just about 500 of its species—a pittance of its total diversity. Leopold probably never saw the Sierra's flora in complete leaf, for his visits were during the cool season, months after the widest range of wildflowers, insects, and birds are at their peak. Somehow, though, that wildlife biologist raised in the more monotonous Midwest sensed that the Song of the Gavilán was filled with many voices.

It is also filled with many tastes, as Leopold himself did recognize: "To the superficial eye the Gavilán is a hard and stony land.... But the old terrace-builders were not deceived; they knew it by experience to be a land of milk and honey. These twisted oaks and junipers bear each year a crop of mast to be had by wildings for the pawing. The deer, turkeys, and javelinas spend their days, like steers in a cornfield, converting this mast into succulent meat. These golden grasses conceal, under their waving plumes, a subterranean garden of bulbs and tubers, including wild potatoes."

I have eaten those wild potatoes myself, along with many of the other 250 wild crop relatives that still occur in the region. Although I love the tastes and textures of the wild potatoes, chiles, tomatillos, teosintes, beans, and strawberries of the Sierra, they are but a small component of comestible cornucopia there. More than 400 plant species are eaten by the tribes of the northern Sierra Madre; historically, the Tarahumara alone utilized at least 220 kinds of native plants as food. But perhaps these numbers mean nothing; Bob Bye has estimated that by the time modern ethnobotanists entered the region with all the tools needed to identify and analyze these nutritional resources, less than 40 percent of the plants prepared as food in previous centuries remained in use.

Just as the forests of the Gavilán have not remained fully intact since Leopold's death, life in the remaining indigenous communities to the south—in a spur range known as the Sierra Tarahumara—has also undergone rapid change in this century. Most of the 66,000 Tarahumara living in the Sierra still converse in their native tongue, but their degree of dependence on the land's diverse plant resources is diminishing. When Aggie, Anne, and I detoured into the heart of Tarahumara country for several days, we were amazed just how deeply this dependence had been shattered.

On a crisp and brilliant morning, we awoke not far from the railroad yards of Creel, a lumber town that is blanketed in wood smoke and fog at this time of year. Shafts of light touched down as the fog broke up, illuminating the piles and piles of pine logs ready to leave the Sierra by rail. Nearly all of the surrounding coniferous forests have already been cut, some as many as four times over the past century. The old growth remaining nearby occurs in isolated patches and is under constant threat. Not far away, in the town of Anáhuac, a massive pulping mill has recently been renovated and expanded to the tune of 350 million dollars; to repay their loan, the mill owners will turn thousands of acres of mixed pine forests into toilet paper destined for American markets.

The loss of forest canopy nearby did much to reduce the abundance of edible plants in the understory, and a recent four-year drought diminished them even further. As we were leaving Creel for the hinterlands, I ran into Padre Verplanken, the priest who had organized much of the food relief effort for drought-stricken communities bereft of both wild and cultivated crops.

"At least 119 communities were affected," Verplanken reported. "We received 190 metric tons of foodstuffs by train, but the hard part was ensuring distribution out to remote areas of the Sierra."

It was hard to imagine that a place with so much natural abundance had been so devastated in just a few years. The drought was obviously not the sole cause of the hunger; it was primarily an aggravating factor once the land's bounty had been depleted. As we drove out of Creel, we saw slope after slope with no more than immature pine saplings on them; the formerly rich carpet of other wildlings had been frayed and desiccated. I have since learned that the Sierra Madre forests are one of seven global hot spots with at least half their area more than a mile high where the endemic plants are threatened by imminent destruction.

We headed out toward the Tarahumara community of Panalachic, stopping now and then to talk with farmers, pottery makers, loggers, and herders, many of them mestizo rather than Tarahumara. Along the way, we kept seeing a car that would pass us, head off on a spur road, and then, later, pass us again. Finally, I flagged the driver down, curious to see what he was up to.

"I'm selling factory-made flour tortillas and white bread to all the ranchos out this way. The maize crops have almost completely failed for several years running; I don't know how it will be this year, but I bet not too good. Before the shipments of dry *masa* and other flour starting coming in, people had hardly any grain. So I started this route that I run every few days. It used to be that just the *Mexicanos* would buy the bread and flour tortillas, because the Indians still prefer corn tortillas. But now they've gotten used to it, and the Indians buy bread as well."

Several hours later, when we arrived at the fields of Manuel Torres Lerma, his entire Tarahumara family was out harvesting what little blue corn his sloping field had produced that season. The women, all dressed in brightly colored skirts, blouses, and scarves, with children wrapped onto their backs, moved between the corn rows, husking the ears and tossing the fuller ones into gunnysacks carried away in a wheelbarrow. Manuel stripped an ear of a corn stalk and husked it to show us what they were up against.

"The rains came too late, not until early August," he explained. "Look, all the grain on the ends of the ears is shriveled up, because we planted so late that they could not mature once the late-season drought came again. See those plants lower down on the slope? They're the only ones with fully filled ears. We fertilized that area with goat manure, and that is the only place where the plants matured before the late-season drought.... Those ears are longer, brighter, richer in blue. The others already look bleached by the sun."

Maize cultivation has gone on in the Sierra for centuries, but perhaps it was done on a smaller scale before the introduction of draft animals and the walking plow. Now, where forests are cut upslope from fields, and fields are fallowed a good portion of the year, soil erosion can be severe. In many of the more extensive fields found near Tarahumara villages, there is a curious lack of terracing to control soil and water flow, although some terracing can be found in small orchards and dooryard gardens. I thought of the ominous warning from the Worldwatch Institute regarding montane farming cultures: "Time-tested mountain farming practices, many of which go back centuries, are being abruptly threatened by population growth, the fast-growing global economy, and the overwhelming cultural influences of the plains."

The infrequency of terracing today is surprising, considering how extensive terrace building was prehistorically. Aldo Leopold was neither the first nor the last to marvel at them. Archaeologists such as Aggie's deceased husband, Doc Haury, along with his flamboyant sometimes-crony, sometimes-rival Charlie DiPeso, were altogether astonished by the extensiveness of the *trincheras* (terracing) left all over northern Mexico and adjacent Arizona by prehistoric peoples. One time, at a conference I attended on regional history where Doc Haury and Charlie DiPeso were the featured speakers, DiPeso went to the podium wearing a bright red cochineal-dyed cape he had purchased somewhere in Mexico, and presented a slide of ruins at the foot of the Sierra, with dozens and dozens of stone terraces reaching beyond them for as far as the eye could discern. Waving his hands up in the air as if he were scaling a mountain, DiPeso cried out, "Not a single drop of water fell within the entire watershed above that prehistoric village without having had its erosive force broken by terraces and check dams, then channeled into canals for agricultural and domestic uses. Every slope of that watershed was managed to conserve water and soil!"

DiPeso's predilection for hyperbole was well known to his bemused audience, which appeared more comfortable with Doc Haury's scientific precision and more modest behavior. But both men had documented extensive water and soil control structures during their half century of archaeological excavations. Why did such a commonsense practice atrophy within the Sierra?

Aggie, Anne, and I knew that we could not answer this question, but we did want to take a look at prehistoric terraces. We headed north toward Casas Grandes, Chihuahua, where DiPeso had devoted much of his career to the archaeological excavation and interpretation of the Paquime ruins. An old friend of mine, Paul Minnis, had been following up on DiPeso's work at the nearby village of Mata Ortíz, situated on the high grassy plains at the foot of the Sierra. He had given me a map showing how to get to some terrace fields a few miles west of Mata Ortíz, but once again, I needed the help of Aggie's good eye and map-reading skills to help us find these prehistoric treasures.

"We go down into this drainage and cross a little wash.... Yes, this must be it.... Then, drive upslope past a corral.... There, I think those may be some rock alignments off to the left! Don't you think they could be what we're after?"

I pulled the van over to one side of the rutted track across the grassy slope, and we opened our mud-caked doors to a fierce wind howling down out of the Sierra. Each of us spotted a different line of cobbles extending across the plain, perpendicular to the prevailing gradient of slope. The wind's penetrating chill found its way beneath my blue-jean jacket as I ambled along the edge of a hundred-yard-long terrace. Nothing had been planted above its lip of volcanic cobbles for several centuries, but it was as obviously a man-made feature as the terraces Leopold had seen many miles west of where we stood. And unlike the Tarahumara fields we had seen a few days before, these had not been plowed or planted with short-lived herbaceous crops; they had been home to thousands of rosettes of hardy perennial century plants, whose roots held soil in place year-round. We were looking at the remnants of one of the steadiest forms of agriculture in the world; it reminded me of how I still sought such stability in my own life.

I turned my back to the wind and stood above the westernmost terrace trying to count the other half-buried linear alignments of cobbles that I could see on the gently sloping plain below. As I turned my eyes to the next row of cobbles, a black-tailed jackrabbit suddenly appeared, as though it had melted out of one of the volcanic rocks. It had been perfectly camouflaged, with its ears pulled back and its white flanks hidden by a furtive crouch. The jackrabbit ran downslope from the terrace, then froze again, assuming an even lower crouch against the ground, blending in with the buff color of the grama grasses surrounding it. Within another ten paces, I scared up two additional jackrabbits, both of which ran downwind and out of sight.

When I rejoined Aggie and Anne, we had all found different paths to the same dry watercourse, which showed evidence of hand-dug canals jutting off from it, draining toward the terraces themselves. Along the widest portion of the watercourse, there was an island-like bench of extremely fertile soil set in the midst of one drainageway;

the entire "island" had been carefully terraced and partitioned into irrigable patches, each lined with larger, broader cobble borders than the ones we had seen up on the grassy plains. We marveled at the careful reading of contours and flow patterns that the prehistoric agave farmers must have made to ensure that this field mosaic captured sufficient moisture for its crops year after year. And although no agaves remained and no humans fed themselves from these terraces' bounty, I was gratified to know that the lush grassy cover resulting from the soil and water conservation accomplished by the terraces still fed a few jackrabbits and sheltered them from the winds.

For millennia, the forests of the Sierra have offered the same ecological services that the terraces provide on a microcosmic scale: keeping soil in place, slowing the flow of water and filtering it along the way, and offering an abundance of food to wildlife and human inhabitants alike. The rivers that flow out of the northern Sierra Madre provide irrigation water to several of Mexico's major breadbaskets: the Yaqui Valley of Sonora, birthplace of the Green Revolution; the coastal plain of Sinaloa, where most winter vegetables destined for the western United States are grown; and the lower Rio Grande, which provides the Midwest with many of the tomatoes and salad greens blessing its grocery shelves every winter.

Should more of the forest cover of the Sierra be reduced to stubble, these ecological services will dry up with the same rapidity as the understory edibles. In the early 1990s, I assisted my Native Seeds/SEARCH cofounders, Mahina Drees and Barney Burns, in their efforts to halt a massive forest-harvesting project in the northern Sierra that was being promulgated by the World Bank. Fortunately, prominent ecologists in Mexico—Exequiel Escurra, Luis Bojorquez, Robert Bye, and others—marshaled considerable evidence to convince the World Bank that the Sierra Madrean forests were more valuable when managed intact than when cut down and flushed away.

When I received a call from a scientist inside the World Bank who confided that the multi-billion-dollar project was being scrapped indefinitely, I was elated. The same type of logging that had impoverished the Rio Gavilán since the time of Leopold's death would be halted—or at least, postponed—in the Sierra Tarahumara. But that assumption was naive, for it did not take into account that many

American industries had heard about the Sierra's forestry resources in the meantime.

Over the past five years, since the World Bank was forced to scrap its grand plan for the Sierra, one remnant forest after another has been placed on the chopping block. The kind of integration of human activities within the forest community that Aldo Leopold envisioned in the Rio Gavilán is less and less possible, for small-scale uses of non-timber resources are being overwhelmed by massive private-funded extractive industries.

Not long after Aggie, Anne, and I returned home, I began to receive notices of new field surveys determining that more than 99 percent of the old-growth forests of the northern Sierra Madre have now been cut—forests that once covered an area the size of Denmark. The thick-billed parrot is retreating farther and farther south into Mexico as more and more Chihuahua pine stands are felled. The Mexican government has recently established El Carricito as Mexico's first Important Bird Area in the southern Sierra Madre near the Durango border, in part because it offers a refuge for the thick-billed parrots, Mexican spotted owls, and other birds now under siege in Chihuahua.

From the terraces on grassy plains near Mata Ortíz, the Tarahumara gardens near Panalichic, and the protected wooded canyon below Basaseachic Falls, I could triangulate to feel what the Sierra must have been like when human settlements still had the capacity to contribute to ecosystem health. But by the time of my visits, something was missing from these northern Sierra habitats, something that Aldo Leopold believed to be essential:

> It is easy to say that the loss is all in our mind's eye, but is there any other ecologist who will agree? He knows full well that there has been an ecological death, the significance of which is inexpressible in terms of contemporary science. A philosopher called this imponderable essence the *numenon* of things. It stands in contradistinction to *phenomenon*, which is ponderable and predictable, even to the tossings and turnings of the remotest star.... Be that as it may, I here record the discovery of the numenon of the Sierra Madre: the Thick-Billed Parrot.

Leopold recorded that numenon late in his life—and late in the life of healthy forest habitats within the Rio Gavilán. His son, Starker

Leopold, and many others who have entered that watershed since then have not had the same opportunity to hear roistering flocks of such velvety green, scarlet, and gold-ornamented aerial delights. The Chihuahua pines are more even-aged today than they were before, and old ones are tougher to find. In some places, I am told, the prehistoric terraces have been blown out by floods and, in others, buried by layers of sawdust and silt.

I have a gut feeling that the old partnerships between nature and culture have momentarily slipped out of our reach. It is the same feeling I have about the shattered intimacies and tattered landscapes that haunt my own home.

I am one of many biologists who simply hope that we have not surveyed such areas well enough to know that the likes of thick-billed parrots and imperial woodpeckers are truly gone for good. If they are, I only hope that those who venture back into the Sierra will hear another kind of call in their stead: the ghost of Aldo Leopold wailing in the wind, mourning the loss of a large tract of land that once had its ecological health intact, a health in which humans formerly played an essential part.

TWO

Growing Up with Others

Our grasp of the blessings of diversity begins
in childhood and predisposes us to accept
or reject different cultures and habitats
for the rest of our lives.

Children in Touch, Creatures in Story

Simply stated, the loss of neighborhood species endangers our experience of nature. If a species becomes extinct within our radius of reach (smaller for the very old, very young, disabled, and poor), it might as well be gone altogether, in one important sense. To those whose access suffers by it, local extinction has much the same result as global eradication.
ROBERT MICHAEL PYLE, *The Thunder Tree*

We were gathered together for the New Year, friends and members of an extended family on a Mexican ranch, tucked back into a desert valley three hours south of the U.S. border. The elderly grandmother kept all the women busy sorting and cooking beans, stuffing tamales, and patting out tortillas. Her husband, a mestizo Sonoran cowboy, was not too old to do hard work, but he let his sons and sons-in-law do most of the wrangling, woodcutting, and hay hauling that week, quietly guiding them through the tasks at hand.

When chores were done, though, the adults had little else to do. And so they told stories all day long, while drinking coffee, *pinole*, and chocolate and watching a pack of two dozen children run wild through the house, ranchyard, and desert. Because the nights were so long and the ranch was without electricity, we would build a bonfire just before dusk; then we'd hunker around it for several hours, nursing more hot drinks, roasting marshmallows, and swapping tales.

The preparation for this ritual would begin several hours earlier. Around three in the afternoon, the grandmother—a tiny woman of Cahitan Indian descent—would tire of the children darting in and out of the kitchen while she was preparing dinner. She would wipe her hands on her apron, walk outside, clap her hands, and start giving commands: "Stay out of the house now, you little ones! You two, come down from that tree! The rest of you, quit that jumping off the haystack, and come over here! I need your help! It's going to be cold and windy tonight! We need extra wood for the bonfire! *Andenles*, get going for some wood, enough wood to keep us all warm!" She feigned a shiver in her sweater and long dress, then dispatched them all for the desert surrounding the ranchyard.

Suddenly filled with purpose, the older adolescents quickly organized the troop—right down to the three- and four-year-olds—and marched them out the wooden gate into open country. I straggled along behind them with another parent (keeping well within earshot). We could not help but be curious about these children as they rambled and playfully argued their way through the desert scrub, paying us no mind.

I soon realized that I was witnessing the most comprehensive environmental education lesson I had ever seen. Geography, plant ecology, hydrology, archaeology, history, and ethnobotany were all wrapped into one roving seminar, offered impromptu by a team of field instructors—none of them over fourteen years of age. As the children gathered kindling during the next hour and a half, they also accumulated places and stories for their mental maps of their grandparents' ranch.

"Where can we get enough wood?" one girl visiting from a Baja California town asked her country cousins. "There are hardly any sticks near the house anymore."

"That's because Grandma gets any wood near the house during the times when we're not around to help her. We have to go farther away to get what we need today, maybe over there where Grandpa built their first adobe house."

"No, that wasn't their *first* house. He made one out of mud and sticks when they first came to the ranch a real long time ago. It's over by those dead trees—that's where the first well went dry, so they had to move…"

"I've never seen an empty well," one little boy cried. "Let's go over there!"

"Why not? Maybe some branches have fallen down off of those old trees." And they were off, like a herd of goats seeking some palatable forage.

A few minutes later, each child was busy looking for a branch that he or she could drag or carry away. The local ruffians-in-residence directed their city cousins toward deadfalls of mesquite and cautioned them against the remains of an introduced eucalyptus tree. "That wood is no good, it's too smelly. It makes the bonfire stink like medicine."

"Yeah, mesquite or ironwood are better. Mesquite smoke is sweet. And you can always tell the ironwood, even when there is just one piece left by itself on the ground. It weighs a ton!"

"Let's show them that place where the old chunks of ironwood sit on the ground like stones. It's over there, at the bottom of that rocky *bajada*."

Suddenly, the herd veered off course, farther away from the house, over a small rise, and down the slope. There, where the slope met a small sandy wash, they found fossilized fragments of ironwood chunks; among these fossilized chunks lay old pot shards as well.

"Grandpa says that these are from water *ollas* that Indian ladies used to balance on their heads, no hands, like I ride my bike."

"You ride your bike with clay pots of water on your head? No wonder all this pottery is broken!" one of the older kids teased.

"No, I didn't break the potteries. I'm better that those Indians. I never drop a thing!"

The smaller kids had already gone back toward the ranch house with one of the older girls; when the boys were done teasing each other, they ran to catch up with the rest of the mob. They noticed that one of the youngsters was dragging a bright red spray of branches. "Where did you get that?" they inquired.

The child pointed. "From that bush by the side of the wash."

"That's *yerba de la flecha*. The Indians used to use it for poison. It's no good to burn." The child shrugged, dropped the branch, and picked up another under a mesquite tree. They all headed in to the ranch-yard as the sun went down behind their backs.

There, under the supervision of their parents and uncles, they sorted the wood: paloverde and small kindling for heating tortillas on the *comal*; mesquite for the bonfire; ironwood set aside for the moment. As the boys stacked the wood, they asked their grandfather when he had built the different houses on the ranch and why he had located them where he did; one of the girls went over to her grandmother and whispered to her, "Nana, what kind of Indians used the poisons in that *yerba de la flecha?*"

"Who knows? Apaches or Seris, I guess."

"What did *your* people do with it?" she whispered, not wanting to call her own grandmother an *Indian* but sensing her nativity nonetheless.

"Well," the grandmother sighed. "It's been many years...I remember when I was a girl, my uncle would gather little white cocoons off the stems of the *yerba de la flecha*. I would help him. He called them *teneboi'im*. He was a *pascola* dancer—you've seen them, haven't you? Like the deer dancer, they wear hundreds of these cocoons tied around their ankles, and this makes a rhythm as they dance. I grew up with that sound..."

The stories for the night had been chosen: about the grandmother growing up in southern Sonora, moving to the new ranch as a young bride, and helping her husband build a house to begin a new life. The children listened wide-eyed as the tales touched down in the places through which they had romped just that afternoon. Abandoned houses became homes again, as the family re-membered its origins. And as the elders shared with the youngsters the memories lodged there, the family renewed its membership in the land.

What I witnessed among those children is nothing unique to Indians, Mexicans, ranch families, or desert dwellers. The playful exploration of *habitat* by cohorts of children—as well as the gradual accumulation of an oral tradition about it—has been essential to child development ever since the emergence of language allowed stories to be told to express kinships with the land. Through such informal means, tens of thousands of generations of children have become ecologically literate about their home ground. They have gradually learned hundreds of specific guidelines and rules about how to respond to particular plants and animals—not only the ones with which they have frequent contact but the seldom seen, mythic ones as well. The qualities of firewood, the songs of birds, the identities of floral fragrances and mammalian musks all filtered into their consciousness.

This was what *environmental education* was like before indigenous children were pulled out of their homes to go to boarding schools in distant lands; before *environment* was partitioned off as a concern distinct from that of simply learning to live well with the "others" around you. *Story* had not yet been sequestered in books, nor had pertinent knowledge about the natural world been reduced to "facts" ritually presented only by the members of some scientific priesthood.

Southwest Indian storyteller Leslie Silko reminds us that considerable biological knowledge is embodied in oral narratives, for most land-based cultures perceive "the world and themselves within that world as part of a continuous story composed of innumerable bundles of stories.... Thus stories about the Creation and Emergence of human beings and animals into this world continue to be retold.... Accounts of the appearance of the first Europeans...were no more or less important than stories about the biggest mule deer ever taken, or adulterous couples surprised in cornfields and chicken coops."

Such stories were not merely intended for adult ears, nor were they turned into innocuous "fables" sanitized and simplified for the sake of children. Silko observes that "everyone, from the youngest child to the oldest person, was expected to listen and be able to recall or tell a portion, if only a small detail, from a narrative account or story. Thus the remembering and retelling were a communal process. Even if a key figure, an elder who knew much more than others, were to die unexpectedly, the system would remain intact."

When children encountered plants and animals with which they were unfamiliar, the stories informed them of the roles that these beings played in their culture. Unlike our own society's preoccupation with charismatic megafauna, such stories were not restricted to cuddly, big-eyed creatures and frightening predators. For instance, my Cahitan Indian neighbors still fill their oral literature with more than twenty-nine kinds of plants, thirteen invertebrates, eighteen birds, twenty-seven mammals, and fourteen kinds of fish, reptiles, and amphibians. Only a tenth of these nonhuman inhabitants of Mayo and Yaqui stories are domesticated—the tame livestock and cultivated crops that Cahitan speakers have tended. More than 90 percent of the characters in their stories, songs, and speeches are wild plants and wily or woolly creatures that predate agriculture as part of Yaqui existence in the *huya ania*, or "wilderness world."

Traditionally, certain metaphorical expressions in a native tongue depended on having a sense of those characters. To be lazy or lascivious like a coyote, to stand firm like a stalwart saguaro cactus, to be distant and uncontrollable like a mountain sheep—these qualities provided the metaphors for human behavior.

There are still many children in this world who live where they have primary contact with wild nature, who still hear the old stories, and who have uncles and grandfathers or grandmothers and aunts to guide them through their gender's rites of passage. Yet the percentage of children who have frequent exposure to wildlands and to other, undomesticated species is smaller than ever before in human history.

The traditions of animal stories and rites of initiation in the wild have no doubt declined in northern Europe, urban America, the Far East, and the Mediterranean over many generations. However, the rupture of such traditions has been far more rapid and severe in native North America, South America, Africa, and the Australian outback. Since World War II, television, formal classroom education, and urban migration have dramatically disrupted oral traditions and reduced most children's exposure to and involvement with other organisms. There has been a greater intergenerational atrophy of such traditions among indigenous peoples during the past three decades than ever before. Among the mountain tribes of Bolivia, children today cannot comprehend even a third of the natural history information encoded in their native tongue that anyone over forty-five years of age knows intimately. Their communities may suffer a time lag in understanding the consequences of this loss; but once their reservoirs of knowledge have been dissipated, it is increasingly hard to replenish them. Their culture of habitat is diminished.

Fundamental to this cultural loss is the phenomenon that Robert

Michael Pyle has termed "the extinction of experience," or the termination of direct, hands-on contact between children and wildlife. While many children may visit zoos, watch nature films, or cuddle with pets and stuffed animals, their responses to other species have become more "politically correct" but less grounded on their own visceral experiences.

Studies have demonstrated that this vicarious view of nature has developed among urban, suburban, and even some rural black and white children in many parts of the United States. I became curious to know whether such a devastating trend had yet reached into the rural cultures of the desert Southwest. After informally interviewing dozens of Mexican and Indian children during the winter and spring of 1992, I began to see that such trends were indeed evident among parts of the desert-dwelling populations of southern Arizona. But why, I wondered, had they become evident even among the children who lived in or near wild places, in communities where at least some of the elders still knew ancient stories and songs about animals and plants?

Concerned that profound shifts had begun in the way children were growing up in the desert, I decided to enlist the help of Sara St. Antoine in figuring out what was going on among the kids who seemed to be some of the most likely of any I had encountered to sustain their involvement with nature and ancient cultural traditions. I could not have found anyone better to help me with this task. Sara is an accomplished writer of children's novels and environmental education curricula. Her graduate work at the Yale School of Forestry and Environmental Studies had been under the guidance of Steve Kellert, who had pioneered "wildlife attitude" surveys among children and adults in five countries around the world. Sara had both a familiarity with this brand of environmental sociology and a great sensitivity to children of all colors and all ages.

Together, we interviewed another fifty-two Anglo, Hispanic, O'odham (Papago/Pima), and Yoeme (Yaqui/Cahitan) children during the summer of 1992, in towns such as Sonoyta, Ajo, Quitovac, and Marana. The majority lived in the desert beyond the reaches of big cities such as Tucson, in the shadows of two U.S. national parks and one Mexican protected zone. Although all of the children interviewed were between eight and fourteen years old and spoke either English or Spanish as their first language, many of the Indian children lived in households where their grandparents spoke a Native American language as well as a European one.

Sara and I were amazed at the range of environmental education opportunities available to most of the children we encountered, and were heartened by the depth of concern that many had for the conservation of endangered plants, wildlife, and habitat. Nearly all of them had visited national parks, zoos, outdoor natural history museums, or botanical gardens. Most had read books about plants and animals or had seen films about their increasing scarcity and their need for protection.

It was a relief to us that most of the children did claim some direct and pleasurable interaction with desert landscapes and their organisms—either through plant gathering, playful capture of small animals, or pursuit of larger ones. Nevertheless, the vast majority of the children whom we interviewed were now gaining most of their knowledge about other organisms vicariously. The trends were staggering: 77 percent of the Mexican kids, 61 percent of the Anglos, 60 percent of the Yaquis, and 35 percent of the O'odham kids felt that they had seen more animals on television and in movies than they had personally seen in the wild.

Sara said that the children we interviewed seemed to have as much or more access to wildlands and open spaces as any she had ever met. She guessed that the frequency of TV-dominated wildlife watchers would be even higher if we had included more urban dwellers in our samples. Yet despite *access* to open spaces, few of these children were spending much time alone in nature. When asked if they had ever spent even a half hour alone in a wild place, none of the Yaqui children, only 42 percent of the O'odham, 47 percent of the Anglos, and only 39 percent of the Mexican kids responded positively.

The kind of solitude in nature that had instilled a sense of wonder in many naturalists was shared by only a few of the kids interviewed. For a rare few, however, being out in the desert was not the same as being *alone*. A young girl from Ajo, Arizona, was confused by my question when I asked if she had ever been alone in the desert for more than a half hour's time.

"No...well, yes, maybe, well, what do you mean?" she asked me. "Do you mean when I'm completely alone?"

I was disoriented by her vacillation, until she mentioned that she loves to take a riding trail into the desert after school at least a couple of afternoons a week. "See, I ride out into the desert on my horse, and we stop to watch the sunset together.... I don't ever really feel alone, because my horse is there with me."

This made us curious about other activities that kids often do together in nature, such as the casual collection of feathers, bones, butterflies, and beautiful stones, not so much for study as for play. Such involvement with the details of the natural world often leads a child into later study of natural history. As the renowned paleontologist David Steadman once quipped, "every summer, my brothers and I would roam the woods and farmlands, turning over logs to see what was hiding there, catching turtles and picking up bones. Now, after twenty years in formal education, and three degrees, I am paid to do what was my first love as a child."

Again, we were surprised that a significant percentage of kids today were not collecting, carrying around, or keeping such natural treasures as nearly all children used to do. Thirty-five percent of the O'odham, 60 percent of the Yaqui, 44 percent of the Mexican, and 46 percent of the Anglo children have *never* been involved in such a pursuit. While some protectionists might be relieved that we found fewer children hunting or trapping animals and taking natural curiosities out of their habitats, this diminished hands-on involvement with nature is strongly correlated with diminished sensory and intellectual engagement with their surroundings.

What most disturbed us was the failure of many kids to know basic facts about the desert that can be learned only firsthand. Some of these failures would have been unimaginable a century ago: 55 percent of the Mexican kids didn't know you could eat prickly pear fruit, a food that has been a staple in northern Mexico for more than 8,000 years. Roughly a quarter of the Indian kids weren't sure whether the aromatic creosote bush known to them as "greasewood" smelled stronger after rains than cactus did, even though former generations of Indians claimed that creosote gave their homeland its distinctive smell. Nearly a fifth of all kids interviewed could not recall that desert birds sing more early in the morning than at midday. Perhaps these figures are not so unexpected, considering that more than 60 percent of the children we talked with say that they learn more about plants and animals at school than at home—in the communities we studied, "knowledge about nature" seems to be gained more through formal education than from personal observation.

Classroom, museum, and park education programs are not the problem; it's just that they simply cannot enrich kids who don't have much personal experience in nature on which to build. The kids who scored highest on factual questions in our survey invariably had informal interactions with desert plants and animals that whetted their curiosity for classroom and museum studies. A good teacher or nature guide can nurture such incipient naturalists, but they can seldom create them from scratch.

On another level, I have become concerned that formal education unintentionally encourages children to discount what can be learned at home, especially when traditional knowledge about the desert is juxtaposed with that presented in texts by authoritative science experts. Most of the desert children we talked to claimed that they had learned more about plants and animals from school than their grandparents had learned their entire lives. Why? Perhaps most of the students knew that their grandparents had not finished as many years in school as they or their teachers had, so they were obviously not as "smart." I was especially saddened to learn that 58 percent of the O'odham and 60 percent of the Yaqui kids felt this way, because their grandparents have taught me the most valuable information I know about the desert.

Sara noticed that only 38 percent of the Anglo-American children felt they knew more about the plants and animals than their parents and grandparents did! A higher percentage of these Anglo relatives had completed their formal education, so the children probably perceived that their parents or grandparents "knew more" because of that. Sara reasoned that perhaps there has not been such a large intergenerational difference in Anglo education as there has been for Indians. Still, I was most struck by the fact that the detailed knowledge of the plants and animals held by Indian elders was not considered valuable

exactly because it was *not* book learning! It was as though our society's high regard for zoological or botanical "facts" derived from lab
experiments, books, and science films has invalidated knowledge
learned by other means.

Worse yet, the current preoccupation with printed and electronic
media has all but replaced the time that children would otherwise
spend listening to what their grandparents have to tell them. Roughly
half of the children learn more about the desert flora and wildlife from
books than from their elders. Alvron, a Mexican-American boy from
a small Arizona town, shrugged when asked whether his family or his
books were the primary source of what he knew about animals. His
answer to Sara's probing was immediate: "Neither. The Discovery
Channel!" Except for the children in the poorest, most remote desert
communities, nearly all the kids I talked with spent more time after
school watching TV than playing outside or listening to stories from
their elders.

Some might argue that if the "ultimate message" of various kinds
of instruction is the same—in this case, respect for nature—then it
makes little difference whether children get the message via television, books, museum exhibits, stories from elders, or personal encounters. Native American educators Ernie Lennie and Barbara Smith,
however, have taken issue with this claim. When interviewed by Jerry
Mander, Lennie remarked that "the type of learning we get in school
and also on TV is the type where we just sit and absorb. But in family life…learning has to come from doing." The traditional means of
learning his community's "fund of knowledge" were active, not passive.

Lennie may be correct that "just sitting and absorbing" in front of
a book or "electronic screen image" is neither as interactive nor as
healthy as other means of learning. Among Eskimo communities living to the north of Lennie's Canadian homeland, myopia (nearsight-
edness) became commonplace within the first generation exposed to
books and audiovisual media in the schools. Eskimo children were
seldom diagnosed for myopia earlier in this century, even though it
is now suspected that they have a genetic predisposition to this eye
condition. Yet when Eskimo children took to staring at books and
TV sets, myopia increased to the point at which it affected more than

half of all school-age children. No longer exercising their eyesight to read the rich and subtle landscapes of the north country, they did not receive the visual stimuli required to develop their eyes fully during the critical stages of their early development. It is a sad irony of formal education that it may make many native people "shortsighted" within a matter of years.

It is not merely that TV screens are bad for you. As Barbara Smith observed, there is something that makes narrative stories from elders particularly effective for transmitting values as well as knowledge regarding the natural world: "Legends are tools that help people grow in certain ways. A lot of what matters is the power and the feeling of the experience," she concluded, having absorbed Diné legends from her elders in Canada's Northwest Territories. "But when you find something in a museum, or even on TV, you can see it all right, but you're really looking only at the shell."

Yaqui Indian educator Felipe Molina also feels that values can be taught through traditional stories in ways that today's school science classes cannot teach them. "We might learn about plants in science," Felipe told Sara outside his home in Yoeme village. "When I was in school, we learned how to name their parts or how they grow, but we never went the next step, which was to talk about how to *care* for them." This added dimension is one that Yaqui lore could offer to children at home, or even in the schools if the elders were brought in to tell the stories. However, until recently, Felipe has observed that Yaqui parables have never been "uplifted" or given credence in the schools.

Such realizations are not unique to Native Americans. Halfway around the world, a great Italian novelist and naturalist grew up in a world where his father taught him that each tree and each bird has a story to tell. Italo Calvino once wrote that "new knowledge does not compensate for the knowledge spread only by direct oral transmission, which, once lost, cannot be regained or retransmitted: no book can teach what can be learned only in childhood if you lend an alert ear and eye to the song and flight of birds or if you find someone who knows how to give them a specific name."

Our world today is one in which we are losing ways of speaking about plants and animals as rapidly as we are losing endangered species themselves. Oral traditions about plants, animals, treacherous waters, and complex topography depend on specific vocabularies, for these vocabularies encode particularities that may not be recognized in the lexicons of commonly spoken, widespread languages. Half of the 200 native languages in North America will soon die as the last elder speakers fall silent, and then thousands of Indian children will have forfeited the chance to speak of their plant and animal neighbors in ways filled with the nuances and feeling that characterized their forefathers' speech.

Native American poet-linguist Nora Dauenhauer has reminded us that language extinction is "forever" just as much as the loss of species is irrevocable: "If a Native American language dies, there is no place on earth one can travel to learn it. The public statements that some school administrators continue to make in opposition to teaching native languages would not be tolerated if made about some endangered species of bird or snail."

Sara and I wondered if even the most rudimentary knowledge about common plants and animals was still being orally transmitted to O'odham and Yaqui children through their aboriginal language. She pasted together a picture book of desert plants and animals, which we first showed to the Yaqui and O'odham children and then to their grandparents. We simply asked them to name in their native dialect the various organisms illustrated in the makeshift booklet.

Most of the children to whom we showed the booklet bowed out before naming even a single creature in their forefathers' tongue: they had not grown up speaking anything but English or Spanish, or in a few cases, they were too shy to speak their native tongue in front of strangers. But of the dozen children who did try to name the 17 native species shown in the drawings, they averaged only 4.6 correct names. In contrast, their grandparents averaged 15.1 native names for the 17 drawings. The younger generation knew fewer than a third of the plant and animal names that their elders knew and even less of the lore associated with those names and the organisms they represented.

It was not just the children who knew little of their native language; most of their parents under forty had the same difficulty remembering plant and animal names. The ones who had known me from earlier visits with the elders remembered that I had spoken some

O'odham in past discussions; when a name escaped both the children and the young parents, they would ask *me* to remind them of the native term. Even though I had never gained more than rudimentary knowledge of O'odham terms for crops and wildlife—perhaps no more than a five-year-old might have known a century ago—it dawned on me that Indians my own age today didn't necessarily know any more of these native terms than I did.

But why should they? Despite the vestiges of traditional instruction persisting among many Native American communities, Indians of my own generation have been barraged by the same messages from television, radio, schoolbooks, and federally mandated classroom curricula as I have been. We were all brought up with the "news" from the outside world that the traditional knowledge of our own families and cultures was not worth that much; if the words that our relatives used for certain birds, weeds, or foods were not in a dictionary, they probably didn't matter.

Nevertheless, part of what once made my O'odham- and Cahitan-speaking neighbors unique is that both their food and their stories were derived from the desert. No wonder the Tohono O'odham tribe of southern Arizona refers to itself in English simply as "the Desert People"; their very blood, muscles, and minds were made out of molecules from desert seeds, desert meat, desert earth. Today, however, their molecules have nearly the same elements in them as mine: beef from Monfort's feedlots in Colorado; winter apples shipped from Puerto Montt in Chile; potatoes mass-produced by a Mormon millionaire in Idaho.

The plants and animals on which the O'odham once depended are now increasingly out of sight and out of mind. Robert Michael Pyle has spoken of the "cycle of disaffection" that is triggered by the extinction of experience: "as cities and metastasizing suburbs forsake their natural diversity, and their citizens grow more removed from personal contact with nature, awareness and appreciation retreat. This breeds apathy toward environmental concerns and, inevitably, further degradation of common habitat...[leading to] the total loss of rarities. People who care, conserve; people who don't know, don't care. What is the extinction of the condor to a child who has never seen a wren?"

If fables about animals are forgotten, it does not necessarily follow that the animals themselves cease to exist. Nevertheless, as floral and faunal narratives play less of a role in keeping us alert to the fate of other biota, we are more likely to let their existence slip through our fingers without ever noticing the loss.

What can be done to break this vicious cycle of disaffection? As Sara and I drove back from our interviews with the children of Quitovac, Ajo, Marana, and Sonoyta, we deliberated on this dilemma.

Would better funding for environmental education programs in outdoor museums and parks solve the problem? Certainly, such programs, which remain miserably underfunded, are valuable, for they move children beyond the classroom. At the same time, making them bigger will not always make them better. The public gardens and zoos that pump tens of thousands of students down their trails do not always satisfy the thirst for intimate contact. Neither do the computer games and video libraries filled with science and nature themes. And yet, the finest environmental educators I know despair that their own best efforts are being spread too far, too thin. They may pique a child's curiosity for a moment, but they are seldom given the chance to offer deeper follow-through.

Near the end of our summer with the desert children, Sara finally framed the situation in this way: "Formal education programs cannot make up for, and should not try to replace, the spontaneous hands-on experience of nature nor the richness of intergenerational storytelling." Instead, we agreed, they should incorporate such elements of traditional learning about nature into their programs so that the amount of time formerly dedicated to such activities is not further usurped.

Some of these traditional activities are easy for schools, nature centers, and museums to absorb and sponsor; others are not. Sara and I identified three key strategies for staving off the extinction of experience: intimate involvement with plants and animals; direct exposure to a variety of wild animals carrying out their routine behaviors in natural habitats; and teaching by community elders (indigenous or otherwise) about their knowledge of the local biota.

Psychiatrist Aaron Katcher has pioneered "therapy through companion animals" in Pennsylvania schools dedicated to children with learning disabilities such as autism and hyperactivity. He has documented that "dogs, cats, turtles and dolphins have produced speech in autistic children"; that five hours of contact with pets each day "decreased aggression, while increasing peer cooperation and acceptance of responsibility" in children with chronically deficient attention spans.

In discussing the benefits and limitations of so-called "animal therapy," Katcher is candid; some of the children revert to their former behavior as soon as they are removed from contact with the school's animals and are taken home to settings where other animals are absent. Katcher is among the scholars who do not believe that manageable, domesticated pets are a panacea: "Our responses to pets may be clues to our needs for other, more differentiated animals." Unlike those of most pet-therapy promoters, Katcher's programs provide children with time for birdwatching, fishing, and exposure to untamed or wild animals. Katcher told me that once the kids have been given frequent access to animals, the same behavior changes occur time and time again: "The kids who have the opportunity to visit these animals begin to do so spontaneously. When that happens, their learning skills go up and their disruptive behavior decreases."

We need not try to do what television often does, which is to set up the assumption that we can achieve immediate intimacy with all animals, even when this simply is not possible in the field. We need not pretend we are bosom buddies with aloof predators or shower all our appreciation on the rare raptor or hyperintelligent cetacean. Real attention given to a covey of quail, a swarm of termites, or a litter of pack rats will do for most kids I know.

Peggy Turk-Boyer, who runs the Center for the Study of Deserts and Oceans in northern Mexico, elicits more sustained engagement from students in a tide pool rich in invertebrates than she can with a school of surf-breaking dolphins. "Small creatures that stay within reach can capture their attention for hours," she has observed, "while their contact with whales or dolphins can only be fleeting." Similarly, I have watched children in Mexico entranced by the industriousness of leaf-cutter ants. (I too could watch these fungus farmers for hours on end without tiring.)

I recall taking my two- and four-year-old ruffians to a zoo once;

this experience cured me of my assumptions about what would impress them. While I tried to steer them toward tapirs and gators—uncaged but on the other side of ten-foot-wide moats—they spent their time feeding ground squirrels that had "broke into the zoo" to take advantage of the tons of squandered feed. After a while, they discovered one ground squirrel that kept a cache of food under the sidewalk leading toward the "exotic wildlife" area; we sat down and spent the rest of the afternoon on the trailside, watching the squirrel emerge from beneath the sidewalk to pounce on spilled popcorn. No nametag in Latin, no interpretative message about his role in the "chain of life" was needed for this creature to capture the attention and hearts of my escorts for hours.

Once children have seen the behavior of a variety of animals in their natural contexts, it is easier to engage them in balanced discussions of the values, ethics, and spiritual responses of humans to the non-human world. They tend not to dismiss all predators as evil killers, all scavengers as uncouth, all wide-eyed furry herbivores as benign. Such stereotypes tell us more about ourselves than about the animals around us.

In a Salish tale told by tribal storyteller Johnny Moses, we learn that "long ago, the trees thought they were people, long ago, the animals thought they were people." Then he adds, "Someday, they will say...long ago, the human beings thought they were people."

Tohono O'odham Nation education director Rosilda Manual once said to me, "For a long time, whenever I heard someone talking about environmental education, I thought they were just wanting to upgrade science education about the environment. Then last year, I realized that environmental education can be *cultural* education too. I was fortunate to grow up with a grandfather who taught me to respect other ways of life—those of animals, plants, whites, blacks, other Indians. He taught me that we have a special way of looking at the world, but others do as well."

While an O'odham Indian grandfather was Rosilda's mentor, the abolitionist Harriet Tubman has served as Kamau Kambui's guide to the world of diversity and human dignity. Trained in social work, therapeutic recreation, and Outward Bound leadership skills,

Kambui developed the Underground Railroad reenactment at Wilder Forest in Minnesota in 1986. In the years since, various forest staff members have played the role of Harriet Tubman, who guides the inner-city black, white, or Native American youth who are willing to experience what it feels like to escape slavery by a passage through unknown wilderness.

"The reenactments are as authentic as possible," Kambui claims, rather than glossy, historic dramas. "Superman is make-believe," Kambui says to the kids as they decide whether or not they'll go out into the woods after dark, "but Harriet Tubman is real."

The Wilder Forest staff has transformed the traditional nature walk into something far richer emotionally: "Dogs howl in pursuit; chains rattle as slave catchers close in; and fear spurs the footsteps of slaves as they thrash through the dark forest in desperate attempts to reach freedom."

The guidance of Harriet Tubman helps pull them through. She first escaped the bonds of slavery in 1849, traveling at night from Maryland to Pennsylvania, using only the North Star and her own cunning as guides. She later made eighteen trips into the South to help more than 300 African slaves find food, shelter, and medicine in the wilderness on their way to freedom. Now, the example of her work is reminding urban African Americans and other people that wilderness is part of their legacy; that the skills of gaining an orientation in the world, of knowing how to feed, shelter, and protect yourself from danger are skills needed in both urban and rural settings.

Daniel Pablo, a high school student at Indian Oasis on the Tohono O'odham reservation, is a youthful preserver of nature and culture. I have known Daniel since he was four, when I would visit his grandfather Delores Lewis, one of the hardest-working and most knowledgeable farmers in the O'odham community. As Delores and I would walk to his floodwater-fed field in the desert over a decade ago, Daniel was already following in his grandfather's footsteps, literally and figuratively. When I kid Daniel about this now, he laughs and explains, "Wherever he went, I used to follow him around. They called me the Shadow. I thought I was following him to get out of my parents' way.

Actually, what I was doing was learning how to plant seeds, how to take care of plants. This is how I learned."

In July of 1992, when the first gathering of the Traditional Native American Farmers Association was convened in Gallup, New Mexico, Daniel had the honor of being the youngest farmer present. His grandfather Delores Lewis was also present, traveling beyond the Sonoran Desert for the first time in his life. After Delores gave a blessing in O'odham, Daniel was among those who explained how he came to farming:

One time I was playing with my cousins. My cousins asked, "Where's Grandpa?"

"He's probably out in the field," I said. "Do you want to go see him?"

"Yeah, let's go see him." So we went, and sure enough, he was sitting under a mesquite tree. He was getting his seeds together, getting ready to plant them.

There were three of us. Next thing you know, Grandpa said, "Line up. Line up!"

He gave one of us kids a hoe, one the seeds, and another the shovel. "All right, start walking. Take two steps and dig a hole. Take two more steps, and dig a hole. And you follow him and put three seeds in the hole. The next hole, next hole. You go along with the shovel, and bury it up, bury it up!"

So he put us all to work, and I thought it was fun. I guess my cousins didn't really take an interest in it. So they figured out they better not go to see Grandpa or he would put us to work.

I used to think my grandpa was a real brave guy (I still do!). When the monsoons come to Arizona, there's lots of lightning with the storms. Sometimes when it rained, I would see my grandpa with his metal shovel on his shoulder walking into the fields when it was still raining...and making lightning! He would go out there and direct the water, or fix one of his dams if it was broke. He taught me how to do that—how to irrigate, how to have water sit in one area and soak in. He taught me lots of different things about how to harvest and thresh various crops....

I didn't really plant for myself when I was young. But when I turned ten, my father gave me a little plot of my own. He went ahead and tilled the ground, really working at it. He got my cousins out there working on it with us for a long time. All day. The time finally came to bring in our harvest: corn, beans, squash, melon. I was pretty proud to see it, and my father was proud to see it.

Two years ago, he passed away. I was isolated for a while, and I didn't know when to plant—my father had always helped me, making sure that I planted at the right time. The ground had turned hard, so I didn't plant that first year, the year he passed away.

The next year, I went out and started planting. I used my hoe and shovel to turn the ground over, and I put my seeds in the ground.

About that time, a traditional dance group formed, the Cultural Exchange Youth Dance Group, set up by Save the Children on our reservation. They asked me if I wanted to join because they'd be taking a trip to Philadelphia, Mississippi, as an exchange with another Indian community, and they needed some dancers. I said, "Sure, I'll go."

I had already told them that I would go along when I realized that no one would be there to take care of my plants. My younger brothers aren't really interested in the garden. I didn't think my mother and grandparents would be able to watch over my garden.

So the time came for me to go. Where I live, the ground is dry and everything is a dull brown color. But when I got over there to Mississippi, I saw *all these trees*—always green and always wet. I wished it could be like that at home.

Then, one of our chaperons called home—and learned that it was raining! It had started raining when we left, and it hadn't stopped yet, two weeks later!

When I got back home, it was dark, too dark to look around. In the morning, I finally got to look around outside and saw green all over! Hey, my wish came true!

Daniel paused here for a moment, looking over at his grandparents, Delores and Margaret, who chuckled, then shifted their glances downward, as if focusing on the garden scene Daniel was describing.

"Grasses covered the ground, the trees were all green! I ran outside—around back to my garden—and looked. My corn was *big*—tall corn! My squash was *really big!*" Then he doubled over, laughing uncontrollably. "The other thing that was really big was the weed cover—*lots of weeds.*

"I was looking around, thinking it was good to be home. I had thought that my garden wasn't going to come out very good...but I was wrong. I guess my father—who had taught me how to do it—was still watching over my garden. I never really said this to anybody before..." His voice cracked, and he looked down at the floor, the earth, just as his grandparents had, "but I think that every time I go out to the garden, he's still watching over it."

Everyone in the room let the silence linger, let the tears fall where they would. Daniel looked up again, finally. "I'm thankful for what he taught me, and I'm thankful that my grandfather is still here to teach me even more."

When I go out to the desert village of Big Fields and see Daniel working with his rototiller or helping his grandfather with the harvest of crops and wild foods, I feel relieved that the generations can still *regenerate* agriculture, culture, and story. But to do so, they must work together at it, keeping the land in front of them and the background noise of television out of earshot. Ironically, it was during a filming of an O'odham garden for Phoenix television that such a connection between cause and effect first entered my consciousness.

I had been asked to introduce a Phoenix filming team to the famous O'odham educator Laura Kerman, who for years has taught Indian, Anglo, and Mexican children about desert gardening and gathering traditions in school, park, and museum settings. Laura sometimes had difficulty hearing and getting around—she was in her late eighties by that time—so I decided to go along with the filming team in case Laura requested any assistance.

When it came time to turn the cameras on, the bouncy blonde news celebrity, Jan d'Atri, appeared out of the remote broadcasting van, wearing fresh make-up and looking for a picturesque setting in which to situate Laura, who had her gray hair tied back with a big ribbon, and a lovely old full-length skirt on. Jan instantly decided that they should not sit down but should stroll around the garden that Laura and her brother have tended for decades.

"You'll have to hold onto my arm, then, and help me walk," Laura cautioned, "and make sure you say things loud enough for me to hear." Jan shot a worried glance at the film crew, but as the two women began to walk arm and arm, Laura's teetering did not appear too awkward. The cameras began to roll.

"Well, Laura, you and the other elders out here on the reservation have made your living from the desert for a long time, gardening and gathering wild plants," Jan's scripted speech went. "Tell me, why do you think the younger generation is not keeping up these traditions?"

Laura listened, stopped dead in her tracks, let go of Jan's arm, and pointed straight at the camera, frowning. *"It's that TV!* They're all watching *that TV!* They just sit around in front of it, they hardly go outside anymore, so how can they plow or plant or gather the fruit? That's the problem, *right there!"*

Making Places Close to Home
Where the Soul Can Fly

*Finally, the deceased dies a second death in the underworld,
and becomes a butterfly, bereft of human memories. As the dead
drift inexorably away from living toward butterfly-hood,
they become increasingly inaccessible and unknowable.*
PIERS VITEBSKY, "Dialogues with the Dead"
(on the shamanistic beliefs of the Sora tribe of India)

One morning not long after my father's funeral and burial, I awoke from a nightmare in which I found myself on the kindergarten playground where I had first learned to swing, wrestle, and flirt twenty years before. The image reminded me of how bleak that playground had been compared to our own backyard in the Indiana Dunes, where I grew up among peach trees, burr oaks, marram grasses, butter-and-eggs blossoms, dragonflies, and cardinals. In my dream, I was running on the barren cinders of the bulldozer-leveled schoolyard with a mob of cousins and brothers, across a space devoid of any plant life larger than a tumbleweed. At first, I could not see what we were running toward.

Then I saw it: a butterfly, spreading its wings to dry. It had recently emerged from a cocoon. Its tranquillity held my attention for a second, and then I realized that all fourteen of my kin were recklessly careening toward the spot where the butterfly was sunning itself. One

of my cousins spotted the butterfly. "Smear the queer," he yelled, referring to the neighborhood game that was an inverted version of king-
on-the-mountain: we'd chase a vulnerable soul, gang-tackle him, then
the entire mob would jump on top of him.

Just before two of my cousins smashed the butterfly into the cinders, I dodged between them, lunged, and cupped my body over the
butterfly. My cousins and brother all leapt onto my back, making a
perfect pile. They tumbled off just as quickly, romping away to chase
one another. The butterfly glided a few feet and landed on the bars of
a jungle gym. I slowly got up and brushed myself off. I noticed that
my older brother Norman had not run off with the rest.

"Why did you keep us from smushing that butterfly?" Norm asked,
frowning, as if I had spoiled the game. I nodded for him to come with
me. I scooped the butterfly off the metal bar, holding it for a moment
in my hands.

"It's Dad," I whispered to him matter-of-factly. Norm shot a star-
tled glance at me. "It's his time to fly away from us. I needed to protect him so that we could let him go."

And we did.

Another twenty years passed before I fathomed how this dream-
sighting of a butterfly on my kindergarten playground had offered
me a means of making peace with the spirit of my father. I was in
Oklahoma, among a group of scholars, all old friends, who were discussing certain flowers and insects that metaphorically bind together
the cosmos for the Tarahumara Indians. Among our group were
Enrique Salmon, an anthropologist of Tarahumara descent, and Bob
Bye, a forester and botanist by training, who had learned much from
Tarahumara families while living with them for three years in a
rancheria in Chihuahua. I was enjoying the cadence of my friends'
give-and-take but not fully listening, until one of them mentioned
something that reminded me of that playground dream: "Among the
Tarahumara, the soul is said to metamorphose into a butterfly."

Enrique then wondered why it was that butterfly and flower
imagery seemed so pervasive among the songs and stories of Uto-
Aztecan cultures like the Tarahumara and Yaqui. Bob could not tell
him why exactly, but he agreed: "You're right, the butterfly is a man-

ifestation of the soul not only among the Tarahumara but all the way down to Central Mexico, among Nahuatl speakers there. It's even in prehistoric Aztec imagery on sculptures, and it's in the Florentine Codices of New Spain."

"How *odd*," I blurted out. Bob and Enrique glanced over at me, wondering *what* was odd. "I've never read nor heard anything of that metaphor, but when my father died, I dreamed he went away from us as a butterfly."

Bob flashed a look of empathy in my direction, and then admitted, "And after my father-in-law passed away a few years ago, he appeared to me as a butterfly in my dreams."

"*Tso'api*," Kay Fowler chuckled; she is a fine linguist who has worked for decades among the Paiute and Shoshone of the Great Basin. "It's a Northern Paiute term, polysemous for butterfly and for transmutated soul, used by all the people from Pyramid Lake in the north down to Mono Lake and Owens Valley."

"I usually don't discuss such things," Walter Lewis said quietly. We turned to the corner of the room where Walter was sitting. The elder among us, Walter had become famous in some circles for his discovery of potential AIDS treatments derived from rain-forest plants in South America. He began again, with considerable hesitation, "I usually don't discuss such things, but a Jívaro herbalist made a comment to me once that I have never forgotten. And I thought it was unique to his people: when the soul goes to its third and final resting place—where everything is tranquil, after everything has been achieved—it is as a blue morpho butterfly."

We sat in silence, trying to reconcile in our minds and hearts how scientists of such varied training could all have stumbled independently on the same metaphor for the metamorphosis of the soul, one that was evidently vital to so many peoples scattered so widely across the Americas.

Had Carl Jung and Joseph Campbell been among us in that room, they might have argued that many of the same animals appear in the myths of the world's 6,500 cultures, for such archetypes are deeply embedded in our collective subconscious. But there is another explanation, which E. O. Wilson asked a number of biologists to consider when he brought us together at Wood's Hole several years ago to test his "biophilia hypothesis." Wilson asked us to evaluate available evidence that humans have a genetically programmed affinity with other life-forms—or at least, an intrinsic need for periodic contact with living elements of the other-than-human world. At Wood's Hole, we reviewed experiments demonstrating that people from all corners of the planet have adverse physiological responses to sudden sightings of snakes, even when they have never personally seen one in the wild or even when they have come from countries where snakes do not naturally occur. In fact, the appearance of a snake produced greater changes in blood pressure and heart rate for a longer period of time than did images of knives, pistols, or automobile accidents—all of which take more lives today than do venomous serpents. These experiments documented a hard-wired *biophobia* to snakes; evidence of cross-cultural *biophilia*, however, seems much harder to come by, at least in this day and age.

Could we have a genetically based affinity for butterflies, which are the most salient demonstrations of metamorphosis present in the environments where humans have evolved? If genetically encoded, does the expression of this image require an environmental trigger? Could the archetype remain latent, within our subconscious mind, until some element in our immediate environment calls it forth?

Perhaps there was some luminous moment when, as a child, I had deeply experienced the presence of a butterfly; the trauma of my father's death then brought that moment of tranquillity and wonder back to me, helping me to feel connected to the larger world at a time of immediate loss. That so many other cultures have gained solace in the presence of butterflies is perhaps not surprising; these ubiquitous creatures undoubtedly capture the imagination of any child who comes upon them, from the rain forests of Peru to the austere sagebrush steppe around Pyramid Lake.

There are many people living today who have never had a butterfly speak to them, who have passed through childhood without having ever been enchanted by monarch or morpho fluttering across their path. I might easily have become one of those lepidoptera-free dreamers if my childhood contact with the natural world had been restricted to the playgrounds and lawns of Gary, Indiana, and if remnant patches of the Indiana Dunes had not persisted just a somersault away from my family's back door.

But butterflies were the only animals other than earthworms that I can remember from the thousands of hours I spent on the William A. Wirt school grounds. The playgrounds of the Gary public school system were designed to have the landscape value of battlefields—no life other than humans was welcome in those war zones.

The school playgrounds of the Gary public schools mirrored the mill yards in which many of my schoolmates and I were destined to work when we became adults. The swings were hung on heavy metal chains from oversized stainless-steel scaffolding, cold and unmalleable to the kindergartner's touch. The giant slides were wide and sturdy enough to hold a 200-pound millworker. The cinder surface of the playground may have come from crushed pig iron, a by-product brought in from the nearby mills and foundries where our fathers and uncles worked. I don't remember any trees or flowers. The city itself had the same impersonal rigidity; it was a failure as a planned community that had been touted "the City of the Century" when founded by U.S. Steel in 1906. In less than a century's time, many of its neatly gridded streets and tract houses had fallen into complete ruin.

We've all experienced such overplanned, barren, out-of-scale places that seem to squelch life rather than nurture it. And even now, when playground equipment has become less intimidating and more inter-active, safety-conscious, and resilient, most of it still lacks life. Roben Stikeman of the Evergreen Foundation in Toronto minces no words when she describes the norm for schoolyards in most countries: "Typ-ically, in Canada as well as in other countries around the world, school grounds are usually asphalted, or covered with pounded turfgrass and surrounded by chain-link fencing. These school grounds not only are aesthetically displeasing but also a wasted resource in our education."

Some urban school grounds are now designed by landscape archi-tects to have narrow corridors of saplings or bedding plants along the sidewalks leading to the principal's office or to the teachers' lounge. Do these formal designs attract and sustain the imaginations of chil-dren? Do they entice butterflies and caterpillars? Hardly ever. Should we give credit to school planners who spare the largest, loveliest tree on a site, bulldozing everything else away, when that one tree's canopy must span the daydreams of 500 to 800 schoolchildren each season?

Even when schoolyard landscapers invest heavily in drip-irrigated, low-maintenance landscaping, the composition of their shrubbery remains cut off from qualities of the nearest natural habitats. In fact, such overly manicured, formal designs are not habitats at all, in the sense that other life-forms—wildflower, swallow, hawk moth, gecko—might settle down in them. Nor are they habitats for children, who are hardly stimulated by neat rows of lollipop-looking trees. Schoolyard critics April Baisan and Lauri Johnson of the University of Arizona have asked, "Who 'owns' the site emotionally? Do the kids own it? Do the teachers own it? Does the community feel any ownership over it?" We might also ask, do other life-forms settle in as if it were theirs? It is as if the mere presence of open ground has been the only feature taken into account when attempting to provide children with opportunities for "recreation." But can such "re-creation" occur when children are kept out of touch with the rest of creation?

Fortunately, there is a growing movement of teachers, parents, and most importantly, *children*, who are involved in "naturalizing" schoolyard habitats. More than forty federal, state, and international programs now assist or sponsor schools in their protection of remnant natural habitats, their ecological restoration of degraded areas, or their development of play areas and nature study sites replete with native plants. More than half of these programs specifically list the return of butterflies to schoolyards as one of their goals. Roben Stikeman, who has visited many of the "Learning Grounds" habitats sponsored by the Evergreen Foundation, is delighted to see how many species of animals reinhabit schoolyards once sufficient native vegetative cover has been planted. "It's the unanticipated return of nature," she says. "Biodiversity to some degree is increased on these sites.... By the very act of increasing plant species, you [usher in] the return of insects, birds, and small mammals."

The most important return she has documented is that of the students themselves. In junior high and high schools across the continent, students have become involved in planning schoolyard naturalizations, in researching what native vegetation once grew where their school was built, and in planting trees, wildflowers, and native grasses in newly prepared soil. They then nurse the plantings along, sometimes forming vacation-time work crews to make sure the plants don't die during the summer heat or creating vigilante groups to keep gangs from trashing them. Stikeman has confirmed that truancy rates drop significantly where teenagers are involved in such schoolyard projects. And they spend their time doing more than just "defending turf"; there are gourds to gather, plums to pick, swallowtails to follow.

A quarter century after Nancy Foote began an outdoor classroom habitat planting at Mount Stuart Elementary School in Ellensberg, Washington, she found that the "children" still come back to see the trees they planted when they were in fifth grade. At the time Nancy began the restoration of *Che-lo-han*—"Gathering Place" in the local Yakima dialect—it was hardly more than a "plain grass pasture" next to a dairy, largely devoid of wildlife. Today, it has both native deciduous and coniferous trees forming a forest canopy. Its open pond has gone through several successive stages, as its aquatic life has blended with that of an adjacent wetland where ducks, muskrats, and frogs are commonly seen.

Nancy began by talking to the kids about what they'd like to have in the pasture. "They decided to have indigenous plants—ones that were growing in the area for centuries but are gone now, or ones that are being lost. They planted some of these on a mound that the fifth graders themselves built by bringing from home milk cartons filled with dirt and sand. On Mound Day, all the little kids would ceremoniously take the soil they had scooped up in their milk cartons and pour it out wherever they wanted to shape the mound. Later, we would have ritual plantings of each tree and shrub that was donated to us. The goal was more than teaching the mechanics of planting; we were *building memories*, as far as I was concerned."

The fifth graders were gradually building *habitat* as well as memories. This habitat has passed through several transitions, with animal populations shifting as the vegetation matured.

"I went out there late one summer before the school year began again, and I couldn't believe all the butterflies that were there," Nancy Foote recounts. "They had absolutely increased over the years, filling the air in a place where there was nothing for them at the start of the project. We had held onto any volunteering milkweeds for the monarchs and had attracted in a number of swallowtails."

Nancy Foote allowed a menagerie of animals and plants to become part of her students' memories. Few other schools are as far along in creating such multiple-species gathering places, but some have begun the process. The task is to make playspaces habitable again, not only for our children but for other creatures as well: the sulfur butterflies, the ruby-throated hummingbirds, the feathery pods of a vagrant milkweed or cattail. In this way the creatures of the imagination will also begin to thrive. If we can't accomplish this task, future generations may not have the chance of dreaming that their deceased elders have metamorphosed into other lives.

Growing Up Othered

An Arab-American Childhood

*Feelings crowd in on me; maybe this is what it means to be
in your genetic home. That you will feel on fifty levels at once,
the immediate as well as the level of blood, the level of uncles, of
weeping in the pillow at night, weddings and graves, the babies
who didn't make it, level of the secret and unseen. Maybe this is
heritage, that deep well that gives us more than we deserve.*
NAOMI SHIHAB NYE, "One Village," *Never in a Hurry*

I squinted. Everything was far too bright. White walls, white ceilings, and a chorus of white-haired boys. The choirmaster called us "little cherub sopranos with tiny angelic voices." When I looked around, I could see how all the others could indeed be angels in training. But I didn't feel like one: I didn't look like one. I didn't realize it at the time, but I was the lone Arab-American boy floating in a blond sea of Swedish and German Lutherans.

I was about five at the time. I had been to Bethel Lutheran Church many times before but always with my father and mother, aunts and uncles, who had other olive-skinned curly-haired children in tow. This time my mother had simply dropped me off so that I could sing with the boys' choir. By the time I arrived in the church basement, a dozen blond boys were already jumping up and down, swinging around the posts, and talking as if they already knew one another. I had seen some of them before, but I didn't know their names. None of my Nabhan cousins were in sight.

I wandered over to a wall where there were pictures of all the Bethel Lutheran Church confirmation classes going back to the thirties. I gravitated to the very first one. It looked overexposed. All blonds. The same with the next. And the next. I looked at the names below the photos that I would first hear and later read many times over the following years: Lindstrom, Anderson, Ahlgren, Dreher, Sederstrom, Stromburg.

Then I came to one from the late thirties that had NABHAN written under it. Theodore Nabhan, as I would later learn. I could not decipher the letters at the time, but I knew what our last name looked like, and I knew the picture included my father when he was young.

I looked up at the photo. It was full of tall, bright-faced straight-haired towheads, with one exception. A shadowy spot in the corner: some dark angel, perhaps. So black was his hair, so dark was his skin that I now see how the photographer could not set the camera exposure to capture all the details of the other children and my father as well. His face looked underdeveloped, more like a shadow than a fact.

Perhaps that was the first time I felt "different." Would I look as different in the boy's choir photo as my father did in that confirmation snapshot? Probably not. My mother was Irish and something else, not Syrian or Lebanese, or A-rab, as my father's family alternatively called themselves. My skin was not as dark as his, my hair not as shiny. His always had a sheen to it, like my baseball glove after I rubbed olive oil into it.

The Swedes I knew treated their mitts with saddle soap, not olive oil, but my family put olive oil in and on everything. We doused the wooden salad bowl with olive oil, lemon juice, and fresh mint. We shaped a depression in the top of the hummus, and poured a shallow puddle of olive oil into it, sometimes sprinkling *simmaq* or another spice on top. My father's family sometimes ate their bread with oil instead of butter. I even wondered whether the men greased back their hair with it. Olive oil lubricated the Nabhan clan's lives.

Was there olive oil in the houses surrounding ours? It was proba-

bly in some—but not in all of them. I knew it was in the Sicilian
woman's home next to ours. She was the plump little lady with swollen
ankles who would make deep-dish pizza whenever our parents went
out for the night. Her English was poor, but I never minded that: she
could fill our entire kitchen with the aromas of rosemary and oregano
as her pizzas baked in our oven. Olive oil was also in the Greek lady's
house on the other side. She, like all my aunts, made heavenly baklava.
The towheaded Swedish boys may have looked like angels in the sto-
rybooks, but the Mediterranean family kitchens in our neighborhood
prepared the foods that all the dark angels must have eaten in heaven.

Other families in our neighborhood did not inundate their lives
with downpours of olive oil and waves of filo dough, but they too had
special foods, special rites. The Polish family hung sausages and
smoked meats in their big kitchen. The soups and cookies and potato
dishes and rye breads of the Russian Jews and the German Jews did
not taste like ours. Their children would invite me over for Hanukkah
or Passover rites, and if for some reason I could not come, they would
offer me leftover foods the next day, foods whose names I could never
remember afterward.

But the names did not sound like *kibbe*, *hummus bitahini*, *koussa*,
baba ganoush. When my grandfather said these words, they always
seemed to come from deep within his throat. They were words he had
first spoken in Zahle, near the present-day border between Syria and
Lebanon.

"Cultural diversity" of a sort was all around us, but I never heard
anyone in my neighborhood say those words. There were at least two
dozen ethnic groups represented in the Indiana Dunes, where we lived
along Lake Michigan, most of them manifest in a few extended families recently emigrated from the "old country." Not many of them
had strong ties to the Dunes themselves, and they had only vague
notions that Indians preceded them as inhabitants of the Dunes. One
street crossing our own was called Miami Place, but the last speaker
of Miami in Indiana had died about the time I was born. In Gary,
Indiana, U.S. Steel had attempted to amalgamate this ethnic melt-
ing pot into a unified workforce for its furnaces and foundries. No
one knew then that the Dunes which survived this industrial

onslaught would become the third most biologically diverse national park in the continental United States. But like cultural diversity, the value of biodiversity was not yet recognized.

Most of my neighbors were more concerned about the "old country" than about their new homelands. Yet they did not signal that they thought there was anything "bad" about my family being Arab until the Six Days' War in the Middle East. By that time, we were living in a house where two roads came together in a Y, and each branch of the Y had many Jewish families living on it. I remember, as news of the war splashed onto our TV screens, that one of my Jewish friends told me his father was afraid that all Israeli Jews would be annihilated. He said that his family and others were sending money to Israel to help the cause. Were we?

"I don't think so," I stuttered. "My family's Syrian. I don't think my dad sends any money to the old country."

My friend must have told his family or one of his neighbors what I said. Not only were we not Jewish but we were Arab. The next day before school, an older girl from down the street came up to me at the bus stop to sneer, "We're at war with you." Then she turned and walked away. My Jewish friends didn't know what to say. My ears burned.

Fortunately, the war was over quickly, and "they" won. In a few days, it seemed that most everyone had forgotten that my family had been part of "the enemy." Our conversations before school or during sandlot football games or while riding bikes reverted to the routine banter. For a while, I didn't feel so different around any of the Jews or Swedes or Greeks, as long as we were out on the streets and the trails through the dunes surrounding our homes.

A couple of years later, though, it happened again. I developed a crush on an Israeli exchange student who happened to be staying at the home of my first girlfriend, Ilene. By that time Ilene had begun to date older Jewish guys. I, on the other hand, had not worked up the nerve to date anyone, but I would sometimes ask a girl if she would walk somewhere with me—to the beach, to a game, to the ice cream parlor. I loved this exchange student's accent, her quiet, crisp way of making brief but funny statements; I was intrigued by her stories of kibbutz life in the Israeli desert and of her having already undergone

ROTC-like training with rifles. I had been shooting .22s weekly at a nearby Izaak Walton range and had never been able to talk about rifles with any girl I knew. We would have tantalizing, flirtatious conversations; yes, she said, she would walk to the beach with me sometime soon.

And then someone told her: I was Arab. No, she couldn't go, she said, eyes glancing down at the ground. Her family back home would be angry with her and her American Jewish hosts if they ever learned that she had even spent this much time with me.

For the first time in my life, my heart felt closed off from the exciting potential of knowing someone so intriguingly different from me, closed off by abstract rules that I did not understand. I had been "othered"—set aside for reasons I could not fathom. One by one, over the course of the next three years, the Jewish girls who had been my sweethearts, my confidantes, and my best friends all began to date older Jewish boys. How had they even met these guys? I wondered. I had never seen them at the parties I had been invited to. Some of the girls remained close to me; we'd walk, we'd talk on the phone for hours on end, we'd exchange secret notes through all of our classes. But they would date Jewish boys, and not me.

I turned to dating Irish Catholic girls. A Japanese girl. One Swedish girl I'd known from my days in the Lutheran youth group. A Scottish Methodist. A Greek. For me, cultural diversity was a latent curiosity, expressed in terms of which girls were the most interesting dates.

As my teenage years ended, I began to spend more time trying to learn the history of my family and of the Indiana Dunes and less time trying to fit in with my peers. I grew less attached to my high school friends and more involved in picking grape leaves and bittersweet from the dunes. The Nabhans and the sand were what attracted me back to my birthplace. However, my growing sense of place and ethnicity did not lure me into seeking either a hometown girl as a partner or a distant Lebanese cousin as a wife in an arranged marriage.

I never met a Lebanese girl who wasn't also my cousin, however distant. Some of my aunts had married their cousins, but that had to be arranged. In fact, one of my great-aunts had at one time arranged for my father to marry one of his second cousins who lived in Massachusetts, but "the deal fell through." Once, when I took my first wife, a German girl, to a Nabhan family celebration, the cousin whom my father was to marry had been there, slightly inebriated, very animated. When she realized who I was, she hung on me the rest of the night, telling me hilarious family stories of arranged marriages that did and didn't work. I liked her, this almost mother of sorts, who seemed youthful and confident and very Lebanese despite her dyed blonde hair.

On the way home, my wife blurted out, "You two just sat there all night telling stories, like you were flirting with one another. I felt left out, like you had gone off the deep end into some family thing." I looked at her and remembered the first time I had brought her home to meet the Nabhan clan. We were married by that time, she was pregnant, and her countenance was absolutely rosy as we entered the holiday party. I led her past younger cousins and older uncles and aunts who kissed me on the mouth and hugged her as if they had known her all their lives. And then, we arrived at a couch where all five of my father's lovely black-haired, olive-skinned, baggy-eyed sisters sat with one another, laughing, arms draped over each other's shoulders.

"This is my wife Karen," I said proudly. And just as proudly, I said to her, "And these are my aunts: Mary, Emily, Rose, Violet, and Mabel."

Aunt Rose signaled her, "Come on over here, honey; sit and talk with us for a while."

I let go of Karen's hand, but then I realized that she wasn't moving toward them. She paled.

"Where?" she stumbled. "Where would I sit?" She looked at them. There was no chair nearby.

"Here," Aunt Emily cackled, and at the same time, she rolled her left hip toward Mabel while Rose, to the right of her, squeezed toward Violet. It was like the Dead Sea parting; a small opening appeared on the couch between the fannies of two of my five aunts.

Karen stood frozen, hardly able to imagine herself wedged between my Lebanese aunts with their hairy, tattooed arms and hands cascading over her shoulders. I realized then that Karen might learn to love them but she would never *feel* like part of the Nabhan clan. Kinship is something visceral, not an abstraction I could offer my wife like a gift-wrapped present.

Lately, I've been reading other Arab-American writers: Joseph Geha's fine stories in *Through and Through*; Greg Orfalea's immigrant history, *Beyond the Flames*; Diana Abu Jaber's *Arabian Jazz*, and Naomi Shihab Nye's *Sitti's Secrets* and *Never in a Hurry*. My daughter, now twelve, with lovely olive-tinged skin and dark wavy hair, noticed that I was reading one of Naomi's works that she was sure I had read before.

"Are you hung up on that?" she said coolly. "It seems like you're always reading her stuff."

"Well," I replied, surprised that Laura was taking an interest in my reading, "I like seeing the world through another Arab-American's eyes. It's good to know that to someone else, all of America doesn't look like the same—"

She cut off my sentence with one of those looks that twelve-year-old girls master: not exactly impatience or exasperation but an expression that says, "I should have known you'd say something that foolish, so why did I even ask?" Yet she paused for another moment, the look changing into one of tentative curiosity. I knew that she secretly liked Naomi's book, *Sitti's Secrets*, about the time the author had spent as a child with her Palestinian grandmother in Jerusalem. Laura knew it reminded me of my aunts, my family, my home.

"Does it make you feel different?" she asked quietly.

It struck me that the last thing in the world most twelve-year-old girls want to feel is "different"; all the social pressures bearing down on them force most of them to try to "fit in."

I couldn't tell her all I wanted to say right then: *this story*. I looked at her skin, her eyes, her hair, and that of the people walking nearby. Unlike my father, who looked as Arab as they come, those genes were dilute enough in Laura and me that we could "fit in" most anywhere in America that we wanted to. We could look like, act like, and eat like whites, those pasteurized, homogenized "mutts" we see on TV who don't eat falafel, *lufsa*, or hominy; who don't drink mint tea, goat's milk, or mescal; who don't dance the *dupke*, the *cumbia*, or the *schodiche*; who don't smell of garlic, olive oil, or cumin; who never kiss their aunts and uncles on the mouths or sleep several children in a single bed.

I didn't want to tell her so bluntly that we're *all* different, that subsumed within that garbage-can term "white America" is as much ethnic diversity as there is under the politically correct term "people of color." There is as much prejudice toward those of us who stand for immigrant America, as there is toward Native Americans, and as much of a search for identity. Somehow, we each need to reckon with the legacy of our ancestry, and remember the many ways we are also enriched by contact with others from completely different backgrounds.

I closed my book, patted Laura on the back in a fatherly way, then shut my eyes and tried hard to fathom how much of this Lebanese-American "difference" she would come to recognize and embody as she sought out her own identity.

Embody? My mind changed scales then and, like a microscope, tried to focus on the very genes and cells found in Laura's body and in mine. I imagined that each one of them was shaped like those clear plastic food containers they sometimes give you for take-out food at a Middle Eastern deli, transparent rectangular cartons with snap-on lids.

Laura's body and my own had a certain number of such cells that were filled with hummus, tabbouleh, goat cheese, grape leaves, and mashed eggplant saturated with spices and olive oil. Such cookery did not fill all her cells, but enough to color her skin olive, to make her eyelids bulge and fold, to shape and tinge her hair. I could be sure: there was no way she could end up anything but "different." In the desert where we live, ancient rivers may appear dry, but below the surface they run deep and strong. Such a river would run as a vital undercurrent through her life, and, I hoped, she would one day sense the way its power enriched her own existence.

Behind the Zipper

Discovering the Diversity around Us

Like a lot of people, we were wondering just what is going on here
on Planet Ocean, why is it that carbon atoms born in the fires
of stars have careened through eons of time to produce Sibelius,
rap music, joy, sorrow, child abuse, baseball, art,
poetry, television, passion, automobiles, Yo-Yo Ma,
money, Republicans, birds, and steelhead.
BRAD MATSEN, *Planet Ocean*

I have a wish for humanity: that all of our children would become field naturalists as they grow up. Imagine living in a society where every youth has the chance to explore the earth on foot and in hand, getting to know its creatures on a first-name basis.

This is not a death wish, mind you. I am not trying to inoculate the masses with *Giardia* microbes, Lyme disease, poison ivy, or chigger bites.

The reason that I want everyone to become field naturalists has nothing to do with financial or professional rewards—or, for that matter, with the hope of advancing science. To the contrary, ecology seems to be *the* field in which I am most likely to fail to prove any scientific hypothesis I attempt to test. And that's why I like it: I am constantly reminded how wrong I can be about how the world works.

That's half the problem: most of us need to be humbled more often, to be reminded that nature is not only more complex than we think, it's more complex than we *can* think.

The other half of the problem is that most children today grow up robbed of the chance of discovering anything at all on their own. They are told early on that scientists in little white coats discover all the world's "facts" in neat, antiseptic laboratories. These facts are then handed to an ecologically illiterate public on an equally antiseptic platter filled with pasteurized, homogenized truisms to nibble on as stale appetizers empty of much of their former nutrition. Trouble is, all those tidbits taste far more bland than any wild fruit plucked right off the tree.

And so I wish to champion the fine art of *discovering*, a process far different from the heroic act of *discovery*. Through the process of *discovering*, we seldom achieve any hard-and-fast truth about the world, its cornucopia of creatures, or its cultural interactions with them. Instead, we are inevitably assured of how little we know about that on which each of our lives depends.

I started down this bewildering trail of misinformation when I was quite young. My first failed field in biology was the human body. When I was four, I often wore corduroy pants with an elastic band gathering the waist. Whenever I had to urinate while out on a hike with my older brother in the woods beyond our neighborhood, I would simply pull my pants down far enough to relieve myself. One day, my older brother—who already wore regular blue jeans—asked me why I pulled my pants down instead of opening my zipper. I told him that I didn't know that's what the zipper was there for.

"Sure," he said. "Everyone's got their plumbing right behind their zippers."

I didn't give my brother's explanation that much thought until one afternoon as I went along with my mother to some local social function. I grew up in a family with no sisters, only brothers. Suddenly, I looked up and realized that every woman in the room had a zipper on her *hip*—whether wearing a skirt or a pair of stylish pedal pushers, the rave of the midfifties. I had no idea what kind of plumbing women had. All I could do was envision them riding sidesaddle on a toilet seat, pants, pedalpushers, or skirt unzipped, staring at the wall between two bathroom stalls. That was the first time I was dumb-struck by the mysteries of women. My awe remains undiminished.

I didn't really learn how biologically wrong I could be until I was fourteen, when a girl from school invited me down into her basement to do "homework" with her one night when her parents were away at a PTA meeting. I was already well versed in one theory of mate selec-tion: in order to optimize the potential for sexual activity, high school boys should seek out partners whose parents go to a lot of evening meetings. As we went downstairs into her basement, she made her intentions known to me when, with a complaint about how hot their furnace was, she tossed off her vest and unbuttoned her blouse.

And that's when I began to sneeze. My eyes began to water. My voice dropped four octaves (the only reassuring sign that I might be reaching manhood as I reached toward her womanhood). Just before all our clothes molted off in a would-be metamorphosis, I was struck with a sneezing attack so fierce that I had to excuse myself. From her embrace, from the basement, and even from her household.

The next day in school, my eyes half-swollen shut, I caught a glimpse of my girlfriend briskly ducking down a hallway to avoid me. I was crestfallen. I had been so close to achieving every teenage boy's wildest dream, and yet... Could I be allergic to my sweetheart? To girls in general? To love? *La différence?* There was no one to ask. I had to find out painfully on my own.

My mother soon dragged me off to another one of her social func-tions. Such events are typically fates worse than death for a teenage boy. This gathering should have made me particularly self-conscious, since my ex-girlfriend's mother was there as well. Yet it didn't mat-ter to me at the time. Nothing did. I had become a zombie in the weeks following my failed homework assignment. Somehow, I mus-tered the fortitude to leave my room that Saturday. And it was for-tunate that I did, for I inadvertently made the biological discovery that would redeem my existence.

The hostess, I noticed, had a long-haired cat, almost identical to the one my girlfriend's family kept locked up in their basement. A new possibility revealed itself to me. "Here, kitty-kitty," I whispered. The cat came near me. I sneezed. I picked up the pillow lying on the couch next to me—a likely place for a cat to lounge for hours on end. I brought the pillow up to my nose, sniffing it. I sneezed again.

That was enough to confirm the nature of my allergy. Spontaneously, I let out a war whoop, but sneezed in the middle of it. My mother and her friends turned abruptly toward me, peeking in from the other room. "Are you *okay?*" my mother blurted out, obviously embarrassed by my disruptive behavior.

"Yes! I *am* okay! I'm okay! I'm allergic to cats!" Tears came to my eyes. "I can't stay here though, or I'll keep on sneezing. If it's OK, I'll get back home on my own."

"Go home, *please,*" she urged, obviously embarrassed by my outbreak. Her friends' eyebrows all tilted, sympathetic to Mother's distress. I shot a glance at my girlfriend's mother, who looked as though she would be glued to her chair for a while longer.

"I will," I said as I ran out the door.

Home was not my destination.

My first formal field studies in natural history took place during that period of zombiehood following the allergy attack. At that point, as a hormonally charged teenager, I could focus on nothing (other than girls undressing in my imagination) for more than seventeen seconds at a time. And yet I had to deal with a biology teacher who had the annoying habit of pretending that freshmen could keep something in their heads for the entire semester. He would give us homework assignments that would take months to do, as if biology were the only pursuit filling our after-school hours.

During the autumn semester of my freshman year, he commanded us to identify twelve different kinds of trees in our neighborhood and then record how long it took each to change color and lose its leaves. We cringed when he announced that the fall project had been so satisfying "for all of us" that he had decided to assign a similar task for the spring: "Go to the lake and to the swamps between the dunes, and find which migratory birds pass through here. I'd like you to identify *twenty* different kinds and record when they first arrive, then when they depart."

After the first time I went out on my own, searching for birds, I was stinging with indignation. There were only four kinds of waterfowl on a pond near my home, and one of them, the mallard duck, could be seen there year round, so it didn't count. If it took me an hour just to *identify* these first few birds, how long would it take to complete the entire assignment? Had this joker of a teacher ever done this himself? What if only eighteen kinds of birds showed up all spring? Would he flunk all of us?

I was furious, so furious that the day the biology teacher scheduled us to dissect pigs, I decided to play hooky so that I could find some birds during school hours and have my after-school time to myself. I sneaked home at lunchtime, grabbed the binoculars my uncle had loaned me, and hightailed it for Long Lake.

Long Lake was a chain of interdunal lagoons, marshlands, and bogs not far from my home, perhaps a half mile back from the Lake Michigan shoreline. From the vantage point of a small dune, I could see that something peculiar was happening that day, or at least, something that I had never noticed before. The entire area of open water was filling up with birds—not hundreds but tens of thousands of them.

At first, when I glassed them, I was disappointed if not downright frustrated. They all appeared to be Canada geese, a species I had already checked off my list the weekend before.

"I found thousands of birds," I moaned to myself, "but they're all a species I don't even need."

But just as I voiced this sour note, a thousand honkers rained down from the heavens, drowning out every other sound. They had come in behind me from Lake Michigan, so I hadn't seen them until they were nearly on top of me. Now, as they glided in for a landing, the other waterfowl already present raised up an even more deafening racket. They seemed as indignant as I was: "DON'T YOU LAND ON ME, YOU IDIOTS! I don't care if you're on your way from Mexico to Upper Michigan, I don't need any webbed feet in my face!"

The formerly comfortable flocks decided to get up and get out of the way. With a thunderous beat of wings, tens of thousands of geese levitated above the water for a split second, then slowly rose to the west and sailed away. I watched as they circled and landed across the county line road, in a far less occupied leg of the lake.

Stunned, I lay back against the sloping dune and surveyed the scene. Even without peering through the field glasses, everything seemed to have come into sharp focus: each white cheek patch, each black stocking stretched across the head of a Canada goose floating on the water. Every pale breast and paler chin stripe flashed above me as they took flight, forming undulating wedges of two to three dozen birds at a time.

Sooner or later I spotted a few snow geese and their darker morph, the blue geese, amid all the honkers. Their pale bills were a giveaway; their short muffled notes were an obvious contrast to the high-pitched honks of the longer-necked Canada geese.

Between spurts of identifying a few other waterfowl species, I just sat back and watched the swirling flocks arrive and leave, as flock after flock V'ed away toward more distant wetland sanctuaries. Then, as the sun began to drop, I left for basketball practice back at my high school.

Even though it was an hour after classes had let out, the first person I saw as I walked up to the court was my biology teacher, talking with one of my friends who had been practicing layups. When the teacher noticed my approach, he grinned at me, just to make me a little uncomfortable about seeing him so soon after skipping his class.

"Hey, mon, if you ditched me class to get out of dissecting pigs, you're in bad luck. The pickled pigs didn't arrive in time, so you'll have to be in on the dissections next Monday. I just let everyone have a free hour to catch up on their homework."

"Well, that's...that's just what I was doing.... I mean, I was working on the assignment about the birds. I went out to Long Lake to see them migrating through."

"See anything special?" he asked.

"I added four kinds to my list: snow goose, blue goose, and the common goldeneye and bufflehead ducks. But the most amazing thing: there were tens of thousands of Canadian honkers! They overwhelmed the rest of them, but I got such a good look at every detail: how they land, take off, everything. And even though there weren't many of 'em, I could still hear how the snow geese didn't even sound the same as the Canada geese. I never thought about goose voices at all before."

My teacher looked pleased that I had finally paid some attention to the natural world, but I noticed that he kept glancing at my friend who was dribbling the ball behind me. When I turned, my friend shot me a look that said, "Great! You ditch classes, then win over the teacher by telling him you've seen a bunch of birds that none of the rest of us will ever see. But if we ditch out, we'll catch hell for it…"

The teacher sensed that he should let us get on with basketball. But he asked me one more question as a parting shot.

"Now that you've seen them, would you go back there on your own?"

"Yeah. Of course. It's cool." I glanced over at my friend, but he had moved downcourt and was now out of earshot. "I'm thinking of hanging out over there this weekend."

The teacher glanced at me. "I don't give a crap how many birds you can name and check off your list. I just want you to *see* them, to hear them, to watch them move. There's amazing stuff going on out there."

Some twenty-one years later, I spent a day with my children peeking at teal and coots through the bushes surrounding Quitobaquito, a desert oasis on the Mexican border. Dusty had been baptized at this oasis, and he had recently gone with me to Australia where all the novel birds had fascinated him. Laura had been dazzled by toucans in Guatemala and had loved the sounds of lowland rain-forest birds on the Yucatán peninsula. Both the kids were still in grade school, but they had been around naturalists of various sorts all their lives, and now they, too, were good with binoculars and quick at thumbing through field guides. A favorite pastime was counting hawks whenever we drove between Organ Pipe Cactus National Monument, where we were temporarily living, and their grandmother's house in Phoenix.

As we sat together on a Park Service bench at the end of the day, I remembered that I had once marked in my field guide the names of birds that Dusty claimed he knew when he was four. There were some eighteen names that he gave me as we turned the pages and looked at all the pictures. Some names he had made up or hybridized in his mind from hearing adults talk about desert birds: Gila woodpeccaries, for instance, and yellow-bellied cactus thrashers. Now, with his age having more than doubled since the first time we listed all the birds he knew, we went through the book once more. More than forty-five common names for American birds quickly spilled out of his mouth as I turned the pages; he retained in his head the names of another dozen Australian birds.

It did not matter whether or not the names were scientifically correct. It mattered whether or not my children felt connected to the lives around them. And one morning at Organ Pipe, when they announced that they had built a secret "nest" for themselves in a wash where only the birds knew they were there, I knew that *biology* was more than an assignment they were given in school. It was a way of looking at and listening to the world.

Some of the most rapturous moments in natural history field studies come when we haven't a clue what we're really looking at. I recall the experience of a friend of mine, a successful advertising artist born and raised in Chicago, who decided to forsake her urban career and move to the desert when she fell in love with a mining engineer. Three days after their honeymoon, he was called out on emergency to inspect an accident, and she was left alone for more than a week in their ranch house set in the midst of the desert of the lower Colorado River Valley.

After two days of reading magazines and watching birds come to the windowsill, she decided to go out and explore the wildlands of their "backyard," which extended seamlessly into a Bureau of Land Management primitive area. Her first discovery was something that looked like a fossilized egg cracked in half. Her second discovery— which made her wonder whether the fossilized egg had recently "hatched"—was slowly sauntering across the desert pavement a few feet away. It was some kind of reptile she had never seen before: with beaded black and orange skin, a slow primitive gait, and a knowing, ancient look in its eyes.

She gasped: it seemed to her that this was just what a baby dinasaur would look like—perhaps this was the first dinosaur to hatch in millions of years! Thinking it might not survive in such a changed climate, she decided to follow it and study its behavior for as long as it lived. Running back to the house, she grabbed two canteens, binoculars, a journal, a colored pencil set, and some food. She left a message on the phone in case her husband called. Then she took off on foot, following the belatedly born monster wherever it went.

As it plodded along through the desert, she mapped the route it followed, keeping a running account of what it ate and where it defecated. Whenever it stopped, she would take out her colored pencils and sketch its sunning postures, trying to capture how the desert light reflected off its beaded skin. When night fell, she went back to the ranch house, fixed herself a sandwich, and brought her sleeping bag out to a place within thirty feet of the slumbering reptile.

Fortunately, the Gila monster's home range was not that large—her husband found her within a quarter mile of their back door a few days later. As she excitedly described to him what she had been doing, he first thought to correct her, to tell her that the "egg" was just a geode he had left in the backyard himself and that the animal she had been watching was a kind of beaded lizard that was characteristic of her newly adopted home. But then, as he listened, he began to envy her: she had been immersed in the process of *discovering* a new life, an experience that had originally drawn him to the natural sciences twenty years before. For the past few days, while he surveyed mining accidents and filed paperwork, his wife had been out exploring the world with freshly opened eyes.

Trained scientists need their eyes opened to the unexpected just as much as laypeople do, for we too often carry in our heads theories, models, and constructions that prevent us from seeing the obvious. Our understanding of the natural world—however imperfect that understanding will continue to be—can only grow if we are willing to shed those old notions when reality rips them to shreds.

Today, it is common for scientists to be so involved with the techniques of "remote sensing"—the use of satellite and low-flight videos processed for data analysis—that they hardly have time to hit the ground to spot-check their study areas for phenomena not discernible from the air. We can digitally count geese using color-enhanced, digitized time-lapse photos without ever setting foot in a squishy wetland. We can collar a Gila monster with a radio transmitter to get "real-time" reports on our computers of where he has ambled while we cool off in the air-conditioned shade of a Winnebago-turned-travel-lab. We can even get all the sex education we'll ever need via CD-ROM, thereby sidestepping panic attacks like the one brought to me by feline allergies. But what have we lost by not keeping our eyes open and our feet firmly planted on the ground?

I have made fewer anatomical mistakes in assessing the human body of late, but I remain a novice when it comes to knowing the earthly body that is our home. I can only hope that I will continue to make the kind of mistakes that will help me to see what is in front of me. And that I will retain a capacity for rapture, as I felt when I finally discovered what was "behind the zipper."

Finding the Wild Thread

The Evolution of a Naturalist

A playful curiosity about the world is surely one of the motives
that people have in attending to biological diversity.
JAMES BOSTER AND JEFFREY JOHNSON, "Form and Function"

I was gandy dancing, maintaining tracks for an industrial railroad not too far inland from the Lake Michigan shore. Perhaps it was that moment when I first noticed how long the wild thread has been woven, how my own life was still somehow connected to primordial events. As I glanced up from my work of driving spikes into the ground, a half-dozen migrating great blue herons captured my attention.

Half of my life has passed since that sighting, but those herons still loom as large in my mind's eye as Jurassic pterodactyls. I can see them flying low in the heavy air above the steel mills of Gary, Indiana. I can hear their deep wing beats and their hoarse squawks as they called to one another over the mechanical cacophony of the factories. The herons appeared oblivious to the mills and railroad yards built over the sand swales and interdunal ponds so well-described by Edwin Way Teale's *Dune Boy* and Donald Culross Peattie's *Flora of the Indiana Dunes*. But as the herons loped along, I wondered if they were searching for some feature beneath the blast furnaces and pig-iron piles that had usurped their former habitat. I guessed that they had been pulled to this place along their migration route by the racial memory of interdunal lagoons that had served their ancestors since the last minor Ice Age advance about 10,000 years ago.

The herons inspected the slag heap nearest to me, where a shallow marsh had once lain between two ridges of dunes. They slowly flew on to the next debris-filled depression...then the next and the next...until they passed out of sight and off the mill's property into the tenuous refuge of Indiana Dunes National Lakeshore. I stood still on the railroad tracks, seeing them off to other primordial pit stops strung along their ancient migration route. I felt my own weight as I stood there, and yet my heart flew with them.

That was when I discovered how to see the world as freshly as a naturalist, even in the most damaged of habitats. With my safety goggles on instead of binoculars, an iron spike in my pocket where a field guide might fit, a sledgehammer handle propping me up as a rustic walking stick might, and in a pin-striped cap and tar-stained coveralls, I didn't fit anyone's image of a naturalist. But like the herons I watched, I was feeling an urge to find a place in this world, a place that had been buried deep by industrial development.

Our evolutionary history has equipped us with a peculiar kind of nature sensing. We have come to some of our senses as hangers-on in the arboreal heights of the tropics; we have acquired other senses as land-walking hominids in subtropical savannas; still others have come to us as free-running hunters ranging through a variety of habitats. For four million years, our frontal vision and increasingly upright posturing have allowed us to "look around," to focus on the horizons before us.

Our midspectrum color vision, which came to primates early on, is rare among mammals. The coolness other creatures only feel, we also see as the dark blues of the coming night deepen in hue. Yellows cue us to the intensifying warmth arising with dawn. Flowers pop out from their backgrounds—but not as vividly as they do for the bees, which can see farther into the ultraviolet range. Flower petals offer these bees landing tracks and nectar guides that are beyond our capacity to notice.

As we gave up tree swinging for life on the ground, our eyes and hands took over chores that whiskers and noses had once managed. Our olfactory sense can still lead us to a night-blooming cactus hidden in the shadows of a desert shrub, but compared to other mammals we are little fazed by the many floral fragrances and faunal pheromones spewed out around us every day. Once we let our grip relax on the branches above us, our hands became free to accomplish the many manual maneuvers that naturalists now take for granted: picking up an armload of firewood and carrying it back to camp; sorting fruit and pulling out the worms; prying open crab shells and plucking out the meat; tying knots and weaving nets with which to trap other animals. Our long, flexible thumbs, opposable to the rest of our fingers, now enable us to hold onto binoculars and focus them to see even further. This we do instead of remaining absorbed by what is immediately before us, the scents and textures of our most intimate surroundings. We may resonate with the bugling of elk across the opening from us, but do we ever hear or feel the ectoparasite crawling through the tangle of our own body hair?

The world is filtered through our network of senses. It is a network that has been woven together and shaped by our evolutionary history of food gathering and hunting in particular environments. Despite the smells and sonar signals that we fail to pick up, we have found more than enough to eat, to drink, to entertain, and to shelter us as we've tumbled and sifted through the rank and verdant growth of the earth's cover. The physical and mental agility of our species has been honed by the harshness and primed by the richness of the wild. We are preadapted to endure a number of challenges that our minds and bodies have encountered since the time when our ancestors began to cultivate, manage, and manicure our surroundings.

We have tried to remove wildness from the context of our daily lives. We have worked to simplify the natural communities around us, hoping to make our environment more manageable, hoping to be more secure. That has not happened, for a simplified environment is ever more prone to what we call "wild fluctuations"—wild, in this sense, meaning uncontrolled or reckless.

But some people remain who associate wildness with wellness. Piman-speaking peoples of the American Southwest use the terms *doajig* for "health" and *doajk* for "wildness." Both words are derived from *doa*, "to be alive" or "to be cured," as are *doakam* for "living creatures," and *doajkam* for "wild and untamed beings." Taken back to their roots, Piman terms for restoration and recovery convey a sense of becoming wild and whole again.

Piman-speaking farmers are practitioners of farming and foraging traditions in which the relationships between wild plants and domesticated ones are both understood and respected. Wild plants often volunteer in Pima Indian fields. Some are allowed to persist in light of the benefits they provide to the soil or to the crops themselves; others are utilized as food or fiber much as the crops are. Piman speakers recognize wild relatives of domesticated plants, which can contribute genes to cross-compatible crops, thereby renewing traits in the crops' gene pools that may have been lost due to artificial selection. They also understand that the fields' nutrients have washed in from the watershed above the field, along with the wild seeds. When Piman communities pray and sing for summer rains, they are asking that the desert watersheds be moistened and replenished with wild organisms as much as they are asking for water to irrigate their crops.

In the past, the Piman-speaking peoples would go into the desert wilderness to renew themselves, to have dreams in which sacred songs were given to them. In many parts of the world, wilderness has served as a temporary sanctuary for sad, disturbed, or diseased people troubled by their society. Medicine men and hermits, homesteaders and monks, biologists, herbalists, and artists have sought cures to their sicknesses and sorrows in deserts, jungles, and tundras. By letting other elements and organisms into our lives, we dilute our poisonous human preoccupations with status, security, and social acceptance.

Wild habitats challenge us to be alert and agile, so we must despair over the conditions in which we find the planet and its peoples today. Many places that formerly engaged us in rites of passage are now tamed. Uninitiated to the power of wilderness, a large percentage of our present human population remains in an arrested, immature stage of development. In worked-over, manicured environments, we are simply not as much in touch with the wild stimuli that originally set us on our path. We must find our way along an obscure trail, hoping that someone has not already kicked down the cairns.

Not too long ago, I found myself working on the floodplain of the lower Rio Colorado where the once wild river had impulsively changed its course several times over the centuries. It rarely has enough water now to drive its meandering, since upstream dams have tamed its flow. Where farmlands have replaced its grand riparian forests, where levees have sharply separated its water from the land, the floodplain has a static, almost petrified feel.

One hot August, however, I watched this frozen landscape thaw before my eyes. After a week of work in remnant mesquite forests, I found myself in a small plane, flying over the desert river valley. By the dawn light, I saw that its earthen history, buried alive, was still breathing beneath the fields of monocultural crops. Passing over miles of cotton, I could still make out the patterns of ancient river trails, oxbows, and backwater sloughs. Each old land feature was marked by a soil of another hue. The cotton plants had emerged from the soil as evenly spaced seedlings, but they could not retain that uniformity on such heterogeneous substrates. Each piece of earth was marked by the way the river had run through it. Even the narrowly bred, lavishly tended strands of domesticated plants could not hide that fact.

Edging one of the fields that spread out across the soils of a former slough, a concrete irrigation canal ran in a straight line far into the distance. From the shallow standing water of that newly irrigated field, a great blue heron took flight. I recalled the meandering path that had led me from the Lake Michigan herons years ago to this one, rising from the abused desert floodplain. I knew that the heron would not set its course along the concrete canal. It would be guided by the wildness that was still visible in the curvilinear meander, the sinuous path.

Hummingbirds and Human Aggression

He goes buzzing from branch to branch, from flower to flower....
At times he's a little drunk from all the honey he has sucked....
As the captain of the Chontals, he glides over the camps
of the enemy, assesses their strength, dive-bombs
them, and kills their chief in his sleep.
EDUARDO GALEANO, "The Hummingbird," *Memory of Fire*

This is not what I'd call a resort, nor have I come here for sport. I've pulled into a pit stop on the Devil's Highway for a reckoning. I've come to see if anything grows in the tank tracks scarring the desert floor, to watch creatures battling for riches in patches along dry washes, and to reflect on human aggression.

My camp in Arizona's Stinkin' Hot Desert is more than twenty-five miles from the nearest permanent human habitation but less than four from a stretch of international border. That borderland, one of the hottest on earth, has pulled me into its camps six winters out of the last sixteen. This year is subtly different; I feel a new tension in the atmosphere. This weight in the air is somehow balanced by the war in Kuwait. I am not sure whether I am the one bringing the tension or whether it is endemic to this land of scarcity.

The origins of this tension have become my consuming passion. Like a lab scientist peering through a microscope in order to identify some debilitating disease, I've fixed on a global issue through concentrating my attention on this desert microcosm. I hope to discover a morality that is not an abstraction, one that emerges out of the local ecology, one I can adhere to in this place. This morality must address a fundamental issue: "Are human societies fatally stuck in a genetic script of aggression against one another, whether or not such behavior is now adaptive?"

With every step I take around camp, I seek clues. I find myself kicking up bones, grave markers, ammunition shells, old warheads, and missile debris. At night, I glimpse vapor trails of desert nomads, coming in for a little water; the cliffs echo with the calls of owls.

Maybe I can echo-locate myself for you. I'm below an ancient but remote watering hole along the Devil's Highway, where more than 400 travelers have died of thirst or ambush over the last century and a half. Some of these wayfarers became crazed from desert drought and heat, some from broken dreams. Here it's not hard to imagine hunters in pursuit and the hunted in hiding or in flight. Tribes have converged here as their migration routes intersected: O'odham, Cucupa, and Quechan among them. They bartered, haggled, and battled over scarce resources. Over the centuries, they shifted the boundary lines of their territories. My camp below the High Tanks is full of the disembodied spirits of these encounters, for the historic cemetery and much of the prehistoric archaeology once evident here have been bulldozed and tank-trampled by more recent military maneuvers.

There are two sorts of tanks. One kind—armed and armored all-terrain vehicles—belongs to the U.S. Marines. The other, the High Tanks, are usually called *Tinajas Altas*, as they were named in Spanish when this land was still part of Mexico. The High Tanks form a series of nine plunge pools, water holes no bigger than bathtubs, naturally carved into the bedrock of a shady drainage that cascades 500 feet down an abrupt granitic ridge.

Such cascades are seldom covered by waterfalls here in southwestern Arizona, where precipitation is so variable from year to year that talk of averages and ranges is meaningless. Rain may fail twenty-six months at a stretch, but bombs fall out of the sky frequently. This is because the tanks lie in a bombing range jointly administered by the U.S. Air Force and the Bureau of Land Management. The area is closed to "public access" during periods of bombing exercises, tank maneuvers, and mock battles. Here, in the late 1970s, the U.S. military reputedly prepared for the ill-fated helicopter raid into Iran's arid turf to free American hostages, and more recently it used this land to prepare its troops for Operation Desert Storm.

I ponder those conflicts in the Middle East from my perspective as an Arab-American. A week before missiles were exchanged across the border between Saudi Arabia and Kuwait, a Middle Eastern geographer sent me a few pages from Sir Arnold Wilson's 1928 history, *The Persian Gulf*. I was intrigued to read how, eleven centuries ago, a state of anarchy prevailed from Oman to Basra. Taking advantage of the general chaos, Muhammad bin Nur wrested control of the region: "He cut off the hands and ears, and scooped out the eyes of the nobles, inflicted unheard-of outrages upon the inhabitants, destroyed the watercourses, burnt the books, and utterly destroyed the country." Nur's tyranny was met with "the vengeance of an infuriated people," who disposed of his deputies. They then went through seven imams of their own in less than thirty years. The area continued to be fraught with "intestine quarrels," Wilson tells us; then, "about the middle of the twelfth century, the *Nabhan* tribe acquired the ascendancy and ruled over the greater part of the interior of the country until the reestablishment of the Imamate in A.D. 1429; this tribe, however, continued to exercise considerable influence for…two centuries longer…until finally suppressed."

I learned how my Nabhan kinsmen fought off Persian invaders, skirmished with a petty sheikh from Hormuz, and then fought the Mongols who, at one time, held nearly all of Asia Minor. During this epoch, at least they introduced a few lasting monuments: underground *qanat* waterwork technologies, stone dams, arid-adapted crops, and Persian-influenced temples. To be sure, the long chronicle of Nabhans involved in bloodletting, upheaval, and desert destruction dwarfed these material accomplishments. My paternal ancestors had no doubt been as absorbed in the warring, the warding of territory, and the hoarding of resources as any of their predecessors. How much of this aggression is genetic, in myself and in others?

I ask this question of the desert, not rhetorically but literally. This desert, like others, is an open book waiting to be read, to show us its scars. I ask this question of the Sonoran Desert, since it is hitched to

every other desert in some essential way, hoping that the answer I hear
can help me understand why the deserts surrounding the Persian Gulf
have so often served as battlegrounds.

The sound of dive-bombing jars me from my slumber. Some hummingbirds call this place home, others migrate through it, but they
all fight tenaciously for its resources. I hear metallic shrieks and
zings—the latter not unlike the sound of glancing bullets—as they
dive or chase one another. I try to roll over and cover my ears, but the
high-pitched chittering has penetrated the tent walls. I must get up
and face the music.

The morning sun has not yet appeared over the Cabeza Prieta range.
The fighting began well before daylight. I am camped in a wash that
is a haven for hummingbirds, but to get here they crossed a veritable
hell of sparsely spaced, low-growing scrub, virtually devoid of the
nectar their hyperactive metabolisms require. For miles in any direction, the surrounding desert flats and rocky slopes have little to offer
the migrants of late winter. But along a couple hundred yards of super-
ficially dry watercourse leading down from the *tinajas* into the desert
valley, the shrubbery is unusually dense. The native bushes form nearly
impenetrable hedges of foliage along the banks of the wash, and some
of these verdant walls look, at first glance, to be splattered with blood.
That color is in fact supplied by thousands of crimson tubes of *chuparosa* flowers for which the shining warriors battle.

Chuparosa simply means "rose sucker" or "hummingbird" in Spanish. I am speaking of flowers so custom-fit for pollination by hummingbirds that they bear the bird's name wherever they grow. The
floral tube of a *chuparosa* is elongated, but not so much that it exceeds
the length of hummingbird bills and tongues. It is a chalice filled to
the brim with nectar each dawn. The bushes bloom through late winter in frost-free zones, tiding the birds over until the coming of spring
stimulates other plants to blossom. Their bright color can attract hummingbirds from some distance away. In turn, the winged creatures
transport the sperm of floral sex from one bush to the next, ensuring
cross-pollination. The birds' iridescent heads become discolored by
the thousands of pollen grains plastered onto them as they probe the
flowers, hovering at the entranceways.

As I marvel over the perfect fit between hummer and blossom, another bird comes along and a high-speed chase begins. A rufous hummingbird and a Costa's hummingbird fight over the flower. Meantime, I wonder how their belligerence is viewed by the "Bambi bunch," those who see all animals as cute, cuddly, or constantly in balance and at peace. In the blazing sun of a Tinajas Altas morning, I take a hard look at the desert, its creatures and flowers, trying to keep my own rose-colored glasses from tainting the picture. I concede that nature behaves unlike model members of either the Tooth-and-Claw Hunting Club or the Benevolent Sorority of Nurturing Networkers.

I walk up and down the wash looking for hummingbirds and soon catch a flurry of avian activity in a dense patch of *chuparosa* bushes. I sit upslope between two battlefields, not far away from a third *chuparosa*. A male Costa's is perching on a mesquite branch overlooking a mound of flowers. He darts out to hover in front of a blossom or two and sucks up their nectar. Then he suddenly turns to chase away another small bird. I watch as he whips away after another Costa's male. Minutes later, he chases an Anna's that ventures too close to his treasure. Although Costa's adults are somewhat smaller than these other species, they are roughriders, well adapted to such desert conditions. It is not surprising that they are the most abundant warriors in this wash.

They must already be nesting and mating here. Down the wash a little way, I spot a purple throat on one of the more bizarre dancers in the bunch; a male Costa's is flying a huge U-shape, an arc perhaps sixty to eighty feet from tip to tip. He hovers high up at the end of the arc, then swoops down to the ground with a high-pitched buzz. Soon, he begins again, tracing the same arching pathway. From my vantage point, I can't see a female at the base of his courtship loop, but suspect that this aerial ballet is not being done to flatter *me*.

In the next patch over, I'm having trouble telling who has been holding the territory most of the time. Whenever I can identify the actors in this Painted Desert drama, a rufous male has the upper hand over a Costa's.

Rufous hummingbirds do not nest here; they migrate up through California when the ocotillo blooming begins, and some continue as far as Alaska. The wandlike ocotillos are spread widely over the rocky ridges and flats of the Sonoran and Mojave Deserts. Their populations burst from bud sequentially—south to north—providing migrants with a "drawbridge" extending northward. Sometimes, when cold winter weather has postponed ocotillo flowering several weeks, the hummers try to migrate anyway, in advance of peak flowering. Ocotillo fruit capsules in such years are left with few seeds when their pollinators miss their date.

The ocotillo-flowering fest is an event that will begin here in another week or so. In most years, I've seen migrants such as the rufous arrive in late February just prior to the ocotillo bloom. They pack into the *chuparosa* patches already occupied by Costa's and Anna's, adding to the territorial tension. My colleague, physiologist William Calder, has documented that rufous individuals are allegiant to particular stops and nest sites along their normal migration route. Even though rufous hummingbirds do not nest at Tinajas Altas as do Costa's and Anna's, their stake in this place is more than a one-shot deal. They lay claim to sets of resources en route to their breeding ground, unlike other birds that become territorial only around courtship. Accordingly, they fight tenaciously to keep other hummers out in the cold.

This fact strikes me as curious, for I had supposed that birds become territorial only to exclude other males of their own species from access to potential mates or to guard enough food to raise a brood. Melees between migrants didn't make sense at first. I weave my way down the wash, wondering about this seeming incongruity. Then I recall that a mentor of mine, avian biologist David Lyon—who had introduced me to the subversive science of ecology two decades before— had probed this very problem in the Chiricahuas, a half day's drive east of Tinajas Altas.

When I recently discussed hummingbird territoriality with Lyon, he responded to my questions on their behavior with the specificity that characterizes the best ecologists. "Where were you?" he asked. "There are great differences in territoriality in the winter depending on the area. But all of these little rascals are opportunistic and will set up territories any time of the year if rewards are sufficient."

If rewards are sufficient. Lyon considers the defense of dense caches of food during times of the year when there are few alternative energy resources to be the driving force of hummingbird territoriality. Because hummers must consume close to half their weight in sugar each day to maintain normal activities, finding a concentrated source of food for their fifty to sixty meals per day is a serious problem. Territoriality at the Tinajas, then, should be most pronounced when *chuparosa* nectar production is sufficiently high to make the exclusion of other birds worth the price of the energy expended in defense. Imagine a *chuparosa* patch as an oil field thick with wells, in a country with few other energy resources developed. That's where the troops will hover.

I have a chance to explore Lyon's notion a month later when I return to my camp, not long after the peak of ocotillo flowering on the surrounding flats. The wash so aggressively and noisily guarded in early March is, in April, as quiet as a reading room. There are still hummers around, but no frenzy of flowering attracts them as before. Most of the resident birds have dispersed to draw on the widely scattered ocotillo blossoms that remain. The migrants have moved on, so the number of competitors for any single patch of flowers is low. Territorial shows, for the most part, have been canceled. Hummingbirds put their guard up only when they are faced with stiff competition for scarce resources.

Lyon also verified that territoriality among different species of hummers was truly adaptive and not simply a misdirected means of venting innate aggression on other species when a male has mistakenly identified them as competing for his potential partners. For his test, Lyon enticed a blue-throated hummingbird to establish a territory in an area circumscribed by ten sugar-filled feeders, two placed in the center of the area and eight in a circle on the periphery. Over the test period, he held constant the amount of sucrose available to the bird, but once a day he moved the eight on the periphery farther out from the midpoint, enlarging the area over which the sugar sources were distributed.

Lyon was not surprised when the blue-throated male took to chasing other hummers out of the artificial territory, regardless of the area it covered. In fact, this male at first spent twice as much time in dogfights around the hummingbird feeders as males typically spend defending natural patches of flowers. The trouble came as the feeders were spread over a larger area. The blue-throated initially attempted to defend the expanded arena, but the number of competitors entering it increased to two and a half times what they had been in the original small territory. In the smaller arena, the territorial male chased after the majority of all hummers trespassing into his turf, regardless of their species identity. When the sugar was set out over the largest area, he was forced to become more selective in his combat maneuvers; he needed more energy to pursue competitors across the longer distances between feeders, and more time flying to reach the various feeders to refuel himself.

The blue-throated male shifted his strategy. Rather than wearing himself out with incessant jousting, he opted for adaptability. He had tolerated the presence of females of his kind all along, but now he also permitted black-chinneds to forage on the periphery. Although they outnumbered the other hummers at this time, black-chinneds were small and therefore the easiest competitor to expel when resources became scarce. Magnificent hummingbirds, another species slightly larger than blue-throateds, posed more of a threat. And yet, by afternoon, most of the magnificents in the oversized territory were tolerated as well.

At last, defense against all comers became tenuous. A few competing blue-throated males were allowed to feed without being ejected. Still, whenever other blue-throated males were chased, they were pursued a greater distance than that flown to repel other species. If another bird was seen as a competitor for *both* food and sex, the aggressive tendency of territorial males toward him remained in place.

Place *per se* is not what the birds are defending. They are after a finite amount of nectar, pollen, and bugs required to stay alive and reproduce—that is, to pass on their genes. If they can glean those foods without much territorial pyrotechnics, they will do so, whether from a small area or a large one.

Their lives cost something, as do ours. On a late winter day, a hummingbird must spend one minute out of every nine feeding in order to fuel its metabolism. Its hovering and flying demand ten times the calories per ounce of flesh that people need when running at full clip. If you give a hummer a feeder full of "junk food," it will reduce its foraging effort to a tenth of what it would be otherwise. Nonetheless,

a male does not fill up all this newly found "leisure time" with warfare. Even when you give him a territory literally dripping with sticky-
sweet sucrose water, his foraging effort decreases tenfold, while his
time pestering intruders only doubles.

Put in terms of an ecological maxim, a male hummer will defend
a patch of riches only to the extent that it is truly "adaptive" to do so.
When battling becomes too costly relative to the food security it
brings, he will relax what many observers have assumed to be unre-
lenting, genetically determined hostility. Here is where the genetic
determinists (and fatalists) have led us astray: they claim it is our "animal nature" to be aggressive, yet even animals considered relentlessly
warlike can suspend their pugnacious territorial behavior. They give
peace a chance whenever their essential needs are met or when the
cost of territorial behavior becomes too high. Moreover, as ornithologist Amadeo Rea has pointed out to me, "hummingbird fighting
and warfare are not really homologous to human activities of the same
name. How many dead hummers do you find in the *chuparosa* patch?
How many bloodied, maimed victims? Their fighting…is probably
only to exclude, not to destroy, a rival male."

The Aztecs called the hummingbird *huitzitzil*, "shining one armed
with a cactus spine." Yet for all their feistiness, hummingbirds do not
embody the incessant irascibility attributed to them by certain historic and modern observers. Do such ascriptions actually tell us more
about the Aztecs—or the sociobiologists—than they do about the
birds themselves? If human warfare is not homologous to that found
in other animal species, what is its derivation? Is it somehow peculiar to the genes of *Homo sapiens*, or is it false to claim fatalistically
that human aggression is genetically determined? I go back into the
desert to answer these questions, a color-blind botanist seeking clues
that those with normal vision may not be able to detect. And I turn
my attention from the hummingbirds—most of which have taken
flight by this time—to human beings, whose tracks are still evident
all around me.

It is April. I'm above the desert floor on the ridge overlooking the
High Tanks. Last night, I tucked my sleeping bag into a cavelike rock
shelter. I shared the night with an old friend, a scorpion under my

pillow, and a few pack rats scampering through the deep recesses of my dreams. We had hoped to see desert bighorn come in for water. This niche in the granite once kept O'odham hunters out of sight until they were ready to trap the wild rams and ewes in the canyon below. I dreamed of seeing sheep approach, imagining myself a hunter from centuries past, hot in the pursuit of big game.

Suddenly, I am jogged from my reverie by the realization that we are being pursued. My friend Susan has noticed that an armored vehicle has lumbered up out of a wash, heading straight toward our parked pickup truck on the desert floor below us.

We watch, silent, hidden in the rocks, as the tanklike all-terrain vehicle stops fifty yards away from our truck. Its passengers do not immediately get out to breathe the fresh morning air. We wait for their doors to open. More than a minute passes.

Simultaneously, all the doors swing open, and six soldiers spring forth to land on the ground, automatic rifles in hand. They spread out. They slowly stalk the truck, scanning the area around them. Forming a semicircle ten feet out from the back and sides of the truck, weapons aimed at all openings, the men ready themselves to move in for the kill.

"Campers!" I yell, immediately regretting it. In the folk taxonomy of the military, the word *campers* does not necessarily exclude "drug runners," "wetbacks," or "undercover agents." It does not bring the same sigh of relief that "garter snake" brings when the other choice might be "sidewinder." Half the armed men now point their weapons toward the wash from which they sense my yell has emerged. I wince, remembering another time on the Devil's Highway when a border guard held me at gunpoint, my hands behind my back, belly to the ground, badgering me with half an hour of questioning. He had been sure I was a drug smuggler; he couldn't believe that anyone who arrived on his borderline beat at dawn was there merely to watch birds. From that distasteful experience, I knew that I had to assure the boys below that they were not stalking aliens from another planet, continent, or country.

"Campers! It's OK! It's OK!" I yell again, waving my Panama hat back and forth, in case they need a moving target. The echoes must have confused them, as they have confused me when I have tried to locate a calling owl while standing near its position below the cliffs. Then, one of the GIs raises field glasses to his eyes, spots my movements, and gives Susan and me a quick once-over. Another lowers his rifle and raises his binoculars as well. There is some talking, largely below earshot, all beyond our comprehension. They radio back to base, no doubt to check out my license number. Soon an order is given, they reset the safeties on their firearms, and reenter the armored vehicle. Before another minute passes, they are gone.

The season of heightened hummingbird aggression has passed, but my preoccupation with human aggression is bursting its buds. Although the military visitors to Tinajas Altas have departed silently, without incident, I feel little solace. As Susan and I descend into camp we feel the same sense of violation that one feels after one's house has been robbed; physical violence may have been avoided, but *psychological* peace has been shattered.

I feel foolish for expecting humans in a place such as the High Tanks to have any taste for tranquillity. As my mind rolls over just a few of the incidents that have been staged here through the years, I realize that there are few fifty-mile stretches of desert that have hosted as many deaths as has this stretch of the Devil's Highway. Teddy Roosevelt's son Kermit described Tinajas Altas and its desperadoes during a hunting trip in the August heat of 1910:

> This is a grim land, and death dogs the footsteps of those who cross it. Most of the dead men [buried below the tanks] were Mexicans who had struggled across the desert only to find the tanks dry. Each lay where he fell, until, sooner or later, some other traveller found him and scooped out for him a shallow grave, and on it laid a pile of rocks in the shape of a rude cross. Forty-six unfortunates perished here at one time of thirst. They were making their way across the deserts to the United States, and were in the last stages of exhaustion for lack of water when they reached these tanks. But a Mexican outlaw named Blanco reached the tanks ahead of them and bailed out the water, after carefully laying in a store for himself not far away. By this cache he waited until he felt sure that his victims were dead; he then returned to the tanks, fathered the possessions of the dead, and safely made his escape.

Add to the human corpses at least twice as many livestock carcasses, and you've arrived at paradise for vultures. When carrion feeders were not enticed to dine in such an out-of-the-way place, the flesh slowly sizzled to beef-jerky consistency on the skilletlike desert pavement. I've measured temperatures of 170 degrees at ground level near here, on a summer day that did not seem unusually hot. In 1861, when New York mining engineer Raphael Pumpelly rode the Devil's Highway during a period of great heat, he wondered (as described in his *Across America and Asia*, published in 1870) if he had stepped beyond the familiar into another world:

> We were approaching the Tinajas Altas, the only spot where, for a distance of 120 miles, water might at times be found. It was a brilliant moonlit night. On our left rose a lofty sierra, its fantastic sculpturing weird even in the moonlight. Suddenly we saw strange forms indefinable in the distance. As we came nearer our horses became uneasy, and we saw before us animals standing on the side of, and facing the trail. It was a long avenue between rows of mummified cattle, horses, and sheep.

Pumpelly's handwritten journal, not published until 1918, gives the same incident in more detail:

> The pack animals bolted and Poston and I rode through with difficulty. Ten or twelve years before, during the time when meat was worth in California almost its weight in gold dust, it paid to take the risk of losing on this desert nearly all of the herd, if a few survived. If no water was found at the Tinajas, most or all of the animals and some of the men would die. In the intensely dry and pure air there was no decomposition. All the dead simply became mummies. The weird avenue had been made by some travelers with a sense of humor and fertile imagination which had not been deadened by thirst.

Thirst of another sort drove miners and buckaroos across the desert and moved Blanco the Bandito to empty all the water out of the plunge pools: greed. Life did not matter as much as money or material possessions. Those who rode down the Devil's Highway did not care about the places they were passing through or the life that they might encounter along the way. Some of the native O'odham, first recorded in residence at Tinajas Altas in 1699, had adopted the same attitude by the mid nineteenth century. They had made a pastime out of robbing and sometimes killing forty-niners en route to California.

Such conduct disturbed their neighbor Tom Childs, the first white man to marry into the Sand People or Hia C-ed O'odham. Tom finally asked one of the Indian bandits, José Augustin, "Why did you kill the Camino travelers?"—and Augustin responded with matter-of-fact brevity: "For their sugar, tobacco, and coffee."

This answer must have struck Childs as strange, for all O'odham—especially the Sand Papago—had been known for a century and a half before Childs's time as "the Peaceful People." In anthropologist Ashley Montagu's global search for cultural models of nonaggressive behavior, the O'odham were included among the two dozen societies least prone to violence.

Despite recent rises in family violence fueled by substance abuse, the O'odham people as a whole can still be characterized by their pacific temperament. I have been befriended by several O'odham families over the past sixteen years, and I have been moved by their peaceable nature. Their humility and their live-and-let-live commitment to conflict evasion underscore most of their interactions with neighbors and visitors. Historic literature on the "Pima, Desert Papago, and Sand Papago," as they were formerly called, consistently emphasizes their aversion to violence.

During World War II, with the support of their elders, the young men of an entire village refused to be inducted into the military. Other O'odham, of course, have dutifully participated in the armed services rather than raising a ruckus, the best known being the Pima Indian hero at Iwo Jima, Ira Hayes. Like Hayes, however, many came back from the service profoundly disturbed by what they had participated in, and some died from the alcohol or drugs taken to deal with such cultural collisions. Anthropologist Ruth Underhill has argued that for the traditional O'odham, "war...was not an occasion for prestige as with the Plains tribes nor of booty as with the Apache. It was a disagreeable necessity. The enemy...or anything that had touched him, was taboo. Therefore all booty was burned and the man who had killed an enemy or who had been wounded by him had to go through a long ordeal of purification."

These words are echoed by those of ethnohistorians Clifford B. Kroeber and Bernard L. Fontana, who worked together for three decades on the major work—*Massacre on the Gila*—concerning intertribal warfare among Southwest Indians: "While they were perfectly capable of taking the offensive, Pimas and Papagos [O'odham] seemed to have done so only when revenge was called for or as a counteroffensive to protect lives and property. There is little to suggest that northern Pimans ever made raids for the sole purpose of obtaining booty.... Neither does it appear that northern Pimans engaged in ritualized formal battles with their Apache and Yavapai enemies [after] 1698."

Indeed, the first O'odham raids on Devil's Highway migrants may have been in response to finding that these travellers had consumed a year's supply of water in a single visit. Cattle, horses, and journeymen could go through such scarce resources during a day's stopover. When Padre Kino came into the area around 1700, his livestock drank dry one tinaja after another. Able-bodied O'odham men did not immediately fight him, but fled instead, leaving only the smallest children and infirm elders to be baptized by the Jesuit father. It was not until Anglos and Mexicans began draining the plunge tanks of the Devil's Highway with considerable frequency—during the California gold rush—that the O'odham had little choice but to discourage travelers along the route.

Like the !Kung bushmen of the Kalahari and Australian Aborigines of the Red Centre, the O'odham of the Sonoran Desert developed traditions that reduce aggressive behavior and encourage cooperation. In *Anger: The Misunderstood Emotion*, psychologist Carol Tavris describes desert nomads so dependent on unpredictable environments that "their only insurance against hard times is each other. No individual can lay-in a supply of frozen pizzas and beer in the event of famine and drought, and no individual could long survive on his or her own.... Under such conditions, any antisocial or angry outbursts threaten the whole group; so it is in the [desert dweller's] interest to avoid direct physical confrontation or violence, and to be suspicious of individuals who cannot control their behavior or their tempers."

Tavris sees nothing innately aggressive in human beings: "It is the world, not the genes, that determines which way it will go." This point has itself become a battleground within academia. Sociobiologists such as E. O. Wilson still ardently maintain that "human beings have a marked hereditary predisposition to aggressive behavior." Wilson does concede that aggression is not tied to a single gene, adap-

tive syndrome, or racial lineage. He has also expressed other ambiva-
lences. In one place, he has argued that our territorial expressions often
respond to the same problems of resource scarcity that direct other
animals toward territoriality. Elsewhere, he has maintained that our
aggressive expressions are peculiar. "The human forms of aggressive
behavior," he wrote, "are species-specific: although basically primate
in form, they contain features that distinguish them from aggression
in all other species."

I have been surprised to find a scholar and writer as clearheaded as
Wilson shifting between two parallel ruts. First, he argues that we
are inexorably tied to a genetic heritage of aggression. Then, he pro-
poses that our scholars and political leaders can lead us into more
diplomatic resolutions of conflict if they consciously choose pacifi-
cism as their ultimate goal. Wilson's often delightful scientific parables are typically fixed on the notion that our behavior can be explained
by understanding the evolutionary history we share with other species.
While he has rightly emphasized that we respond to many social or
environmental stresses and conflicts much the way other organisms
do—there are only so many options—could it be that he has inadvertently shifted our focus away from one critical difference between
humans and our fellow creatures? That difference is *intent*—a difference that ethicists, not sociobiologists, must evaluate for us.

Nevertheless, one of Wilson's paradigms may shed light on the
hummingbirds that become territorial around dense patches of *chuparosa* in the middle of nowhere, as well as on the O'odham who do
the same with plunge pools:

> A territory invariably contains a scarce resource, usually a steady food
> supply, shelter, space for sexual display, or a site for laying eggs.... Ter-
> ritorial behavior evolves in animal species only when the vital resource
> is *economically defensible:* the energy saved and the increase in survival
> and reproduction due to territorial defense outweigh the energy
> expended and the risk of injury and death.... In the case of food ter-
> ritories the size of the defended area is at or just above the size required
> to yield enough food to keep the resident healthy and able to repro-
> duce. Finally, territories contain an "invincible center." The resident
> animal defends the territory far more vigorously than intruders
> attempt to usurp it, and as a result the defender usually wins. In a spe-
> cial sense, it has the "moral advantage" over trespassers.

Wilson would agree that it is "natural" for indigenous desert people to defend a water hole from intruders, much the same way we accept the territorial tenacity of hummingbirds. But because such aggressiveness is often relaxed when resources become more abundant or widely dispersed, for both the hummers and the hunter-gatherers fighting seems a variable rather than a fixed behavior. Cross-cultural comparisons suggest that most societies fight for reasons other than those obviously related to their immediate physical survival. Only 10 percent of so-called primitive cultures apparently maintain a constant peace with their neighbors. For the 64 percent that skirmish with neighbors at least once every two years, their conflicts are not necessarily concerned at all with competition for basic resources. Cultural evolution has left us with tensions not easily explained by addressing only the driving forces of natural selection: the need for food, water, and shelter; the urge to reproduce and keep our genes "alive" in the form of offspring.

That is why there is something profoundly disturbing—almost unprecedented in mammalian evolution until 10,000 years ago—about Blanco the Bandit. By draining the plunge pools, he left all later travelers without access to an essential resource. If there is something peculiar about us latter-day human beings, it is our willingness to destroy a resource essential for everyone's survival. As the resource vanishes, all potential users are inevitably vanquished; they can survive only if, like Blanco, they have hidden their own backup supplies nearby.

For weeks, the tension had mounted. Young, hormone-charged men stood on the south side of a line, like so many hummingbirds waiting for the ice to break up north, waiting for the season to burst with activity. First Lieutenant John Deedrick likened the mood on the front lines to that of men waiting in a blind while hunting deer: "Just like being in a tree stand. You're cold and miserable and you just have to wait."

Then the Desert Storm was let loose, and after an all-out war of some one hundred hours, it was done. The troops were coming home, having freed the oil fields of Kuwait from a despot's control. American soldiers were regaining that solid manly image that had been deflated during the sixties. "By God," George Bush exclaimed, "we've kicked the Vietnam syndrome once and for all!"

Lingerie sales in America reached a new all-time high, as women swooned for the victors. The boys were a bit embarrassed; one returning GI told reporters, "I think it's kinda shallow that a girl might want to make it with me just because I was over there....Fun, but shallow."

As anthropologists Fontana and Kroeber see it, ever since farming overtook hunting as society's primary means of support, young men have been trying to figure out at what activity they can excel over women. The hunter's prowess and tenacity, which once won him the most attractive and fecund mates, seemed weakened when men and women began to share in the chores of agrarian society. Women had been tending plants for centuries, domesticating them and possibly bringing in far more calories than male "breadwinners." As habitats became tamed and men spent less time on the mythic wild proving grounds, they abdicated a primordial connection that had given them their meaning. The feeling grew, according to Kroeber and Fontana in *Massacre on the Gila*, that "women could do all the work necessary for society's physical survival. Males were potentially persons of great leisure. Or," as they rather bluntly state, "...males were all but useless."

Men swerved off course, shifting the balance from the sacramental, ritualistic, or nutritionally justified bloodletting of hunting to that of warfare, even when the gains did not justify the risks. Another hunger grew in men that made them want to taste blood, to be on top. And this hunger, rarely satisfied, sticks with many men today.

No boot camp or campus fraternity hazing has ever quenched this deeper hunger. And far from the mythic rite of passage that it once was for males in many societies, military service has now become an objectified routine of monitoring computer printouts and calculating missile trajectories to strike at distant locations. The bombing of targets has become so depersonalized by the jargon that one might as well be playing Pac-Man. The young technicians of the Gulf War simply "took out targets" and euphemistically referred to any civilian presence in those devastated places as "collateral damage."

American audiences responded to the Gulf War with much the

same fervor they normally reserve for the Super Bowl. Arab-bashing became a new spectator sport; "Operation Desert Storm" trading cards came packaged with bubble gum.

Even though the government's lies about the war disturbed some Americans, it was fortunate for Bush that Saddam Hussein seemed downright evil. Of course, that perception was largely influenced by the White House media machine. Who else could be better cast in the role of Blanco the Bandit than Saddam Hussein? Rather than emptying out the *tinajas* of all their water, he set fire to the scarcest resource underpinning our global economy: fossil fuel. While more than 500 wells burned like battle torches day after day, enough oil was going up in smoke to meet a tenth of the world's daily consumption.

"If hell had a national park, this would be it," mourned the Environmental Protection Agency's director William Reilly on the *Today* show just after his return from Kuwait on May 7, 1991, just two months after the Gulf War "cease-fire." The fires, of course, had not ceased. It would take months to extinguish all of them, and as each month passed with the fires still burning, the atmosphere absorbed as much as a million tons of sulfur dioxide, 100,000 tons of nitrogen oxides, and 25 million tons of oil soot—the latter amount being more than four times the monthly emissions from the entire United States. And those gross estimates of contaminants do not include nerve gasses and other toxins to which soldiers and civilians alike were exposed.

President Bush puffed up whenever he spoke of Desert Storm's swift victory, and he has maintained until this day that the long-term damages were minimal. Unfortunately, his antiseptic war was never that at all; more than a 100,000 were dead within a month, with twice that many wounded, crippled, or contaminated with toxins. Many more people were deprived of potable water and food for months. It is now estimated that only one tenth of all deaths resulting from the conflict occurred during the "official" war. Environmental destruction proceeds on an unprecedented scale, and unsanitary remains will persist indefinitely.

William Reilly assured us that "President Bush cares as much about the environment as he did about winning the war." But the current condition of the fragile desert left damaged by a million troops does not give his assertion credence. Scars left by military vehicles will be seen in the vegetation patterns and soils for a hundred to a thousand years. In some places, observers found the desert biologically sterile following the war; elsewhere, the plants remaining were covered with a crust of soot oil and wind-drifted sand. Massive defense berms and countless bomb craters interrupted watercourses. Further, the U.S. Air Force admits that it left behind nearly 9,000 tons of undetectable explosive materials in desert areas. The culpability is blurred. "Who knows who set what off?" asked Tony Burgess during a telephone interview. Burgess is a desert ecologist who spent three weeks with Friends of the Earth in the Persian Gulf assessing environmental damage. "The country was so trashed. It literally was a vision of hell."

We have only an inkling of how far that hellish apparition will spread, but Burgess assured me that the oil fires are bound to have profound, pervasive global ramifications. Using the greasy soot particles resulting from the burning oil fields as but one example, Burgess told me that "effects from the Kuwaiti smoke plume have already been picked up in Australia and Hawaii," more than 8,000 miles away from their source. From the snows of the Himalayas to the headwaters of the Blue Nile, acid rain and carbon soot have been accumulating at unprecedented levels.

Petroleum engineer John Cox regards the magnitude of carbon soot from Kuwait, Iraq, and Saudi Arabia to be more concentrated and therefore more devastating than what would be expected were a nuclear winter to occur. He explains why the Kuwaiti smoke plume has already been so widely dispersed: "If you are in a rainy area, a very high proportion of the smoke is going to be washed out. If, however, you are in an area that is already dry—and the microclimate around Kuwait is very dry—and you have an intense temperature, then the chances are that the smoke cloud will go to a much greater height than the nuclear war simulations suggest.... [There will be] a major effect upon the growth of vegetation and crops."

This is not the maverick opinion of one self-styled expert but that of the Greenpeace organization as well, which claims that the Gulf War already ranks as one of the most ecologically destructive conflicts ever. According to André Carothers, Kuwaiti officials have begun to concede that the environmental damages of the war have been more crippling than any material losses incurred during the hundred days of armed conflict. And that, to my mind, is the fatal deviation, the divergence of our path from that of our occasionally bellicose biological ancestors and neighbors on this planet. Although some sociobiological scholars still argue that we are far from being the world's most violent animal, the damage our kind has done is without equal.

Hummingbirds skirmishing over *chuparosa*, O'odham and Quechan Indians vying for a water hole, or Kuwaitis and Iraqis battling over an oil field may appear to be parallel parables of territorial disputes over scarce resources in the desert. But the Persian Gulf battle has the capacity to damage a broad range of resources required for life now and in the future—indeed, to damage irreparably the capacity for life support within a particular place on this planet. Gone are the days when ritualized warfare was waged for control over a single water hole, food-gathering ground, or territory.

The verbal sparring between Saddam Hussein and George Bush was a pathetic throwback to esoteric jousting by medieval sportsmen who lived in a time when the stakes were low and the damage local. We can no longer speak of competition for a single, concentrated resource; a life-support system dependent on widely dispersed, vitally important resources is now under threat. Compared to other centuries, the number of wars within and between nations has increased during the past one hundred years, despite pacifying efforts by the United Nations and other mediating bodies. If Bush or Hussein had the mentality of a hummingbird, it would be clear to them that the resources crucial to our survival are no longer economically or ecologically defensible through territorial behavior. These resources are too diffuse, too globally interdependent, to be worth the risks both leaders have placed before us. But what a hummingbird can surmise with its senses in a matter of hours or days, our species must muddle through, argue about, and even shed blood over for decades.

I am back, in the dead of the summer, on a desert wash near the international border where hummingbird bushes like *chuparosa* exhibit a few last, ill-fated flowers withering in the heat. A fire has burned a patch along the border today. Dusty whirlwinds are everywhere, turning and churning in the drought-stricken air. A hummingbird whirs by me. I turn one direction to see if he is being chased, then back in the other to see if he is in hot pursuit of another. He is not. I stop on the other side of the wash, which is wide enough to let me pause for a moment without losing sight of the hummer.

As I pause, I think of the O'odham names for the Tinajas Altas: *U'uvaak*, "where the arrowhead sunk in," or *U'uv Oopad*, "where the arrows were laid down." The Sand Papago tell a story about one of their fellow O'odham who climbed to one of the ridges overlooking the steep-sided canyon where the precious pools of water are found today; he saw an Apache warrior on the ridge facing him. One of these two warriors challenged the other to a contest: the task was to shoot an arrow all the way across the canyon to the opposite ridge.

As my O'odham friends tell it, the first man's arrow cleared the canyon, but the Apache's did not. Instead, it glanced against the bedrock in the drainage, skipped along, then sunk into the granite. Wherever it had struck the rock, however, a pool of water formed, offering the O'odham and their neighbors a much-needed water supply ever since. Retelling this story, my friends express their gratitude for the unlikely appearance of water, and note the irony that it came from someone they had initially perceived as an enemy.

I turn to the hummingbird and think, "Who, then, won the contest? The warrior demonstrating the greatest facility with weaponry or the one who helped make a lasting resource for people?" Laughing at myself, at the long and winding trails my answers take, I leave the wash with one last gesture to the hummer. "You must be my teacher," I offer, palms open in his direction. "We're here together." I am beginning to learn what we have in common—this earth—and what differences in behavior I cannot bear to let come between us.

THREE

The Ancient Connections: Rooting, Hunting, and Gathering

For most of our species' existence,
we have been hunter-gatherers tied to specific
habitats for our sustenance. What happens
when these ties are unraveled?

Searching for Lost Places

Just where one ventures in the country of the past sometimes
depends on where one has ventured before on personal predilections,
nurtured over time, for congenial pieces of experiential terrain: the
terrain of one's youth, perhaps, or of where one's forebears lived,
or of decisive events that altered the course of history.... Yet what-
ever these preferences are...the past has a way of luring curious
travelers off the beaten track. It is, after all, a
country conducive to wandering, with plenty of unmarked
roads, unexpected vistas, and unforeseen occurrences.
KEITH H. BASSO, *Wisdom Sits in Places*

For years, I had heard of a place way out in the Mexican desert where various tribes would come to trade with one another: Coyote Well. There, just a dozen miles from the Sea of Cortez coast, they would barter, banter, gamble, and occasionally take a partner from another cultural community. Coyote Well was truly a crossroads, where coastal Seri Indians would meet Sand Papago, Lowland Pima, and Yaqui travelers from the desert interior. The convergence of trails allowed them to exchange stories, songs, goods, and genes. I knew I had been close by it, but I was never sure exactly where this multicultural mall had been located. At last, my collaborator Janice Rosenberg and I asked some Seri Indian women from Desemboque, Sonora, if they would take us there.

"Pozo Coyote. Pues, ¿cómo no?" they responded. *"Vámanos."* They had no qualms about going; it sounded like they thought it would be a good diversion from the daily chores. Before joining us for the outing, they ducked into their houses, where Amalia changed her scarf while Angelita and Lolita traded skirts and sweaters; each of them added a purse or duffel bag to their take-along gear. At last, they piled into my van, ready for the journey.

Janice sat sideways in the front seat to pass along any directions the three women would utter that I might not hear. "We've never been there," I hollered in Spanish, as I headed down the dirt road running out of their coastal village, "so you'll have to show us where to turn."

They looked at one another, puzzled. Then Amalia, the eldest of the women, waved her hand in front of her and replied, *"Derecho, derechito, no está lejo. Sigue.* (Straight ahead, right ahead. It's not far. Go ahead)."

I had been working for years with both the Hia C-ed O'odham (Sand Papago) and the Comcaac (Seri), so I was excited by the prospect of visiting the one now-abandoned village site where the two tribes had lived together. At Pozo Coyote, the Seri had apparently shown the Sand Papago how to make baskets out of limberbush. In turn, the Sand Papago showed the Seri how to harvest the underground stems of edible broomrapes from sandy washes; the Seri even nicknamed one of their Sand Papago brothers-in-law *Motar* ("broomrape") because of his fondness for this food. Pozo Coyote had been the territorial boundary for the groups; it therefore helps establish the range of their aboriginal land claims. I was eager to walk around to make sense of the stories about its earlier inhabitants.

On the way, Amalia granted me half my wish by telling us tales from her childhood there. Her father, José Astorga, lived at Pozo Coyote for more than a decade so that he could hunt the wildlife needed for his clan's ceremonies and sustenance. There, he regularly sang the hunting songs that brought mule deer, javelina, and desert tortoise within his grasp.

I asked Amalia if any Sand Papago families came to trade or camp during her residence there.

"No, that was before my time," she began, "perhaps in the era of Coyote Iguana, the powerful Seri man whom a few of our people think the well is named for. He did pass through, but he lived mostly on Isla Tiburón. Some people think he was Papago or Pima because he could speak their language, but he was one of us." She was referring to a Seri Indian medicine man prominent in the 1850s, but she spoke as though he had been a neighbor during her own lifetime. There was more than a half-century gap between his death and her birth, yet, as we learned from historic documents written during his era, the orally transmitted stories about him were as accurate as any could be.

Almost as an afterthought, Amalia tossed out another comment. "Of course, my mother could understand Papago, although...could only speak a few...of their dialect.... She...."

I thought I had heard her correctly, but the background noise of driving the washboard road had robbed my ears of certain words. I asked Janice if she could ask Amalia to say it again.

"Your mother could understand Papago?" Janice beckoned. It seemed incredible, since Seri and Papago are in different language families; their sounds, syntax, and deep structures are as distinct from one another as Mandarin Chinese is from Czech.

"Well, yes," Amalia replied, nonplussed. "My grandmother was Papago married into the Seri. Have I not told you I have Papago blood running in me?"

I looked at her through the rearview mirror. She had always seemed to me to be the quintessential *cmique cmaam*—as Seri as a woman could be. She knew more Seri songs than any woman in her village; she knew the local herbs, the traditional dances. It had never occurred to me that she could be of mixed cultural heritage.

I was jarred out of my reverie by the sight of a ridge that I had assumed to be past the turnoff to Pozo Coyote. We had nearly reached the paved highway, and still Amalia had not told me to turn.

"Have we gone by Pozo Coyote? The highway is not far away...."

The three Seri women broke out in giggles.

"How many times have you traveled this road when you've come to visit us? Here comes Pozo Coyote now. *Ya viene, mihijito.*"

I shifted my gaze from the rearview mirror—where Amalia's eyes continued to dazzle me beneath the snakeskin pattern on the scarf drawn tightly over her brow—to the modern Mexican ranch house poised on the side of the road. Janice and I had passed this ranch, with its windmill, corrals, and planted palm trees, more than a handful of times just within the last year and many other times prior to that. Janice looked at me and laughed, surprised that I had not figured out "the mystery" of Coyote Well before.

"This is Pozo Coyote?" I moaned, embarrassed that I had not realized that Coyote Well, like many other water holes in the desert, had been usurped by non-Indian ranchers.

This time, the Seri did not give my question an audible response. They wished to alert us to the fact that it was somewhat uncomfortable for them now to return here. This place, where Amalia had been born, was now someone else's. It was the property of a Mexican rancher who decades before had obtained legal papers for terrain that had long been an intertribal commons. Since neither the Seri nor the Papago had claimed it exclusively as their own, a rancher with any savvy at all could easily gain title to it as "open country belonging to no one."

A grizzled Mexican man stared at us from the porch of the ranch house; the three women glanced at him, then whispered something in the backseat, seeming to know who he was. He stepped down off the porch and staggered toward our Dodge van. It was clear that he was inebriated. When he got close enough to see Amalia, Lolita, and Angelita in the backseat, he smirked drunkenly and nodded to me, "You've brought my girlfriends from Desemboque to see me."

Angelita sneered, and Amalia muttered something under her breath. In case I hadn't noticed, Janice touched my knee and whispered, "I don't think they like him—keep us as far away from the drunk as you can."

"Excuse me, sir, is it OK to park the van over there in the shade by the corral?" I pointed to a large mesquite tree a full hundred yards away from where he stood.

"What do you want to do that for?" he asked, unable to figure out why we wouldn't park in front of his house if we were to stay a while.

"These ladies are going to show us where some old Indian camps are," Janice cut in. "We'll be over toward the mountain somewhere," and she waved her arm so widely toward the range in front of us that he'd be discouraged to follow.

This made no sense to him in his semi-stupor. "Go ahead. Do what you want. Your car will be safe anywhere you leave it."

As we left him behind to park in the shade, Amalia filled us in on grizzled old Pedro.

"He's just caretaking while the *patrón* is away. He sometimes runs a store in our village, where he bothers all the women with his come-ons. We won't have anything to do with him."

After we had parked and locked the van, Janice asked the women, "Can you show us some of the places where your people used to stay?"

We watched as Amalia, without even a word in return, began walking in the opposite direction from the ranch house; Angelita and Lolita fell in behind her. Janice and I hurried to catch up with them—they were dressed in their finest clothes, but they still made rapid tracks across the desert floor.

Finally, Amalia paused for a moment on the other side of the corral, looking at all the piles of dried cow manure, broken-down pumps, cracked plowshares, and roasting pits for the clandestine production of ironwood and mesquite charcoal.

"We had brush houses and campfires all along through here." There was more mesquite and ironwood then and no cows, I imagined. Few Seri have ever kept livestock for long. Amalia glanced down at the ground and walked on. I looked to where she had glanced and spotted a pottery shard. I held it up to the three women who inspected it for a moment. "It's Papago pottery," Amalia said matter-of-factly. "Seri pottery is much thinner and never black inside. We never used cow manure to fire it."

The women walked on across the shrub-choked floodplain, casually pointing out medicinal herbs to Janice, who was eager to learn their Seri names. They would correct her if she mispronounced them, laughing with delight when she enunciated the names so well that she sounded like a Seri herself. All the time, however, Amalia's eyes scanned ahead, as she picked a way through the burrowweed and cholla to the base of a rocky ridge on the other side of the floodplain. She led us over to a large boulder just above the dry stream channel and nodded, encouraging us to stand on top of it. It was pocked with bedrock mortar holes, hand-carved for grinding mesquite pods into flour—a Seri and Papago staple in the old days.

"*Son morteros para machacar la pechita, ¿no?*" I asked her, motioning as if I were grinding mesquite pods on a mortar.

"*Azj,*" she replied simply. One of the seven terms the Seri use for the different stages of ripeness of mesquite pods, this one signified the driest stage, when the pods are easiest to grind into fine flour. The Spanish term for mesquite pod, *pechita*, lacks that precision.

Amalia stood with her back to us, looking over the fertile flood-plain that had been her home—now a deforested, pitted, trashed landscape.

"At least the rocks are still here," she said at last, referring not merely to the boulder but to the grindstone *manos* we had found under the bushes on the slope behind it. Then she added perfunctorily, "Everything else has been washed away."

Not everything, I thought to myself. Some of it has been plowed and bulldozed away. Some of it has been burned and fire scarred, broken or buried. But that ancient place where the Coyote came to drink water—*Hathajc Ano Ziix Cooco* in the Seri language—rose again in her memory as she surveyed the land: the crackle of campfires, the smell of meat being grilled, the singing late into the night, the taste of ripened cactus fruit juices lingering on the tongue. From there, she had once walked overland to a cave at *Hast Ihiajaxo*, where she swung a bullroarer around her head at its entrance until the cave opened its spirit to her, just as it had empowered the first Seri who came to this desert. No, not all was gone—not until Amalia herself died.

After a bit, I asked Amalia why the Seri let a Mexican rancher take over a place that meant so much to them. She looked out over the volcanic landforms for a long time and smiled faintly.

"Well, he doesn't even know it, but his great-grandmother was a Seri woman named Virginia. During the time of Coyote Iguana, Virginia had many daughters, one who married a Papago, another a Yaqui, and another a Castilian; that daughter was to be this rancher's grandmother. At some point, his family got papers claiming ownership to the well in what used to be our home, but there was a reason we never fought them: it is a distant memory, but his family was one of ours."

She stopped talking for a moment. "My husband and the rancher, they are friends. But I see him bring hunters here to kill the mountain sheep and the peccaries that are ours. I am not so sure I am as complacent about all this as Adolfo is."

Amalia's neighbor Evangelina López Blanco later told me that she too is uneasy about the Seri legacy at Pozo Coyote. "It's all over for us there, our time is finished," she said. "All of the great old-timers have died. Now it is in the hands of the descendants of a man who called himself the king of Coyote Well. We had no way to defend our rights there; now they've all gone."

Amalia and Evangelina's wrenching reflections propelled me a hundred miles down the coast, and back in time a half dozen years. I had been invited to talk to the "Environment Committee" of the Arizona-Mexico Governors' Commission, which was having its meetings that year in the booming tourist town of Bahía San Carlos. The North American Free Trade Agreement (NAFTA) had recently passed, with the blessings of both governors and most members of the binational commission. They were using their annual meetings to celebrate the victory and to begin scheming on transboundary economic developments. I was one of the minority that was concerned that NAFTA's passing had already begun to hasten new woodcutting, mining, and tourist development along the coast, before proper environmental protection measures had been put into place.

The pollution-abatement engineer who chaired the Environment Committee warned me against giving too pessimistic a talk at the meeting, for fear of alienating government officials still giddy from NAFTA's passage. He asked that we chat before the environment session, which, he informed me, had been moved from the old Playa de Cortez hotel where we were staying to another hotel down the road.

"How do I find this other hotel?" I asked.

"Don't worry—there will be buses to take all of us over there. It is where the NAFTA celebratory banquet will be as well. I'll see you in the lobby there."

I had been pouring over my notes when the bus came to a halt. I looked up from my notebook and glanced out the window. A wave of disorientation washed over me. I had been coming to San Carlos Bay on camping trips for almost twenty years, but I could not recall ever having seen this hotel.

As I disembarked and looked around me, I saw a familiar landmark on the horizon. Then another—*Teta Cahui*—a famous peak on the boundary between Seri and Yaqui country—marking the other horizon. I triangulated from their positions and realized where I was: the hotel parking lot was situated in a former cactus forest where I had first camped on New Year's Eve, 1973. Since that first memorable night, I had camped there with friends at least another dozen times. And now it was paved over and marked with a banner welcoming the Govenor's Commission to "NAFTAlandia."

Perhaps neither of these coastal places had been truly lost: the landmarks surrounding them could still be seen on the horizons, and their underlying landforms were still intact. When I grumbled to another member of the Governors' Environment Committee that I used to camp where the hotel now stands, he scoffed:

> So what do you want to do? Turn back the clock? To when you first came to San Carlos Bay as a tourist? Now thousands of other guys can see the sunsets, feel the breeze, and smell the cactus flowers....Aren't they lured by the same attractions hooking you into coming here again and again? Why should other folks be kept from enjoying what you've enjoyed here just because they prefer beds to your sand-filled sleeping bags?

I did not argue with my fellow committee member. I have never felt smug enough about my own peculiar relationship to a particular place to shut the gate behind me, repelling every other mortal curious about the same spot that fascinates me.

And yet, I wondered, haven't there been places that have been literally wiped clean off the map? Who, in that case, would not feel some remorse?

All too soon after asking myself that question for the first time, I was confronted with the challenge of relocating a place that had been lost from most maps. Over a dozen years, I had collected archival notes and oral histories about an ancient village that I will call Hanging-on-by-a-Thread. It has long been considered to be a "mother village"

of the Sand Papago—that is, an ancestral community from which the
Sand Papago migrated in order to establish new settlements. As far
back as their oral histories go, the Sand Papago would periodically
return to Hanging-on-by-a-Thread from wherever they had gone, in
order to renew contact with their kinsmen. Although written histories document their presence in the area as far back as 1699, I have
stumbled on more ancient sleeping circles there. Archaeologists
reckon that these bedding areas for prehistoric pilgrims date from eras
prior to the local adoption of pottery making in southern Arizona—
at least two thousand years ago.

Despite ample archival evidence regarding the cultural significance
of Hanging-on-by-a-Thread, its specific location had been obscured
by a number of unfortunate circumstances. First, the forty-niners discovered gold in its immediate vicinity, and soon a boomtown grew
up in its midst. But the boomers quickly came to bust, while the Sand
Papago who survived their onslaught remained in place.

Forty years later, however, a hundred-year flood scoured their plantings out of the river valley and washed away their seasonal field houses.
All inhabitants temporarily moved to higher ground, some of them
concentrating their construction of new houses on an island-like ridge
in a side canyon above the fertile floodplain. There, they persisted for
another thirty years, panning for gold, foraging, and fishing along an
intermittent river in a desert where barely four inches of rain fell most
years.

Then, an unprecedented tragedy struck—one much harder to
recover from than a mining boom or bust or even a flood. In the 1920s,
their river dried up. Irrigation engineers miles upstream from the
ancient village had dammed and diverted its entire water flow. There
was suddenly not a drop available to flood-irrigate native crops as they
had been for centuries. Without the ability to farm, forage, or mine
nearby, nearly all the Sand Papago left the area.

One pair of brothers did not leave. Their elderly sister lived off and
on with them. One day in 1963 a man who was later to become a
teacher of mine happened on these three survivors.

"I suppose they were remnant Sand Papago," he told me thirty
years later, as we chatted and drank around a campfire one clear cool
desert night. "They seemed unclear about what to call themselves,

but they took me to an old village where they had grown up. Only a brush house or two were still left standing. No one lived in the old village anymore."

I was anxious to rediscover the village, but I knew it would be hard to find amid the scatter of mine claims, railroad dumps, flood-control levees, and Snowbird homesteads that had accumulated over the last century. Finally, after gathering up my teacher's hand-annotated map, half a dozen oral histories, and a single historic photo, I decided it was time to relocate the mother village on the ground. I invited along a tribal historian and another Native American woman who had extensive training as an archaeological surveyor and mapper. With a few other friends, we left home before dawn, hoping to come upon that ancient place, perhaps even to stumble upon a brush house foundation still intact.

Four hours later, we found ourselves descending toward the floodplain from the precipitous flanks of the volcanic mountain range to the south of it. The archaeologist sat in the backseat of our four-wheel-drive wagon, glancing out the windows, trying to reconcile the map's contour lines with the visible landmarks on the horizons. The historian and I excitedly recalled the names of those families who had originated in this place. She had heard about it since she was a child, she confessed, but had never had the chance to visit it as an adult.

We climbed into a canyon where the floodplain spread out before us. I saw the archaeologist stick her head out the window and glance at the ridges edging the canyon. Then I heard her moan.

"What's up?" I queried. "Are we in the wrong canyon?"

"No, it's not that," she replied, checking the map's contour lines against the scene before us once more. "We're in the canyon right where the map says the village should be. But the low ridge where the village was? The ridge that appears on the map should be right in front of us. Not just the village, the entire ridge—I think they're gone! All of it!"

We were too skeptical to believe that a village could simply disappear. After a couple of weeks, we found an elder of the Sand Papago who had first lived at Hanging-on-by-a-Thread in the 1920s and had visited there off and on for several more decades. "No, I think you went to some other place nearby," he said. "Where I remember the village is just a ways east of there on the other side of the irrigation canal. I could show you where we lived if you want."

On a wintry desert day we left his house a few miles outside of Phoenix and drove three hours through cold rain toward his former home. We postponed our search until the next morning, when the fog had lifted and the dirt roads had dried out. Then we began the slow drive along an irrigation canal, gummy clods of mud sticking to our tires the entire way.

At one point, the old man spotted the adobe walls of the store where he used to buy canned goods.

"Our village, it's just across the canal from here. There should be a little chapel of ours across the way." He nodded toward the east, but all I could see was a thin strip of weedy salt cedar trees clogging the canal banks, and some lettuce fields in the distance.

"There should be a bridge down a half mile or so," he said quietly, tugging his baseball cap visor lower over his eyes.

We drove to where he had known the bridge to be, but it was gone. The irrigation district had apparently decided that there was no reason to maintain a bridge when so few people had any need to cross the canal at that point anymore.

We drove farther, down to a bridge on a major highway between two retirement communities, and then continued on the other side of the canal and dry riverbed, going back in the direction from which we had come. When we could see the tops of the adobe walls of the old store on the other side, I slowed the van down to five miles an hour. The old man scanned the scene before us.

The stand of salt cedar along the irrigation ditch was rather narrow—it hid a few beehives and one rickety tire shed from the sixties, but not much else. Next to it was a small backwater slough ponded with saline tailwater. A couple of cattle egrets lounged in its shallows, and a solitary hummingbird darted out into the sunlight from the shadows of the salt cedars on its banks.

The old man, I noticed, was not looking for the village on that side of the van anymore. He looked out in another direction, his eyes fixing on a place not even five hundred yards from where the adobe store stood on the horizon.

"All this ground, out in the onions..." He stopped himself.

"The village was where the field is now..." Again he stopped.

He got out of the van, walked three paces toward the hundred-acre field of onions, and paused. He pulled his baseball cap down lower over his eyes, then climbed back in.

"We would walk about this far over from the store," he sighed. "But because they put in these fields here the way they did, I don't know if they left anything of the church. There should be bricks..."

He didn't finish the sentence. I couldn't stand the notion of the walls of their sanctuary of prayer atomizing under the onion bulbs. We sat there for a couple more minutes, looking at tens of thousands of onions in perfectly shaped furrows.

The old man spoke once more, his voice just above a whisper.

"The river was over there. The canal is that way. The houses must have been right in here..."

His eyes dropped to the first few rows of onions.

"It's hard to tell where it really was anymore."

The rest of us could not say a thing.

"I guess we can go now."

Disorientation. Is it when you lose your landmarks? Or when you lose yourself, the personal path you are following? Perhaps there is some vicious feedback loop between these two ways of becoming disoriented.

When I first worked around the O'odham in southern Arizona, it was with Tohono O'odham (Desert Papago) families who still foraged for some wild foods but who made their meager incomes off farming, ranching, basketry, and firewood collecting. For this latter task, they often used wagons for hauling loads along sandy or muddy roads, and to pull the wagons they used mules.

In one O'odham village, they named a mule after me. I had helped the villagers purchase my namesake in a Mormon town off the reservation. Before putting him and his partner Cynthia to work, the two mules were broken and trained at an old livery stable in South Tucson.

Every few days that summer, I would visit the stable and check up on the mule's progress. An Okie cowboy ran the stables, but he had three unpaid consultants on mule skinning and horse breaking who did most of the talking when I came by.

One of these consultants had worked all around Arizona, logging and prospecting, and had kept mules most of his adult life. He was dying of emphysema and was obtaining medical services by staying with his daughter, who lived in the middle of the city. He clearly hated the city, hated doctors, and hated dying. So he spent all his waking hours volunteering at the stables. Because of his long, gray, curly beard and loquaciousness, we called him Gabby Hayes.

Another of the unpaid consultants was a Sonoran who had worked ranches on both sides of the border. He was normally quiet but prided himself that he had learned English well enough to understand most of Gabby's jokes. He had a wonderful way of talking to the mules, calming them, reassuring them, when they had blinders first put on them. The others simply called him "the Mexican." I was never sure whether they could even pronounce his name.

The third consultant was the one who seemed the loneliest. He had lived most of his life in Montana and Wyoming and had worked as a blacksmith when he was younger. He also had a knack for repairing old tack—mending leather, reriveting pieces of bridles and harnesses and stirrups. He had sold a small ranch up in the Northern Plains and had moved to Tucson with no prior knowledge of the place. Perhaps his second wife had asked him to do so, and he had naively consented; I cannot remember the details, but it was clear that he was homesick. We called him Montana.

What I do remember is that all three of these men had somehow converged at the stables just when we needed help with the mules. For the next five weeks, those two mules kept the three men alive and relatively sane. When the men were not out working them behind carriages, carts, and plows, they sat on some alfalfa bales watching the beasts, telling tales that conjured up every mule they had ever known. None of them knew firsthand the places the other two spoke of nor the people and animals that became the heroes and villains they shared through their yarns. Yet the telling of the tales made those mythic characters come alive once more and helped the three men fend off the hopelessness they otherwise felt in the city.

They kept the mules two weeks longer than we had originally

planned, but when Gary and Cynthia left one day in a double horse trailer, they were ready to plow, pull wagons, and be ridden.

Two months after the mules had done their first plowing on the reservation, I went to give Gabby, the Mexican, and Montana a progress report. As I drove down the avenue in South Tucson toward the stables, I noticed two bulldozers and a dump truck in a vacant lot. Suddenly, I realized that what was "vacant" had been the site of the stables. Nearly every trace—horse turd, board, and nail—had been removed. Where the corral had stood, where the mules had been tamed, a big white sign announced the new use planned for the site: FUTURE HOME OF THE OLD PUEBLO NEIGHBORHOOD HEALTH CENTER — BRINGING YOUR COMMUNITY THE BEST OF FAMILY COUNSELING, MENTAL HEALTH, AND OCCUPATIONAL THERAPY.

I'm sure that Gabby, Montana, and the Mexican never set foot inside its doors.

It happens to others, right? Indians, Mexicans, cowboys, miners. It happens in rapidly growing cities, sure. On coastlines, and along rivers.

I guess I thought I was immune. Or that my birthplace was immune—after all, it had already been settled for hundreds of years. On the edge of Gary, Indiana, the Indiana Dunes were not exactly pristine—they had been logged to provide timber to rebuild the city after the Great Chicago Fire, and their sand had been quarried by railroads and steel mills long before I had been born. What more could be lost there?

Two decades after leaving the Midwest, I was invited back to Chicagoland to give an evening lecture to the Society for Ecological Restoration. When I received the invitation, I decided to take a couple of extra days in northern Indiana to see my Lebanese relatives and to reacquaint myself with the dunes. The first day I would spend with cousins in my old neighborhood haunts; the day after the lecture, I would join a field trip to look at rare plants in and around Indiana Dunes National Lakeshore.

When a cousin offered to drive me to the new Paul Douglas Environmental Education Center built by the National Park Service, I assumed that it would be out at West Beach—the largest administrative unit of the Lakeshore close to the city. Instead, he drove me two blocks down from where my father grew up, not far from where our Lutheran church had once been, in between two sets of railroad tracks running into the steel mills. It had been wooded dunes and marshes when I had grown up, land owned by the mills and destined for industrial development. Then the bottom had fallen out of U.S. steel production, and the land had been shunted off to the Park Service. A victory for dunes conservation, yes? The Park Service decided to build a state-of-the-art interactive learning center there to teach inner-city kids about the wonders of sand and swamps. Finally, the park planners hoped, the dunes could be appreciated by more than just the leisure class. It was an ideal that I embraced, to be sure.

My reaction to being in the dunes this time was different than ever before. The asphalt lot where we parked my rental car had been a stables where I had first ridden a horse, propped up in front of the mother of this cousin. When I first studied medicinal herbs, I had collected sassafras roots there.

When we walked across a bridge above the street, we came down on the other side into woods I had wandered in for years. With my father, I once saw the police arrest a black man for fishing in one of the swamps on this side of the road. Another time, the same officer wrote out tickets for Polish women picking mushrooms there.

"They were trespassing," I heard the policeman tell my father. "Wild mushrooms, of all things. Most are either poisonous or like dope," the cop smirked. Even if they weren't hallucinogenic, he added, the women had no right to wander past the mill's NO TRESPASSING signs to pick things in the woods. The mills run the show in this company town, he added, and I would not have been surprised if he received something on the side for keeping their interests in mind.

I remember only the image of stocky women in flowered dresses, cardigan sweaters, and babushkas. They were bent over, searching the ground for fungus. They had baskets full of these earthy riches. I wondered why men like my father and his Irish cronies were allowed to hunt rabbits there, or why I could practice shooting my uncle's double-barreled shotgun, but those old Polish women could not hunt their mushrooms, and African-American men could not fish.

When I recalled that scene for my cousin, he asked if the Park Service would now let anyone at all forage, fish, or hunt small game on that land. No, I realized. Of course not. National parks and lakeshores are typically *protected* from all uses—that is, except *recreation and education*.

We made our way through the Douglas Environmental Education Center, guided by a bright young African-American ranger who had an immense knowledge of wetland water chemistry and frogs. The photos and drawings in the Douglas Center showed children of African, Asian, and Mesoamerican descent learning about the dunes. Interactions were confined to the "learning modules" inside. You were not allowed to partake of the dunes. On the edge of a city where racial prejudice had run rampant for decades, it was heartening to see that no ethnic minority was left out of the picture. But they were all expected to act like the leisure class—no mushroom gathering, no sassafras-root collecting, and no hunting as their grandparents (or mine) might have done.

A couple of days later, I joined the Society for Ecological Restoration field trip in the Indiana Dunes. I was surprised when their bus stopped just half a mile from where I had grown up, in a sparsely populated patch of dunes and marshlands that had recently been acquired by the National Park Service. It was not particularly scenic nor a very large tract of land. My friend from college days, Ken Cole, was leading the trip; he was a National Park Service ecologist.

I pulled him aside as the rest of the group was still getting off the bus.

"Ken, why are we stopping here? Most people consider this to be a fairly beat-up patch of dunes. I used to play in it."

"Well, it happens to be one of the few patches with a dynamic population of endangered plants in it. They happen to need occasional fires running through their habitat to keep it opened up, and from looking at historic photos, this is one of the few areas that fires have regularly run through for decades."

I suppressed a smile. "Tell me more."

"There are other patches of this rare plant in older, more scenic parts of the park, but I can't get a fire permit from the local municipality to burn there—too many buildings nearby, they say. Fortunately, this neighborhood has always had a wild bunch of kids that periodically torch the place. Because the plant population is between sets of railroad lines, we can usually stop their fires before they reach the houses."

"I know all about *that* part of the story," I laughed. "I was one of the kids who used to start those fires."

"What?"

"Originally, we just set rocks and tree branches on the railroad tracks to try and derail trains. When they screeched to a stop, they'd throw sparks into the dry brush along the tracks, and very often the sparks would catch. We'd watch it burn for a while until we thought we had something challenging, and then we'd take old doormats and rugs, soak them, and try to put the fire out. Usually, it'd burn toward the marshes and put itself out, so there wasn't much danger."

"Well, that informal practice of pyromania has become a tradition in your old neighborhood, Nabhan. They get to start fires where I can't get permission to do so, and that's the main reason this plant is still surviving here."

The bus had emptied, and Ken had to go and tell the "official story" of endangered plant recovery in the dunes. I stayed back from the crowd, wandered around a little, and found a trail spur that I must have taken on my first hike of more than four miles, a hike I did with a friend one Sunday when we were nine or ten years old. I could close my eyes and recall what the wetlands and sand prairies here smelled like when a wildfire blazed through them. I could remember what it felt like to run down this trail, shoes filled with sand and stinking of burned rubber, chasing the flames. Not all lost places go away for good. Some we carry with us. Some remain hidden behind the most unlikely facades, waiting for us to remember.

Cultural Parallax

The Wilderness Concept in Crisis

"This naturalist I admire," I said, "says that
every species lives in its own sensory world."
The raccoon stared down; he was silent.
"He also said that we may come to know enough about
the human brain to diagnose and correct for the
deformations imposed by evolution on the human senses
and arrive at something like objective truth."
The raccoon was silent.
ROBERT HASS, *Sun Under Wood*

The Sierra Bacatete rises up from the desert plains of southern Sonora like a battleship out of a placid sea; the mountain range is unbelievably rugged, arid, and, at first glance, impenetrable. That is how the Yoeme or Yaqui Indian *guerrilleros* have wanted outsiders to think of it—as a place too formidable for casual entry.

Indeed, from a 1740 Yaqui "rebellion" against the Spaniards colonizing the west coast of Mexico through the Mexican Revolution and beyond, Yaqui dissidents regularly took refuge in this sierra when the political climate got too hot down on the Rio Yaqui floodplain. But it has also been a place where the Yaqui sought the spirit of the wilderness, a power called *yo ania.* No doubt there were a few small Yaqui outposts on the margins of the Sierra Bacatete before 1600, but since then it has been largely uninhabited.

Throughout Yaqui history this region has been considered among the most culturally significant terrain within the wilderness world that the Yaqui call the *huya ania.* They consider it rich not only in vegetation and wildlife but also in power—put simply in terms of their folk Catholicism, it is a place "where Jesus has walked."

In 1987, a Sonoran Yaqui elder known by the name of Miki Maaso, who had come up from his homeland to a gathering of deer singers, told Felipe Molina and Larry Evers that there was no difference between this wilderness and what a Westerner might call a "holy place," be it a sacred mountain or a church: "The holy churches of the Eight [Yaqui] Pueblos, the holy churches that are sitting there in the wilderness world, in the mountains, wherever they are in the desert in the most enchanted world, they are sitting there."

A few years later, while waiting to meet Felipe Molina at the home of his Yaqui relatives in southern Sonora, I camped with Richard Nelson at the base of the Sierra Bacatete. I recall a lovely spring morning at the foot of the Bacatetes, the Tall Cane-reed Mountains. We sat around a small campfire, eating tortillas and salsa, stumbling on ancient potsherds, watching caracaras land in giant *cardón* cacti, and reading historic texts about the Yaqui. Of all the historic accounts I have ever read about the first contact between Europeans and Native Americans, the one I read that morning is most deeply imprinted in my memory.

On October 4, 1533—the day the Yaqui celebrate as the Feast of Saint Francis—an observer recorded the arrival of a slave-trading expedition at its northernmost destination within the Rio Yaqui watershed. The soldiers and slave buyers looked up to see a wave of Yaqui people and animals moving toward them: "[They] began to march towards us very boldly, throwing fistfuls of dirt into the air, flexing their bows and making fierce grimaces.... [Their leader was] an old man more distinguished than the others, because he wore a black robe like a scapular, studded with pearls and surrounded by dogs, birds, deer and many other things.... And as it was morning, the sunlight fell on him, he blazed like silver…the old man drew a line on the ground as a demarcation, threatening death to any intruder who dared cross it."

In this manner, the Spaniards became familiar not only with the ferocity of the Yaqui when defending their homelands but also with the sanctity of their wilderness world, the *huya ania*, with all its attendant creatures.

Nearly 500 years have passed since Europeans encountered the Yaqui and their animal neighbors in the Yaqui's self-described wilderness world. Ironically, there are scholars who believe that the concept of *wilderness* is unique to Eurocentric cultures, whether this concept is used in a pejorative way as a place uninhabitable or taken in a positive light as a sanctuary of immeasurable spiritual significance. In a recent essay by award-winning environmental historian William Cronon, "The Trouble with Wilderness," we are told that "wilderness is not what it seems. Far from being the one place on earth that stands apart from humanity, it is quite profoundly a human creation—indeed, the creation of very particular human cultures at very particular moments in human history. It is not a pristine sanctuary where the last remnant of an untouched, endangered, but still transcendent nature can for at least a little while longer be encountered without the contaminating taint of civilization. Instead, it is a product of that civilization, and could hardly be contaminated by the very stuff of which it is made…. The removal of Indians to create an 'uninhabited wilderness'—uninhabitable as never before in the human history of the place—reminds us of just how invented, just how constructed, the American wilderness really is."

If I read Cronon correctly, he wishes us to believe that all American land masses were completely inhabited by peoples who spared no areas from hunting, gathering, plowing, or home construction. He believes that celebrating wilderness came into vogue only when European civilization invaded America, transformed it, and in retrospect, developed a nostalgic view of our fall from the Garden.

Scholars are not the only ones who feel that there is an inevitable tension between indigenous peoples and the notion of wilderness. Human rights activists and conservationists have also entered into the discussion. Marcus Colchester, director of the Forest Peoples Programme of the World Rainforest Movement, has argued that "the concept of 'wilderness' is a culturally bound one that does not apply well to indigenous peoples' areas, for such [areas are] their home. The concept of 'wilderness' should be re-evaluated or rejected. The concept lies behind a number of the problems inherent in imposing protected area status on indigenous territories."

Clearly, there is a debate raging about "wild nature." It is not merely an argument regarding indigenous people's displacement by national park rangers and game wardens. It is also a disagreement regarding the extent to which habitats have been managed, diversified, or degraded over the past ten thousand years of human occupation.

This debate has at its heart three issues: whether the "natural condition of the land" by definition excludes human management; whether officially designated wilderness areas in the United States should be free of hunting, gathering, and vegetation management by Native Americans or other people; and whether traditional management by indigenous peoples is any more benign or ecologically sensitive than that imposed by resource managers trained in the use of modern Western scientific principles, methods, and technologies. This is not merely an academic dispute. It involves hunters, gatherers, ranchers, farmers, and political activists from a variety of cultures. The outcome will no doubt shape the destiny of officially designated wilderness areas in national parks and forests throughout North America.

Consider the declaration of the 1963 Leopold Report to the U.S. secretary of the interior: that each large national park should maintain or recreate "a vignette of primitive America," seeking to restore "conditions as they prevailed when the area was first visited by the white man"—as if those conditions were synonymous with "pristine" or "untrammeled" wilderness.

Such a declaration either implies that pre-Columbian Native Americans had no impact on the areas now found within the U.S. National Park System or that indigenous management of vegetation and wildlife as it was done in pre-Columbian times is compatible with and essential to wilderness quality. For Native Americans with historic ties to land, water, and biota within parks, the latter interpretation offers a rationale for their serving as *co-managers* of these areas, not merely harvesters of certain traditionally utilized resources, as currently sanctioned by the National Park Service.

On one side of the debate are those who argue that Native Americans have had a negligible impact on their homelands. That is to say, these original human inhabitants did little actively to manage or influence wildlife populations one way or another. These proponents might cite John Muir, who wrote, "Indians walked softly and hurt the landscape hardly more than the birds and squirrels, and their brush and bark huts last hardly longer than those of wood rats, while their enduring monuments, excepting those wrought on the forests by fires they made to improve their hunting grounds, vanish in a few centuries." Yet the Yosemite landscapes that Muir knew so well are now known to have been dramatically shaped by Native American management practices.

Some feel that Native American spirituality kept indigenous communities from harming habitats or the biota. Leslie Silko, of Laguna Pueblo, has argued that "survival depended upon the harmony and cooperation, not only among human beings, but among all things— the animate and the less animate.... As long as good family relations [among all beings] are maintained, then the Sky will continue to bless her sister, the Earth, with rain, and the Earth's children will continue to survive." The implication is that Native Americans practiced a spirituality earthly enough to foster cooperation and harmony rather than competition with or depletion of other animals.

Others contend that indigenous peoples have opportunistically exterminated wildlife and that their farming, hunting, and gathering techniques were often ecologically ill suited for the habitats in which they were practiced. Kent Redford of the Nature Conservancy has challenged the romantic notion of "the ecological noble savage." Jared Diamond, author of *The Third Chimpanzee*, claims that in thirty years of visiting native peoples on the island of New Guinea, he has failed to come across a single example of indigenous New Guineans showing friendly responses to wild animals or consciously managing habitats to enhance wildlife populations. He adds that natives have damaged biota in North America as well.

But Diamond's conclusions have been challenged by many experts. Part of Diamond's problem is his failure to take into account historic and cultural differences in discussions of "the Native American view of nature" and assessments of the pre-Columbian condition of North American habitats. To assume, for example, that the Hopi and their Navajo neighbors think of, speak of, and treat nature in the same manner is simply naive. Yet individuals from two hundred different language groups from three historically and culturally distinct colonizations of the continent are commonly lumped under the catchall terms "American Indian" or "Native American."

Even within one mutually intelligible language group, such as the Piman-speaking O'odham, there are considerable differences in the linguistically encoded taboos with which they honor dangerous or symbolically powerful animals. While the River Pima do not allow themselves to eat badgers, bears, quail, or certain reptiles for fear of "staying sickness," these taboos are relaxed or even dismissed by other Piman groups who live in more marginal habitats where game is less abundant. An animal such as the black bear—which is never eaten by one Piman community because it is still considered to be one of the "people"—is routinely hunted by another Piman-speaking group, which prizes its skin and pit-roasts its meat—an act that would be considered akin to cannibalism in the former group.

Despite such diversity within and between North American cultures, it is still quite common to read statements implying a uniform Native American view of nature, as if all the diverse cultural relations with particular habitats on the continent can be swept under one all-encompassing rug. The same absurdity occurs when "the Eurocentric view of nature" is taken to mean that the Swiss, Swedes, Sicilians, Slovaks, Basques, Lapps, and Gypsies all view and use wildlands in the same manner. This assumption is both erroneous and counterproductive, and it undermines respect for the realities of cultural diversity. Nevertheless, it continues to permeate land-use policies, environmental philosophies, and even park management plans. It does not grant *any* culture—indigenous or otherwise—the capacity to evolve, to diverge from others, or to learn about their local environments through time.

This distortion of the relationships between human cultures and the rest of the natural world is what I call "cultural parallax" of the wilderness concept. *Parallax* is the apparent displacement of an observed object due to the difference between two points of view. Simply put, it is the discrepancy between what you see out of the viewfinder and what the film "sees" through the lens. A cultural parallax, then, might be considered to be the difference in views between those who are actively participating in the dynamics of the habitats within their home range and those who view those habitats as "landscapes" from the outside. As Leslie Silko has suggested, "so long as human consciousness remains *within* the hills, canyons, cliffs, and the plants, clouds, and sky, the term *landscape* as it has entered the English language is misleading. A portion of territory the eye can comprehend in a single view does not correctly describe the relationship between a human being and his or her surroundings."

Adherents of the classic notion of landscape claim that the most pristine and therefore most favorable condition of the American continent worthy of reconstruction is that which prevailed at the moment of European colonization. This is ironic, for as historic geographers William Denevan and William Cronon have amply documented, the continent was most intensively managed by Native Americans for the several centuries prior to Columbus's arrival in the West Indies. Because European diseases decimated native populations through the Americas over the following hundred and fifty years, the European colonists who arrived after the epidemics saw only vestiges of these managed habitats, if they recognized them as managed at all.

Such evidence notwithstanding, ecologists such as Daniel Botkin still maintain that "the idea is to create natural areas that appear as they did when first viewed by European explorers. In the Americas, this would be the landscape of the seventeenth century.... If natural means simply *before human intervention*, then all these habitats could be claimed as natural."

Astonishingly, Botkin equates the periods prior to European colonization with those *prior to human intervention* in American ecosystems, assuming that all habitats were equally untouched at that time. Either the pre-Columbian inhabitants of North America were not human, or they had no significant interactions with the biota of the areas where they resided!

But human intervention in North American habitats began at least 9,200 years prior to the period Botkin pinpoints—in one scenario, this occurred when newly arrived "colonists" came down from the Bering Strait into ice-free country. Regardless of how major a role humans played in the Pleistocene extinctions, the loss of 73 percent of the North American genera of terrestrial mammals weighing one hundred pounds or more precipitated major changes in vegetation and wildlife abundance. By Paul Martin's criteria, North American wilderness areas have been lacking "completeness" for more than ten millennia; that is, they have been playing without a full deck of fauna. To Martin's mind, they now require the introduction of large herbivores from other continents to simulate the "natural conditions" comparable to those under which vegetation cover evolved over the hundreds of thousands of years prior to these extinctions.

Many of the same scholars who grant pre-Columbian cultures more ecological wisdom than recent European colonists deny the possibility that these cultures could have played any role at all in these faunal extinctions, as if that wisdom did not take centuries to accumulate. Do they believe that the pre-Columbian cultures of North America became "instant natives" incapable of overtaxing any resources in their newfound homeland—an incapability that few Europeans have achieved since arriving in the Americas five centuries ago? Conservation biologist Michael Soule has pointed out that "the most destructive cultures, environmentally, appear to be those that are colonizing uninhabited territory and those that are in a stage of rapid cultural (often technological) transition."

Might it take time for any culture to become truly "native," if that term is to imply sensitivity to ecological constraints? It seems plausible that many indigenous American cultures developed increasing sensitivity to the plant and animal populations most vulnerable to depletion within their home ranges. Indigenous cultures probably learned to manage vulnerable habitats and plant populations in response to earlier episodes of overexploitation.

There is now abundant evidence that hundreds of thousands of acres in various bioregions of North America were actively managed by indigenous cultures, while millions of additional acres were scarcely exploited. The entire continent was not a Garden of Eden cultivated or hunted by Native Americans, nor was it all pristine. Many large tracts of the North American continent remained beyond the influence of human cultures and should remain so. Nevertheless, it is clear that the degree to which North American plant populations were consciously managed—and conserved—by local cultural traditions has been underestimated.

Hohokam farmers cultivated two perennial agaves related to the tequila plant over hundreds of square miles of Arizona's slopes and terraces beyond where modern annual crops can be cultivated today. Ironically, the discovery of native domesticated agaves being grown on a large scale in the Sonoran Desert has been made only within the last quarter century, despite more than a half century of intensive archaeological investigation in the region. Earlier archaeologists had simply never imagined that pre-Columbian cultures in North America could have cultivated perennial crops on such a scale away from riverine irrigation sources, for their own society could not pull off such a feat.

In the deserts of southern California, indigenous communities transplanted and managed palms for their fruits and fiber in artificial oases, some of them apparently beyond the "natural distribution" of the California fan palm. Controlled burns were part of their management of these habitats. Such deliberate use of fire created artificial savannas in regions as widely separated as the California Sierra and the Carolinas. In the Yosemite area, where John Muir claimed that "Indians walked softly and hurt the landscape hardly more than the birds and squirrels," Anderson's reconstructions of Miwok subsistence ecology demonstrate that the very habitat mosaic Muir attempted to preserve as wilderness was in fact the cumulative result of Miwok burning, pruning, and selective harvesting over the course of centuries. Is it not odd that after ten to twelve thousand years of indigenous cultures making their homes in North America, Europeans moved in and hardly noticed that the place looked "lived-in"?

There are three possible explanations for this failure. One response, as Cronon and Denevan have suggested, is that many previously managed landscapes had been left abandoned between the time when European-introduced diseases spread through the Americas and the time when Europeans actually set foot in second-growth forests, shrub-invaded savannas, or defaunated deserts. The second explanation is that Europeans were so intent on taking possession of these lands and developing them in their own manner that they hardly paid attention to signs that the land had already been managed on a different scale and level of intensity. A third explanation (as described in Kirkpatrick Sale's *The Conquest of Paradise*) is that Europe was so devastated ecologically by the fifteenth century that Europeans couldn't recognize a healthy habitat.

It was also easier for Europeans to assume possession of a land they considered to be virgin or at least unworked and uninhabited by people of their equal. Columbus himself had set out to discover unspoiled lands where the seeds of Christianity—a faith that was being corrupted in Europe, he felt—could be transplanted into an untainted context. In 1502, well after his own men had unleashed European weeds, diseases, and weapons on the inhabitants of the Americas, Columbus wrote to Pope Alexander VI claiming that he had personally visited the Garden of Eden on his voyages to the New World. He said it was a bump on the globe, "like a nipple on a woman's breast."

We must also keep in mind some other nuances in the argument over wilderness and indigenous resource management. Among those who have condemned Europeans for ecological imperialism, there is a tendency to talk of "conquistadors raping a virgin land." As "subjects of rape," American lands and their resident human populations are reduced to the role of passive victims, incapable of any resilience or response for dealing with such invasions. The notion that before the white man came, North America was essentially a wilderness where the few Indian inhabitants lived in constant harmony with nature is one that oversimplifies a rich and varied history. At any one time during the centuries prior to Columbus, four to twelve million North American residents speaking two hundred languages variously burned, pruned, hunted, hacked, cleared, irrigated, planted, offered prayers, and sought visions in an astonishing diversity of habitats.

Although there is little evidence that late prehistoric indigenous cultures extirpated any rare plants, there are intriguing signs that a few communities did deplete certain small game such as woodchucks and squirrels, local supplies of cottonwood or mesquite firewood, and slow-growing fiber plants such as yuccas. Despite this, it can no longer be denied that some cultures have developed specific conservation practices to sustain plant populations of economic or symbolic importance to their communities. The O'odham are among those who still protect rare plants from overharvesting near sacred sites, who transplant individual cacti and tubers to more protected sites, and who once conserved caches of seeds in caves to ensure future supplies. They have pruned and promoted the fruiting of certain rare food plants, plants they claim to be rarer now than when Native Americans intensively used them.

These practices, maintained for multiple generations, can be called *conservation traditions*. I find in the oral literature of my O'odham neighbors—as I do in the Yaqui concept of *huya ania*—a counterpoint to the notion that conserving wildlands with minimum human manipulation is at odds with indigenous beliefs. The O'odham term for wildness, *doajkam*, is etymologically tied to terms for health, wholeness, and liveliness. While it seems wildness is valued as an ideal by which to measure other conditions, the O'odham also feel that certain other plants, animals, and habitats—those of the people— "degenerate" if not properly cared for. Thus their failure to take care of a horse or a crop may allow it to go feral, but this degenerated feral state is different from being truly wild. Similarly, if the O'odham fail to pay attention to their fields, watersheds, and associated ceremonies, it may keep the rains from providing sufficient moisture to sustain those dependent on both wild and cultivated environments. Many O'odham express humility in the face of unpredictable rains or infrequent sightings of game animals, but they still feel a measure of responsibility in making clear distinctions over what they can manage and what they cannot.

As O'odham poet Ofelia Zepeda has written, "we know where the 'wild' desert ends and the 'other space' begins." She explains that the other, domesticated space is nested within the wilderness that is also part of her people's habitat, even though each is clearly delineated: "We have marked the space within the space that is already ours. This space, I say, is already ours, ours in the sense that it is our habitat: we are the ones who were put here to live. And even though we live here, we continue to remark it, create boundaries. We fence in, and out.... Now because we know where the desert ends, we also know *what* is in that desert.... As O'odham, we know the desert is a place of songs...the place where nightmares hide...a place of power."

The O'odham elders I know best are still active participants in the desert without ever assuming that they are ultimately "in control" of it. This, in essence, is the difference between participating in *untrammeled* wilderness (as defined by the U.S. Wilderness Act) and attempting to tame lands through manipulative management. (My friend Jack Turner explained to me that a *trammel* is a device that shackles, hobbles, cages, or confines an animal, breaking its spirit and capacity to roam.) What may look like uninhabited wilderness to outsiders has within it particular habitats in which the O'odham actively participate. They do not define the desert as it was derived from the Old French *deserter*, "a place abandoned or left wasted." The O'odham term for the desert, *tohono*, can be etymologically understood as a "bright and shining place," and they have long called themselves the *Tohono O'odham*: the people belonging to that place. They share that place with a variety of plants and animals, a broad range of which still inhabit their oral literature.

Within their Sonoran Desert homeland, many O'odham people still learn certain traditional land management scripts encoded in their own Piman language, which they put into practice in particular settings, each in their own peculiar way. But I worry that their indigenous language is now being replaced by English. Their indigenous desert science is being supplanted by exposure to Western science. Their internal sense of what it is to be O'odham is being contaminated by the media's presentation of what it is to be (generically) an American Indian. While I will be among the first to admit that change is inherent to all natural and cultural phenomena, I do not believe that these particular changes are desirable.

In virtually every culture and habitat I know on this continent, similar changes are occurring with blinding speed. Both nature and culture are being rapidly redefined, not so much by our advances in understanding them, but by processes of fragmentation, disruption, and loss.

With more than half the two hundred native languages on this continent falling out of use at an accelerating rate, a great diversity of perspectives on how to sustain the productivity of wildlands is surely being lost as well. Culture-specific land management practices are perhaps being lost even more rapidly, particularly on reservation lands where Bureau of Indian Affairs Land Operations negate or ignore local conservation traditions.

When I recently surveyed the few Native American professionals who assist their communities with managing fish and wildlife, the majority of them could identify particular salmon runs, raptor migrations, medicinal plant patches, or basketry plant stands that have been destroyed during their own lifetimes. This destruction was not usually at the hands of their own people; it was caused by dam construction, mining operations, commercial harvesting ventures, and environmental contamination. In fact, an overwhelming majority of Native American professionals involved in resource management agree that until declining plant and animal populations on wildlands have a chance to recover, their own peoples should practice self-restraint in harvesting them for traditional purposes.

Still, the prevailing sentiment is that their Native American communities have lost contact with wildlife and wildlands that once played important roles in their cultures. This loss of contact further depletes the lexicon of terms commonly used to define and guide cultural relations with the other-than-human world. David Abram writes in *The Spell of the Sensuous*, "As technological civilization diminishes the biotic diversity of the earth, language itself is diminished. As there are fewer songbirds in the air, due to the destruction of their forests and wetlands, human speech loses more and more of its evocative power. For when we no longer hear the voices of warbler and wren, our own speaking can no longer be nourished by their cadences. As the splashing speech of the rivers is silenced by more and more dams, as we drive more and more of the land's wild voices into the oblivion of extinction, our own languages become increasingly impoverished and weightless, progressively emptied of their earthly resonance."

In place of the formerly varied views of the natural world held by the myriad ethnic groups that have inhabited this continent, we are evolving a new, shared viewpoint—one not of experienced participants dynamically involved with their local environment but of observers, viewing the landscape from outside the frame. Because only a small percentage of humankind has any direct, daily engagement with other species of animals and plants in their habitats, we have arrived at a new era in which ecological illiteracy is becoming the norm. Is it any surprise that the deconstructionists' solipsistic assertion that "*wilderness* and *nature* are useless concepts" is in vogue largely within biologically impoverished urban centers where intellectuals tend to ignore any points of reference other than whatever is the current rage in their own circle?

We gain nothing by considering indigenous knowledge and concepts of wilderness to be outmoded constructs. We are losing the cultural perspectives that once maintained the biological diversity of habitats on this continent. I can only hope that future scholars, conservationists, and cultural rights activists will heed Madge Midgley's warning:

> Man is not adapted to live in a mirror-lined box, generating his own electric light and sending for selected images from outside when he needs them. Darkness and bad smell are all that can come from that. We need a vast world, and it must be a world that does not need us; a world constantly capable of surprising us, a world we did not program, since only such a world is the proper object of wonder.

When the Spring of Animal
Dreams Runs Dry

*We are drawn to animals, not just because they are lively and
pretty, but because we think through them. And a world without
an abundance of kinds is bound to be a different world.
A humanity without abundant animals is bound
to be a different humanity.*
PETER STEINHART, "Dreaming Elands," *Audubon*

Where could I go to find ancient bonds between cultures and creatures, connections firmer and stronger than the fragile web entwin-
ing the aspects of my own individual life? After two decades of
following the "environmental movement," I had come to doubt that
any single generation's feeling for wildlife is enough—enough to save
species, to keep their archetypes alive in our minds—if there is not
enough cultural continuity to extend such concerns into future generations. This doubt had sent me out searching for cultural connections with animals that reached back before "wildlife conservation"
became a distinct profession, a concern separate from simply living
well with others in the world. It was then that I began to stumble on
desert Indians who shared a peculiar tradition about bighorn sheep;
they began to teach me something I could not learn from zoology
texts, computerized data banks, or game-management agency files.

Here in the Sonoran Desert borderlands, and nowhere else in the
world, people ritually cremated the bones of their largest prey: bighorn

sheep, pronghorn antelope, and other large game, never bringing the freshly killed animals into their villages. Here, in some of the driest reaches of North America, hunters stacked rams' horns higher than the treetops, and these piles of horns persisted for centuries on the desert floor. It was as if the spirit of wildness had to be kept alive in the desert and outside the confines of domestic life in order to keep wildness itself from becoming endangered.

Thinking of this, I glimpsed a hidden aquifer of uncharted waters. Despite my training as a biologist, I was unsure that I could fathom another, more ancient, way of seeing, dreaming about, and hunting the wild sheep known as *cimarrón* in the desert borderlands between the United States and Mexico. Nevertheless, I began to recognize a sensibility among my O'odham Indian neighbors that had none of the superficial zeal of born-again wildlife protectionists. For an untold number of generations, bighorns had embodied wildness for O'odham dwellers of the Sonoran Desert, and that is what made me look into these waters: the chance of a glimpse at how an oral tradition has expressed the relationship with *wildness*, a relationship of a quality that we may never know again. Although I could never be immersed in their cultural way of seeing and dreaming bighorns—just as I could never see the world as a bighorn sees it—I could at least recognize the existence of a world beyond my vision. Still, I was wary, for in trying to peer beneath the surface, I was just as likely to see my own reflection—my cultural biases—as I was to glimpse the lives within that other realm.

"Ṣa: p u-wua?" I asked, peeking around a wall of dried organ-pipe cactus ribs and cracking mud. I had heard someone working around the corner, in the dooryard garden of cactus, aloes, and canna lilies. It was a young woman, O'odham Indian and Mexican by descent, washing clothes over a scrubbing board perched on wooden legs.

"Estoy lavando la ropa, pues," the young woman responded, drying her hands and holding one out to me for a brief, limp handshake. She understood some of the Piman language and was amused that I was using it. Still, she would not speak it herself, at least not beyond her familiars.

"No ki: Don Luciano?"

"Sí, Luciano está en la casa. Pasale, señor."

"S-ape. Muchas gracias."

We did not go into the house but rather through the yard to the porch. It was actually a *ramada*, a brush-covered shade structure that extended the living area out from the enclosed rooms. There, Luciano Noriega sat in a chair, looking out over the desert, drinking his coffee. He and I spoke a while in a mixture of Spanish and O'odham, catching up. We had known each other for about eleven years.

Our conversation wandered along familiar paths. When it turned to the animals that had been drinking at the lagoon a few hundred feet away, I asked if the *cimarrón* (bighorn) ever came there during the dry months. Before Luciano could answer, one of his nephews working in the yard spoke up: "There might be some in the mountains nearby, but if the *cimarrón* ever came down across the road, they would either be run over or shot before they arrived here."

Luciano was silent for a moment longer, whistling quietly to himself. Then, in a barely audible voice, the old man added, half smiling, half grimacing, "They're far from us now."

My friend and I ambled over to take a look at the *laguna* of Quitovac. It was only a ghost of the spring-fed lagoon I had first seen fourteen years ago, but the specter is still a sight worth beholding. Quitovac sits in the midst of the hellaciously hot desert plain, the only perennial body of water for twenty-five miles in any direction. Located where artesian flows well up along a fault line, Quitovac has served as a magnet for wildlife and human cultures for thousands of years.

Together with other biologists from the United States and Mexico, I had spent years tallying up the number of species found among its wildflowers and its feathered and furred creatures. We had surprised the scientific community by confirming that despite centuries of human "disturbance," Quitovac stands as one of the most biologically diverse localities anywhere in the deserts of North America. It has faced eight thousand summers of hot weather, mineralized waters, and long spans of drought, but still it flourishes with an abundance of plants and animals. Bighorn and other large game may have come to its springs less frequently after the arrival of humans and, later, livestock and firearms, but the life at Quitovac has remained rich.

Then, when a mess of well-meaning Mexican government pro-

grams arrived in the 1980s to "develop and improve" the local economy, Quitovac was suddenly shorn of four hundred acres of ancient
cactus and ironwood forest. Bulldozers and graders demolished the
old houses on the mesa overlooking the lagoon. By *old* houses, I mean
some that had been standing since last century, and all were made
from limestone slabs containing bones of now-extinct creatures that
had lived and died in the marshland there during the Ice Age. Now,
I walked among bulldozed windrows of limestone rubble like so many
graves in a military cemetery.

A D-10 Caterpillar had even started to rip out all the tules and
bushes in and around the lagoon. Someone had had the notion that if
the pond was deepened, it could hold some big fish, so they had
drained the pond down to the slow trickle of seven tiny springs. But
before they could dredge out all the marshy growth to make way for
exotic fish transplants, the D-10 bogged down. The bulldozer nearly
buried itself, another giant body stuck in the muck of the Quitovac
lagoon.

The following year, when the masked dancers of a summertime
ceremony came around to bless all the homes in the village—to bring
good harvests and rains while protecting them from floods—a dancer
paused near the edge of the empty lagoon and inspected the rubble.
He hesitated, then showered blessings on the ruins, giving them their
last rites.

The economic development never materialized; the equipment
needed to turn the acres of bulldozed cactus forest into irrigated alfalfa
did not arrive. The Quitovac locals who had acquiesced to the government's grand scheme found their agricultural acreage reduced,
rather than increased. Fortunately, the government had not let all the
artesian flows be pumped away; those springs had served the locals'
ancestors at the oasis for centuries. Luciano could still gravity-feed
water into his traditional field, but it now stood next to four hundred
acres of scarred land and tumbleweeds too exposed for wild sheep to
venture across, even when potable water beckoned to them on the
other side.

It struck me as ironic that economic "development" had clearly
diminished the local capacity for growth—plant, human, or otherwise. The oldest ways of farming in the desert were being ravaged by

the same forces that were breaking our oldest bonds with wild creatures. Why were wildness and ancient culture so vulnerable?

I shook my head sadly as we walked around the degraded lagoon. With every step, one of us would notice where lime-laden bone fragments had surfaced from the earth, reminders that a rich Pleistocene megafauna must have congregated in the marshlands here for tens of thousands of years. Teeth, ribs, and jaws of extinct fauna appear in the Quitovac ditches wherever there has been water movement or a little digging.

It is no surprise that these fossils have fueled the imaginations of the O'odham—that these bones have become familiars in their dreams. They have often told their children the story of the Ne:big, an enormous creature that emerged from the lagoon, and they have told it to visitors as well, several of whom have recorded the story on paper. The Ne:big's breath was a strong, wild wind, and when it inhaled, the Ne:big created a vacuum. People from a long way off would be sucked into its mouth and swallowed. Although the heart of the animal was slashed and its mouth was finally closed, old-timers still wonder during thunderstorms if the Ne:big is making the lightning strike.

I recalled the time nearly a decade ago when Luciano surprised me by showing me the remains of the Ne:big, which he had sequestered in a place where mischievous kids and casual visitors were unlikely to find them. He unwrapped a protective cloth and showed me the stuff from which legends are made. If I were a paleontologist, I might have examined those bones to discern what species they represented. But I had no such professional inclination. They could have come from an animal unknown to Western science, and they could just as easily have come from Ice Age mammoths or last century's bighorn sheep. All I was sure of was that they were sacred and belonged with the O'odham, where I hoped they would stay.

As I listened to Luciano that day in 1981, I was not so impressed by the bones themselves as by the flesh that Luciano's story wrapped around them. As he talked softly in Spanish spiced with O'odham, the mythic animal came alive. Luciano was restoring animal stories to their central place in what it means to be human. He was letting some creatures run wild again in our dreams.

Now, long after my first view of the fossils, I had been walking around one of the springs, one of the places where skeletal fragments of mythic monsters well up out of the underlying aquifer. I took a quick sideways glance at the spot where the bubbles emerged from the limey mud. I couldn't bring myself to gaze directly at this *nacimiento del agua*, this birthing ground of water. It would be too much like watching a stranger in the throes of spouting forth a delicate new life. I had to turn aside.

Even the smallest spring in the desert is something divinely precious. These springwaters are brewed with the tusks, horns, and bones of ancient wild animals. When I drink from them or winnow out a few bone fragments from their mud, I am reconnected to an animal past—as long as the artesian water flows. A center-pivot irrigation system cannot spray out animal dreams.

Fifty miles due west of Quitovac, center-pivot sprinklers and bighorn poachers have had brief careers near the edge of the Pinacate volcanic shield. From Pinacate and Carnegie peaks, wild sheep could have seen the spray of water rise into the air and evaporate before hitting the talclike soils in the valley below. This is the Rio Sonoyta valley, and the twin *ejido* "collectives" where poachers and pivoters enter the Sierra El Pinacate Biosphere Reserve are called *Ejido Nayarit* and *Ejido El Pinacate*. There, for a period that lasted barely four years, the Mexican government grubstaked the farmers in their attempts to grow 120 acres of alfalfa and ryegrass to feed 370 calves. If well nourished over the winter, the calves could have been sent off to feedlots for the final fattening—and a good price. It looked pretty good on paper.

At present, it does not look pretty at all. The Rio Sonoyta valley grows more tumbleweeds than salable goods, and the only signs of cows are the dried pies they left behind. Some of the farmers, with their fields fallowed, have turned to guiding bighorn poachers into the Pinacate, but the law has caught up with their hunting just as "real world" economics caught up with their farming.

When the federal discount on electrical pumps short-circuited, the *ejidos* could no longer afford to keep a diesel pump running at the pace required to irrigate the ryegrass on demand. Although they irrigated as little as twice a month during the winter, they had to keep the sprinklers on a nonstop cycle during the hotter part of the year. The movable fountain would take a day and a half to make a complete loop around the acreage, and then it would begin again.

But something had been left out of the circle. The "experts" had not factored in the heat, the wind, the blowing sand—the very kinds of wildness you cannot spray, blade, bulldoze, or breed out of a desert. Regardless of how much irrigation water spewed out of an eight-inch pipe protruding from the ground, the crops looked awfully stressed. The aerial sprinkling of this forage—in the midst of black lava cinder plains and shining dunes—faced the most aggravated rates of evaporation of any farmland in North America. Send a blistering wind across barren rock and sand for twenty-five miles, have it hit a wick-like patch of irrigated grass or beans, and you have what meteorologists call "the clothesline effect." With about three-fifths of an inch of water being lost per hour from each square inch of leaf surface during much of the warm season, moisture loss from the Pinacate forage patch probably exceeded all values ever reported in the literature from mainstream agricultural areas. Although ryegrass can be grown under such conditions, it is as water-costly as any ever produced anywhere.

I once visited the Pinacate with the Argentine ecologist Exequial Escurra, later the director of a Mexican environmental protection program and always a master at making quick calculations on napkins. *"Hijo de la chingada!"* Exequial exclaimed, borrowing a curse from his Mexican colleagues and smacking his forehead with his hand. I looked at the numbers at the bottom of the napkin. For the *ejidatarios*, a one-pound steak from Pinacate beeves cost 2,500 to 3,500 gallons of pumped groundwater to produce.

A desert-dwelling ram is lucky if even once during his lifetime he finds a *tinaja* (water catchment) in the bedrock holding a full 2,500 gallons of water. Environmental historian Bill Broyles has estimated that the entire riverless area of five million acres east of the Colorado River delta offered less than 200,000 gallons of water a year to humans and bighorn alike. Desert bighorn have been known to endure droughts in areas where no surface water is discernible, but the *ejidatarios*, after mainlining groundwater for several years, couldn't break their addiction overnight. Following a few years of astronomical pumping costs, the collective decided to dismantle the pipes of its center-pivot system; now they sit, slowly being buried by sand, like the bones of some mythic beast. Some of the *ejidatarios* moved away, while others shifted to cutting local wood for a living.

I have seen animal bones in the Pinacate that were not bleached by the sun but scorched by fire. They had been exposed to high temperatures in a white-hot blaze of specially selected ironwood trunks. Perhaps leaking sheep fat had scorched some of them, for a few of the vertebrae were blackened on one end. The rest looked ghostly white, cemented together by the lime that had leached from the bones themselves. These are called *calcined* bones, and heaps of them abound on the Pinacate lava shield, adjacent dunes, and nearby Cabeza Prieta range. They are most frequently found at old campsites close to *tinajas* that bighorn hunters have used for as long as this land has been inhabited. And yet these skeletons are heaped up apart from the multipurpose hearths and roasting pits found at the same campsites. It is as if someone turned away from the feast and moved over to another spot to burn the leftovers from the main course.

Blanched or charred portions of sheep, pronghorn, white-tailed deer, and mule deer skeletons have been found together in the same heaps. (All are considered kinds of "deer" in O'odham folk taxonomy.) Not far from Tinaja del Cuervo in the Pinacate, one mound of cremated bones approaches the size of a shrine. In fact, it *is* a shrine.

Julian Hayden first heard of such cremations years ago when he was working with Milton Wetherill at the Anasazi cliff dwelling of Kiet Siel. Wetherill had once labored down on the Mexican border, at Rancho de la Osa on the edge of Papaguería. There, he had been told of Indians far to the west who, Wetherill recalled, "had the curious custom of cremating the bones of animals killed for food." Such a practice was not known among any Native American culture at that time.

That casual comment somehow lodged itself deep within Hayden's head, to surface again when he began to see calcined bone piles for himself in the Pinacate twenty-five years later. Was this an ancient but obsolete occurrence, Hayden wondered, or a practice that had persisted into modern times?

Few people have known the Pinacate even half as well as Hayden, but one of them, Ronald Ives, gave him a clue. While visiting the Quitobaquito oasis on the Mexican border, Ives noticed that José Juan Orosco, an O'odham elder—medicine man, hunter, and venerable survivor of the Pinacate band of Sand Papago—was tossing bones into the campfire, bones removed from a recently butchered and eaten bighorn. Ives asked him why he was doing that.

"Sheep bones are burned by the old ones.... It's to quiet the spirits of the dead animals," he answered. "It's so they will not alarm the sheep still living in the area," he added, watching the bones heat up over the ironwood coal and the smoke rise away from the fire.

Ives had stumbled on the ancient connection, still alive in one man's practice. José Juan Orosco died and was buried at Quitobaquito in 1945, but a great-grandson kept up the family connections to that place. Until his death in 1991, Juan Joe Cipriano lived over at Ge Wo'o—the Big Water Hole. Occasionally, he drove around the Ajo Mountains to Quitobaquito to collect medicinal plants, a tradition of gathering that was permitted only if Juan Joe first touched base with the U.S. Park Service, because that oasis is now part of Organ Pipe Cactus National Monument.

I first met Juan Joe when he tracked me down in Papago Park, on the rough edge of Phoenix. Becoming friends as we talked over a heap of Mexican food, we would continue to see each other every so often at his home or down at the oasis. On that first day, I felt comfortable asking him to teach me about bighorn hunting, but I tried to avoid asking anything about cremations—my interest was not archaeology or theology but biology. Just to be clear, I posed one question to guide us away from any potentially sensitive matters.

"Anything special about hunting bighorn? If there is any tradition that is best kept secret, I'll understand…"

"No," Juan Joe answered matter-of-factly. "Nothing special I remember." I breathed a sigh of relief. "Well," he continued, "I guess they were hunted in special places. Like the *cecpo*—what do you call them, *tinajas*? Or sometimes the people would look for them in caves."

Hunting guide turned game warden Ben Tinker observed that there were particular places for stalking bighorns in the Pinacate on his visits there between 1919 and 1926. He had come upon O'odham families who slept in volcanic caves while tracking bighorn sheep around the craters of the Pinacate. Tinker claimed that "bands of mountain sheep descended into [the craters'] depths by narrow trails. The hunters sent their squaws down to drive the sheep up while they blocked the trails' entrance and killed the frightened sheep with spears, arrows, and ironwood clubs."

I asked Juan Joe if he still saw this animal, which his people call *cesoiñ*.

"They stay up in the mountains now, seems like even more than before."

"Before?"

"I haven't seen them lately. Of course, being on kidney dialysis three times a week, I don't get up into the mountains much at all. But when I was growing up at Darby Well, I would see them. When I was a boy, they would come down from the Ajo Mountains sometimes."

"Are they still hunted in the traditional way?"

"Not much hunting nowadays. Except when they go to get deer for the *keihina*, a traditional dance. If they can't get deer, they hunt javelina for it."

"Do they still butcher and divide the game according to custom?"

"When an animal is killed, the hunters still give parts of it to relatives and neighbors. You can eat it right away or make jerky out of it. You know, bighorn tastes different than cow, more mushy. Then, in the old days, I guess they used the bones to make tools, or maybe bows or arrows."

"Did they use the horns, the *a'ag*, for anything?" I wondered.

Juan Joe paused and thought for a moment. "Sometimes when they would bring back the *a'ag*, they would hang them up, outside, over a *ramada*. Sometimes they had to use them to help bring the rains."

I didn't know what he meant. He tried to explain.

"Well, maybe José Juan was the last one to know how to do this. It was after a long time with no rains. Nothing else they had done did any good. So he went to this hill near where we were living." José Juan was said to divide his time between Quitobaquito Springs and an *ak-ciñ* floodwater field in the present-day Cabeza Prieta Wildlife Refuge. I wondered if he had been at the very hill where my teacher Bernard Fontana had found calcined sheep bones years ago.

"What did he do?" I asked.

"He poured water into the sheep horns that he had turned upside down. He did some kind of dance, singing. Then he spilled the water from the horns onto the ground."

"Because the rains hadn't come for a long time?"

"José Juan was the last I ever heard of who knew how to do this." It saddened me to think of José Juan's passing, but not long after the conversation about the old man, Juan Joe followed him. Juan Joe Cipriano died of medical complications related to kidney failure and his longer suffering from diabetes. I wondered if he would be the last O'odham I would ever speak with who had glimpsed this bighorn tradition.

José Juan might have been the last O'odham who knew how to perform that particular rite, but remnants of other old customs are still practiced by Tohono O'odham bighorn hunters. I came across a man who practiced some of these customs, long after I had given up thinking that I would find anyone who knew them as anything but distant memory. I was driving out of Why, Arizona, one morning at dawn when a stocky man in a baseball cap popped up out of the weeds on the side of the road and stuck out his thumb. I pulled over, and he came running up to the car. Panting, he got in.

"My car broke down between here and Gila Bend last night. I got Esker there in Ajo to go and get it with his tow truck. While he's fixing it, I gotta get home. So I tried to get a ride last night but nobody came around. So I just slept over there away from the road a ways."

I glanced at him. Other than a little grass chaff sticking to his shirt and jeans, you could hardly tell he had been out all night. No blanket, sleeping bag, or heavy clothes. This guy must be hardy if he can camp impromptu at the end of winter without complaining, I thought.

"Where you going?"

"Over there, on the other side of those hills," and he nodded toward the northeast side of the Ajo Mountains, on the reservation. "You know, just before the last rains, I saw a herd of sheep over in those hills. They had been coming down from the Ajo Mountains, I guess."

"So they still come down into the desert on that side? They don't stay up high all the time?"

"No, they come down to the hills. Yeah, I got me a ram."

"You did?"

"A bull ram. He was a big one. You know, they find little cubbies, wherever they go in the rocks, but when they see something they don't know, they come out to be sure what they're seeing." He turned to me, adding, "Do you understand? He had to be sure about what he was seeing, so that gave me plenty of time to get in a good position."

"Oh, maybe he was the one that is like a sentry in the army..." The man looked to be over fifty; maybe he had done some time in military service. "You know, that ram could have been their lookout."

"Yeah, I think so. They do that. So I shot him and then had to get some friends to help me haul him out, because I couldn't get my pickup that close to those hills. We butchered him out there."

"When you do the butchering, do you take everything back to the village with you?"

"No, you have to leave those ram horns out, away from the houses for three or four weeks. Then, after that, you can claim them as your own. Even then, you have to put them up high on the *ramada*, I guess, so that the spirits can bless them there."

We were approaching his turnoff, where I would be going the other way. "*Ṣap cugik api?* What's your name? I didn't even ask you who you are and where you come from."

"They call me Woodpecker. Just ask down this road, they all know where I live. Looks like you have to go someplace now, but come around sometime if you're interested in hunting. There are a lot of things you have to do if you are a hunter. Like there is this one kind of deer. After you kill it, you aren't allowed to touch it. Then it's up to the medicine man, not you. So I have to know things like that. Anyway, if you hunt, maybe we can talk sometime. Take it easy."

He hopped out and started walking down the road. I took it easy until I got to the reservation's edge. There, I noticed a barn owl caught in a barbed-wire fence, leg muscles shredded, unable to fly. Out of the corner of my eye I saw a coyote running in for the kill. I drove on toward the Gila River, but my mind was not easy all the rest of that day.

———

"The horns of the mountain sheep were never brought home by hunters," Akimel O'odham chief Antonio Azul told Frank Russell at the beginning of the century, when Russell spent many months working among the Piman settlements along the Gila River. "Each man had a place set apart where he deposited them in order that they might exert no evil influence upon the winds or rains."

The more southerly O'odham also associate violent winds with large game animals, just as they do with the *Ne:big*. One man told me matter-of-factly, "Yes, when you kill a *ceṣoiñ* or a *koji* [javelina], it brings winds. Not whirlwinds, like the *sivuloki*, but regular winds."

The association between wind and sheep has persisted among the Akimel O'odham even though they seldom hunt sheep anymore. When I first climbed the Sierra Estrella with zoologist Amadeo Rea in 1975, sheep were still marginally present there, but only one traditional sheep hunter remained among the Piman villages at the base of the mountain. Nevertheless, elderly Pimas cautioned Amadeo that the hide and horns of the *ceṣoiñ* "must be kept in a safe, respected place, as an insult would result in either violent wind or rain."

That safe place—like the ones where Luciano harbored the bones of the *Ne:big*—could be either somewhere in the house or in an undisturbed place outside. On occasion, the bones would be brought forth for special uses. The late Joseph Giff told Amadeo of one such time when a bighorn hide was enlisted by the Pimas for its power. "Old Tasquinth had a hide. Don't think he killed it. He was never a hunter.... Someone needed to winnow their thrashed wheat but there was no wind at all, and he was waiting. Was afraid the rain would come and ruin the grain.... So this man, he went to Tasquinth, who took out the hide and asked him which way he wanted the wind to blow from." As Joe Giff explained, "we wouldn't want the chaff to blow on our house.

"Tasquinth took the hide in that direction," Joe went on, "and tapped it gently. He said, 'This man wants some wind. Will you give him some wind from this direction?'"

Joe stopped for a moment, remembering the wind. "It came." Then he turned to Amadeo and added, "No one has hides anymore."

Today, the mountain ranges within walking distance of the Pima villages hold few sheep, and those that occasionally descend from the heights are met by myriad treacheries: barbed-wire fences, super-highways, irrigated fields, and retirement subdivisions. Three centuries ago, when Captain Juan Mateo Manje made a visit to the Akimel O'odham along the Gila, there were enough sheep within reach that the entire human population of Tusonimo'o village was out hunting them and gathering mescal. The village name itself, *Ceṣoiñ Mo'o* in modern O'odham, means "bighorn sheep heads."

Two years earlier, Manje learned that the village had been named "for its grand accumulation of horns of wild sheep in the shape of a hill; and for their abundance there, enough to provide for sustenance; and additionally, because the hill itself towers high above the roofs of their low-lying houses. It seems that it consists of more than one hundred thousand horns."

That number is astonishing, for it exceeds by an order of magnitude the highest estimate of sheep living in Arizona in any given year. Although some scholars doubt Manje's estimate, his journals show him to be a consistently accurate measurer of mileage and village population sizes. Even if one assumes that the pile had accumulated over decades or even centuries, the sight of so many horns of an elusive animal, all concentrated in one place, would still be awesome.

The *cimarrón* must have nourished the historic O'odham to a degree impossible to imagine anywhere within the range of desert bighorn today. Of course, sheep habitat then did not consist of ragtag fragments of former range, as it does today. O'odham land uses did not alter *cimarrón* country nearly as much as modern farming, ranching, and urban sprawl have.

The pile of one hundred thousand horn cores stacked at Tusonimo'o was not the only one within Pimería Alta, the greater region. In 1774, Juan Bautista de Anza encountered an O'odham camp near the present-day Cabeza Prieta Tanks, where such a pile persisted until the early 1960s, when it was burned by a white man. Bautista de Anza claimed that O'odham hunters had been careful to preserve the horns. They carried them to a place near the *tinajas*, where they were piled "to prevent the Air from leaving the place." Other horns, since vandalized, were in a rock shelter not far from the water holes.

Additional piles are known from the Tohono O'odham Reservation, where cowboys on roundup sporadically stumble upon them and wonder about their origins. In 1960, Gerald Duncan encountered mounds while monitoring the impact of bighorn hunting around the Sells area of the reservation: "Mounds of desert bighorn horns seen in the vicinity of water holes attest to the fact that these Indians were very active in killing sheep for food and other uses. These mounds of horns have been seen in the vicinity of the tanks in the Cabeza Prieta, Tule and Granite Mountains.... The horns were placed in this particular manner as part of a ritual."

Whether or not Duncan had firsthand knowledge of bighorn rituals, he clearly established that the horn piles that Anza and Manje saw were not isolated occurrences: find an ancient water hole and look for calcined bighorn bones within a few hundred yards of it. Some of these places are the same spots where the O'odham historically hunted, as indicated by arrowheads made of broken glass and awls of cut iron nails found with the heaps of bone. But how far back in time do such traditions reach? How deep is the bighorn connection?

Fastimes. Water World. These do not sound like places you would go to learn about bighorn and human antiquity in the desert. They are, in fact, places where the Bureau of Reclamation has constructed aqueducts that carry water from the distant Colorado River to help farmers who have already squandered the aquifers beneath their farms. During their efforts to keep the desert blooming and nearby cities booming, the bureau is obligated to let archaeologists survey and, in some cases, excavate cultural materials that might be obliterated by federal works. Folks like William Gillespie and Christine Rose Szuter sort bones from these salvages, identify them, and figure out how people butchered the beasts. They also interpret the value of animals to earlier cultures, in exercises Szuter calls "the whys and how-comes of zooarchaeology."

Among the animal bones from Hohokam homes that migrate onto a zooarchaeologist's desk, bighorn, pronghorn, and deer appear now and then. At Water World, twenty big mandibles were found on floors and in pits near cremations. Fastimes yielded another seventeen mandibles. The deer antlers and sheep horn cores found at these Hohokam sites are racks that trophy hunters would give their eyeteeth for, exceeding in size the largest recorded modern specimens from the state.

Chris Szuter is particularly curious about the condition and place-

ment of bighorn, pronghorn, and deer remains salvaged from Hohokam sites. Nearly half the bones show signs of having been burned,
a proportion far higher than that of charred rabbit bones. In addition,
bighorn were much more likely to have their bones reworked into
tools and ornaments than were rabbits or birds. And sheep remains
have been discovered in special wall niches or in corners of pit houses
with other objects of ceremonial import: decorated pottery from Chihuahua, large cardium shells from the Sea of Cortez, rectangular
pumice stones from Lord knows where.

"The bones of bighorn sheep are just burned most of the time,"
Chris explained. "But some are grouped with bones of pronghorn or
deer. It seems that the hunters were taking special care with bighorn
cranial elements, keeping them in pit houses that are different from
all the other pit houses in the village. I've wondered if they were hanging up the horns for ceremonies...or safekeeping them to use later,
to attract living animals as part of the hunt."

Like most careful scientists, Chris notices when her comments start
to slide over into speculation. She cautioned herself, and me: "Of
course, not all bighorn bones are found in special places. Sometimes
there is a scatter of fragments. I've probably looked at reports from
all Hohokam sites where animals have been found, and big game animals have not even been recovered from the majority of them."

I reminded her of the words she had written several years before,
when she said that among the Hohokam, "exploitation of artiodactyls
[such as bighorn], from the hunt through the disposal of bones, is
imbued with ritual."

"Chris," I asked, "do you still sense that the use of bighorn by the
Hohokam was wrapped in ritual connections?"

"Yes. Yes. I would stick by that."

"How long does that go back?"

"Perhaps into the Pioneer Period." That's the period of Hohokam
cultural emergence in southern Arizona that extended up to A.D. 800.
Bighorn rituals may have begun not long after the birth of Jesus in
Bethlehem, in a desert half the world away. But Chris has also found
that Hohokam animal remains from the Pioneer Period look more
like those of the earlier Archaic and less like those of the later Classic and Colonial Periods of Hohokam civilization.

I thought this over. Subsistence during those earlier times

depended more on gleaning wild desert resources and less on the weeds and animal visitors to the irrigated fields surrounding big Hohokam villages. The Hohokam lifestyle was more like that of the wayfaring bands out beyond their frontier, in the Pinacate and Cabeza Prieta. And that's where the bighorn sheep rites may have persisted the longest.

Julian Hayden reckons that sheep cremations began as early as the first Amargosan Period during Archaic times, perhaps three thousand years ago. He sees a relationship between the "bighorn sheep cult" of the Hohokam and the stockpiling of horns by the historic O'odham, but he has never been too sure about how long this deep connection between desert bighorn and people lasted. The last big heaps of cremated sheep bones he came across are those at Sunset Camp, abandoned by 1851.

Camps abandoned, wells gone dry, *tinajas* drained or spoiled by livestock. Sheep populations corralled into smaller and smaller areas, where they are more vulnerable to birth defects rising out of shallow gene pools or to decimation by exotic diseases. And seasonally migratory bands of desert people being corralled as well, told to stay put on reservations or being enslaved to cotton farmers. What is being lost is more than a chunk of desert nature. More than a waning of native culture. What is being lost is a capacity for a long, deep relationship between wild animals and cultural traditions.

Desert bighorn, although no longer abundant, are not truly endangered as a subspecies. O'odham culture, although it has suffered innumerable insults since the arrival of Europeans in the Sonoran Desert, has not reached a vanishing point. But something ancient between these human and animal desert dwellers has nearly disappeared.

I am concerned that we have lost a way of active engagement between a people and another species—the ability of a collective imagination to run wild beyond the confines of its own settlements and constructs. I am wondering about a native artist's propensity to dream of sheep and to take the image wired inside him toward some outward expression—pottery design, petroglyph, dance. I am even thinking about sheep sensing familiar people waiting near the water hole or crater rim—the same recognition of risk they might feel if their range overlapped with that of a puma or a wolf.

I am worried that as wild sheep slip out of sight, then out of mind, then out of dreams, a vacuum is created not only among desert people but among all people. I am worried that if we do not have their nature before us as a standard, we ourselves will grow domesticated and lose the sense of deep-seated wildness that lives within us. It is something that the O'odham say they can smell when coming upon a place where a bighorn, badger, mule deer, or mustang has been moments before: *"S-doakam'o u:v,"* meaning it smells of being wildly alive.

I have smelled that fragrance, seen the movement of *something that is alive* no more than two hundred yards from where I lived in Organ Pipe Cactus National Monument: a young ram rushing over a volcanic ridge. I have seen mountain sheep climbing what looked like a sheer cliff face above Hohokam ruins near New River, Arizona. I have waited days for them to come to *tinajas* in the Cabeza Prieta, and I was once close enough to feel the tension in their haunches owing to my presence. I have waited other times to no avail, learning to respect the fact that their wildness determines that they will behave in ways oblivious to my mind's predictions.

But all my searchings for sheep, all their momentary appearances in my dreams, are like so many brief showers in a desert land where the aquifer has already been mined. The showers are refreshing, and they will help desert life today, replenishing what is at the surface. The deeper problem—the depletion of fossil groundwater set down during the Ice Age that is unlikely to regain its former levels over the next hundred human lifetimes—is not even temporarily relieved. A deep cultural connection is being lost. When it is gone another extinction will have been recorded, an extinction as real and as meaningful as that of any animal on the endangered species list.

Killer, Fire, and the Aboriginal Way

*The constant interaction between {the Aboriginal} firestick and
landscape replenished both.... The banking of fires in large tree
boles, the lighting of heavy scrub, the ignition of larger trees
directly or indirectly, all littered the scene with fire caches, not
unlike food caches or waterholes—temporary sources of an essential
element. Everywhere smoke marked the presence of Aborigines,
whose wanderings traced storm tracks of black lightning.*
STEPHEN J. PYNE, *Burning Bush*

We were at a place that still glowed with the embers of the past. An
Aboriginal band in snap-button Western shirts and cowboy hats had
fired up their generator, amps, and electric guitars. They played Bill
Monroe's "Blue Moon of Kentucky" and Hank Snow's "I'm Movin'
On" over the tiniest of amplifiers, as if the rockabilly fifties had rein-
vaded this planet via some bent sound wave, one that had left the
Louisiana Hayride radio program decades ago, bouncing off the moon,
only to return to Alice Springs just in time for our arrival. The music
had reignited an argument that my partner and I had been having all
day.

"God! This whole scene looks just like Moab, Utah. Those rounded
red ridges…"

"But they're not Navajo sandstone…"

"All the little bike rentals and tacky tourist trinket shops…"

"But they're not selling T-shirts with Anasazi rock art on them…"

"The Aboriginal dot paintings have some of the same designs."

"I haven't seen a single lewd flute player..."

"They're playing didgeridoos—what's the difference?"

"And no one's selling those gawdawful coyotes with bandannas around their necks..."

"Shhh! If there's a store owner in the crowd, he might hear you and put one on a dingo."

In fact, Alice Springs, in the Northern Territory, may indeed be Australia's Moab. Both towns have shifted from ranching to ecotourism economies within the last two decades, but residents in both still pretend they're walking around in Marlboro Country. Both have loads of watchable wildlife; in Moab, you can see desert bighorn and deer come down to the highway just a few blocks from the new espresso bars; in Alice, rock wallabies and euros browse behind the motels where kangaroos are kept tethered near the swimming pools. And both towns have capitalized on their desert mystique, marketing their semblance of remoteness and rough-and-tumble beauty to jet-setters from every continent.

But there is a side of Alice that makes the international tourists uneasy: during certain seasons, Alice is surrounded by Aboriginal camps. Dark, curly-haired men stand around smoldering campfires, singing and drinking all night long beneath the ghost gums. The tourists mumble about how the "blacks" look so pitifully *out of place*— like Thunderbird-drinking Navajos on the outskirts of Gallup—until they remember that the Aborigines have probably been coming to the billabongs here for thousands of years.

They may not have had alcohol back then. And ecotourists did not encroach on their water holes until this last century. But they did have fires. They made them, they moved them, they lived with them and because of them.

So did a number of animals that are rarely seen anywhere near Alice today.

One such animal is the *mala* (*Lagorchestes hirsutus*), a nearly extinct form of hare wallaby. Short, dull-colored, frenetic in its movements, the *mala* does not excite wildlife watchers the way a red kangaroo or emu does. But it has altogether disappeared from western South

Australia, from Western Australia, and as unmanaged populations, from the Northern Territory. Some isolated populations remain on Bernier and Torrey Islands in Shark Bay off the coast of Western Australia, but the last known wild population on the mainland was in the desert areas of the Tanami Faunal Reserve in the Red Centre of the continent. It has declined so precipitously in recent decades that the Northern Territory's Conservation Commission captured all the individuals they could find and brought them into a captive breeding program.

There are a few *malas* left on the outskirts of Alice Springs, but not in the gum-lined dry riverbeds, and not up in the red rocks with the euros and rock wallabies. The *malas* surviving near Alice are all behind bars. The most famous is Killer.

Four of us stood staring into a small cage at the Conservation Commission's compound at the edge of Alice Springs. It was one of several cages used for captive breeding the midsized mammals that seem so prone to extinction in the Australian outback. The wind roared too loudly through the casuarinas—fast-growing trees planted to provide a respite from the desert heat—for us to hear each other, so we were quiet, directing our attention toward the little life left within the cage.

There, under a piece of sheet metal angled up against a chicken-wire fence, hid one of the few rufous hare wallabies left on the entire continent. Known in at least a dozen different aboriginal tongues as *mala*, this animal was the last wild-born individual remaining from a population now extinct in the Tanami Desert.

A dry wind swept through the razor-sharp spinifex grass around us. When the wind died down a little, my son Dusty turned to Don Langford, the senior technical officer on the Mala Project who was showing us around, and asked the inevitable question.

"We call him that because we've had a bit of a problem with him," Don said. "Every time we try to mate Killer, he kills whatever female we put in his cage." Even though *malas* are not true carnivores, the name was a fairly apt one.

Dusty, who was eleven at the time, said nothing.

The wind rose up again. The dry spinifex around us rattled in the breeze. Then all grew silent. Our throats were dry.

In the momentary quiet, I tried to grapple with a couple of facts that Langford had tossed out to us earlier on the walk over to the cage. One: there may be fewer than a hundred desert *malas* left in the entire world. Two: Killer was the last *mala* alive that had been born in the wild from wild parents; all the others on the continent had been captive-bred from parents that have since passed on.

"You mean that Killer hasn't put anything into the *mala* gene pool even though that's why they brought him into captivity?"

My question sounded too bald, set against the vast expanse around us. I tried to cover myself: "But isn't it critical—especially when the breeding pool dwindles down to fifty or so animals—to keep the genetic bottleneck from closing in?"

"It has been one bloody buggerin' bitch of a problem, you're right, mate," grumbled one of Don's coworkers, walking by at that moment. Don frowned.

"Trouble is," he admitted, "Killer probably has some good genes left in him that are not otherwise represented in the breeding pool.... But we've had no luck at all with him. Pretty soon, though, we hope to take him on a little plane ride to the coast, for an all-expenses-paid holiday, where they have a special facility..."

Don shot me a sideways glance, then looked over at my son, apparently wondering whether or not to use euphemisms in deference to Dusty's age. I took Don's lead, and stuck with the euphemisms.

"Oh, you must be taking the guy to a gene bank, where they store a little of the genetic inheritance of endangered animals?"

The conversation detoured into cryptic references to semen extraction, liquid nitrogen storage of sperm, artificial insemination, and even embryo transplants. It appeared that the Aussies were ready to do anything it took to get Killer's genes splashing into the *mala* breeding pool. Inbreeding was the enemy of wildlife biologists.

"No one has ever used those techniques before on behalf of the *mala*," Don offered.

Dusty, staring intently into the cage, ignored us. Finally, he asked quietly, "Is there anyone in there?"

Don and I turned our attention back to the subject at hand. Just then, a tawny marsupial the size of a jackrabbit hopped out from under a piece of sheet metal. It leaped swiftly around the cage a couple of rounds, then rested for a while in the middle of the enclosure.

Killer had suddenly made an appearance. I was struck by the fact that he was shaking. Was the viability of *mala* populations hinging on this high-strung male?

"QUICK, Dusty!" one of Don's technicians urged. "Shoot a picture of him before he disappears!"

The shutter snapped. Killer paused for another moment, erect, forefeet held close to his chest. A tail nearly the length of his body was Killer's counterweight, as he perched on the barren ground.

All the while, the *mala* kept trembling. I tried to imagine what the view was like from inside the cage, looking out through metal to the vast desert beyond.

We kept still, listening to his breathing, hearing the spinifex rattle in the breeze. When the wind waned once more, Killer leaped out of sight. Dusty had had time for two Instamatic photos. And then Killer was gone.

Gone too is a dynamic that prevailed in these deserts for as much as twelve millennia. It was a dynamic that kept vegetation patterns and animal densities shifting, and it was driven by Aboriginal burning. The Aborigines' fire-stick management of open grassy desert steppe favored the *malas* more than current Marlboro Country management practices do.

Aboriginal peoples have lived on the Australian continent for more than forty-eight thousand years, but over most of that duration they clung close to the coasts and kept their hearths full of coals kindled from better-watered trees. Twelve thousand years ago, as populations grew in better-watered regions, they began moving toward the Red Centre around present-day Alice. As they ventured inland, they brought their fire sticks with them, changing not only the density but also the structure of the vegetation.

At first, they may only have torched the razor-edged spinifex clumps to make room for camps or to drive large game toward waiting bands of hunters. Soon, they surmised that certain frequencies and intensities of burns favored the regeneration of desert food plants and their attendant game. Hare wallabies like the *mala* were seldom killed by fires, because they could take refuge in the coolness of underground tunnels while the fires scorched the spinifex above them.

If you could hear naturalist John van den Beld tell it, you'd become convinced that *malas* not only survive fires but thrive because of them: "Aboriginal fire created a mix of old and new vegetation, and therefore of shelter and food.... The *mala's* well-being is very much governed by the right kind of fire. The patchiness of aboriginal burning leaves part of the vegetation untouched. Clumps of old spinifex provide the *mala* with its shelter, from which it moves to new growth to feed on the seed heads and young leaves of forbs and grasses."

The Aborigines were not enhancing hare-wallaby habitat for purely altruistic reasons; as one Warlpiri man told me, bringing an imaginary mouthful of meat to his teeth, "*mala* makes good tucker." Up through the 1950s—about the time that rockabilly and honky-tonk country first reached their ears—a few Warlpiri and Pintubi hunters still brought *malas* into sheep stations for consumption. The hunters had tracked the *malas* back to their burrows, and by stamping on the sand above their tunnels, they had triggered cave-ins. With luck, a hare wallaby or two would be trapped and smothered in the choked-up tunnels. A half hour or so of tedious digging by the Warlpiri and Pintubi would reveal their prey.

The Warlpiri once chased *malas* with the aid of dingoes, raucously driving them toward gaps in brush barriers where men lay waiting to club the fleeing animals.

The practice of fire hunting persisted well into the thirties, when Aboriginal elders were seen catching *malas* some distance from their burrows. They knew how to time the fires to isolate animals when they were out foraging, so that they could not take refuge underground. Once the *malas* were isolated, hunters would throw long sticks at them, sticks to which leafy branches were attached. The leafy branches would make a swishing sound, imitating the flapping of wedge-tailed eagles. This sound can make a *mala* cower and freeze.

The Warlpiri still hunt with boomerangs on occasion, but more to prove their prowess for tourists than for their own subsistence. I once met a Warlpiri man who was fashioning a boomerang out of acacia wood, and when I asked him which acacia it came from, he asked me if I was from some other desert where acacias grew.

"Yes, as a matter of fact, I'm from the Sonoran Desert," assuming he'd have no idea of the place I was speaking of even if I'd called it the American Southwest.

"Been there, man."

"You've been to the Sonoran Desert?"

"As a linguistics research associate for MIT."

"Ken Hale," I rallied back at him. "You must have worked with Ken." (I had learned some Papago Indian grammar from Ken, who had grown up with Papago cowboys in the Sonoran Desert; I knew that he had spent time doing linguistic work near Alice as well.)

"You know Ken?" The man smiled. "He's my 'uncle.' Let me write him a letter in Warlpiri for you to take back to him."

I gave him paper for writing a note to Ken, and later in the day we shared some *goanna* meat that he grilled over a fire. As the rattler rustlers say in Moab, it "tasted just like chicken."

The Warlpiri and neighboring peoples killed *malas* to eat them, but they did not eat them into extinction. In some ways, *mala* meat was considered more of a cure for the hard times than it was a food. Even though *malas* had far less flesh on their legs, rump, and tail than a wallaroo or a red kangaroo, they were esteemed as good medicine. The way it was roasted over coals, the *mala*'s body cavity filled with plenty of blood and meat juices. Aboriginal hunters craved such nutrients at times when they felt that their own blood was "drying up" from too much hunger weather or prolonged drought.

Warlpiri oral history tells how such hunger weather raged from the midtwenties through the early thirties. An ever-worsening drought diminished the edible yields of the desert vegetation in the Red Centre. From 1928 on, Warlpiri bands were forced out of the bush, streaming into Alice Springs and surrounding sheep stations to find something to eat. There, they became hooked for the first time on *damper*—unleavened breads made from finely milled wheat flour. They tasted the greasy meats of domestic livestock. They sampled the grog, the cheapest of alcohol that whites could provide them in exchange for work.

Something snapped. When some families turned their back on the wild bush tuckers that had sustained their ancestors, there was a sudden drying up of the Dreaming Ceremonies. The Dreamings are often ritual reenactments of walking the Songlines—those human migratory corridors recorded in Aboriginal song—and these rituals had held Aboriginal bands together for centuries.

As some Dreamings were lost and others performed less frequently, Aborigines turned to hunting one another. There were drunken brawls and shoot-outs with each other or with the whites. Older Warlpiri still refer to this period as "the Killing Time."

The Warlpiri were not the only ones who had their Dreamings and their fire sticks snuffed out during the Killing Time. A dozen other linguistically distinct peoples fled the bush for good. Without their fire sticks, the frequency of burns throughout the spinifex desert became drastically reduced.

And the *malas*? Already devastated by drought, overhunted for their bloody juices, and outcompeted by introduced rabbits, the *mala* population went into a nosedive. When the fires began to wane, hare-wallaby habitat could hardly recover, even after the rains returned.

The rains did come once more, but they seemed to favor feral introduced animals over the remaining *malas*. European rabbits had been usurping *mala* food and shelter since 1894, and the other exotic critters that were arriving put the final nails in the *malas'* coffin. Feral house cats and European foxes preyed voraciously on all small-sized desert marsupials. From south to north, population after population of *malas* was extirpated, as rabbits, cats, and foxes moved farther inland from the well-watered areas of the coast. The few Aborigines persisting in the Tanami Desert no longer spotted *malas* with any regularity. Most families stopped hunting them and stopped talking about them much.

An ancient relationship had become as imperiled as the animal itself. *Malas* had long been the subjects of "increase ceremonies" to sustain animal populations of symbolic importance to the people. These increase ceremonies could be done only at sacred sites of Hare-Wallaby Dreamings scattered like beads along a Songline running from north of Tenant Creek past Lake MacKay and down toward Ayers Rock—now known internationally as Uluru.

But the *mala* was now largely out of sight and increasingly out of mind. Its scarcity did not bode well for the persistence of the Hare-Wallaby Dreaming tradition. Sure, *mala* tracks would remain on the petroglyph panels at the hare-wallaby sacred sites. But many Aborigines recognized that something unsettling was happening to their living medicines, among them the *malas*.

When a team of Conservation Commission biologists counted the *mala* population near the Granites in the Tanami Desert region, it consisted of fewer than two hundred individuals. Nevertheless, the biologists were elated: as far as they knew at the time, this was the last viable population left on the entire continent. The biologists hunkered down and tried to learn everything they could about *mala* natural history: how these critters used spinifex tussocks for food, how they found shelter, and how they avoided predators. In doing so, the biologists gained a sense of what good *mala* habitat might be. They went looking for similar habitat where other *malas* might have persisted unnoticed. Over a couple of years of searching, they finally encountered a second, smaller population fifteen kilometers from the first.

The Conservation Commission took two actions that were new for desert wildlife conservation efforts. First, they live-captured *malas* to establish a caged colony for captive breeding. The first five *malas* were brought into Alice Springs in 1980, and others have followed since. With the exception of Killer, the captives have been successfully mated, producing more than two hundred offspring.

The wildlife biologists' second action was perhaps unprecedented in the history of conservation. They recruited Aboriginal elders familiar with *malas* from their youth to select sites suitable for reintroduction and to manage and monitor the captive-bred *malas* that would be translocated there.

Don Langford filled me in on the peculiar history of this arrangement. "There's this ethnobiologist on our staff, Peter Latz. Peter had discovered habitat similar to that at the Granites but over on Aboriginal lands to the east. He had been surveying that area of the Tanami because of a Warlpiri land claim over there, and he knew that we had been looking for an additional safe site for reintroduction. He came upon some paleoriver habitat similar to what he had seen at the Granites, and thought to himself, 'If we're going to reintroduce the *mala*, why not do it where the Aborigines can help us figure out burning frequencies and their effects on the food and shelter the *malas* need?'"

Latz was the perfect bridge between modern Western science and Aboriginal knowledge of the *mala*. He was raised at the Hermannsburg mission among Aboriginal people, who call him by his "skinname," for they claim that they adopted and converted him while he was a boy. He has become somewhat of a legend, putting the likes of Bruce Chatwin in awe of his personal knowledge of Aboriginal adaptations to the desert. He has retained a legendary status in my mind, for both times I had been in Alice, he was out in the boonies on extended trips. Latz has described the training in desert ecology that the Aborigines provided:

> I was very privileged [to have grown up among them], and it has had a big effect on my life. In terms of science, it has taught me how to be a good observer. Aboriginal people, of course, are supremely efficient at seeing things that the average White people can't see, things like tracks on the ground or subtle signs of vegetation changes. And, Aboriginal people have been very dependent on managing the landscape with fire in such a way that they were producing gardens of different ages, scattered all over the landscape.
>
> I realized that they were managing the land in a way that we were unaware of, and this led to research that made us realize we have to manage our [critical resources] in the same way as the Aborigines managed them.

Latz convinced his scientific colleagues that this approach to *mala* reintroduction was no heresy. After a number of field trips with Aboriginal elders, a 250-acre site was selected in 1986. That December, an electric fence was erected to exclude exotic predators. Then, in 1987, the *malas* that had been captive-bred were finally introduced.

"The first four years, they bred up wonderfully to about a hundred animals," Don recalled to me. "We had some good rains, and the *pale-pale* spinifex responded incredibly. In those four years, we had no intrusions from cats, dingoes, or foxes."

The Aboriginal elders who still lived in the area would regularly go out to the fenced site and look for tracks of the *mala* inside the fence or for those of predators both inside and out. Several of these elders had previously known the *mala*. They were proud to be part of bringing the animals back to their home range. One of the wildlife biologists, Ken Johnson, recalled first learning what the project meant to the Warlpiri: "It was clear that the *mala* had great importance to them. And now, with the animals back around, we began to hear reports that hare wallabies were becoming more frequent again in their stories."

The rarest hare wallaby had been reintroduced, but more importantly, its habitat could now be restored through Aboriginal burning practices. With these processes back in place, it appeared that Hare-Wallaby Dreaming was on the verge of a resurgence.

Then bad news arrived from the Granites. A feral European fox had arrived on the scene, and in less than three months, it had killed twenty *malas*. The predation continued until not a single hare wallaby was left. Five years after this first catastrophe, the other remaining site was badly damaged by an unusually hot fire out of season relative to Aboriginal burning times; because controlled burns had not fully reestablished a habitat mosaic like those of historic times, this fire took its toll on *mala* food and shelter.

These reports had a sobering effect on the wildlife biologists involved. The animals left caged outside Alice Springs and fenced in the 250-acre refuge in the Tanami were all that stood between survival and extinction for the mainland gene pool. There were no unfenced, natural populations of *malas* left on the Australian continent.

The biologists were not content to have all the remaining *malas* sentenced to living out their lives behind bars. Bolstered by their successes in captive-breeding hundreds of *malas*, the Conservation Commission's wildlifers decided to release some of the captive-bred animals that had already been acclimated in the 250-acre exclosure. They were booted out *beyond* the electric fence to fend for themselves.

Much to everyone's relief, the newly released *mala* herd increased in numbers to about forty. The Aborigines in the area learned to identify members of various *mala* families by their tracks, providing information to the biologists that radiotelemetry alone could not offer.

Nevertheless, some of the Aborigines' observations were disconcerting. At one spot, they stumbled on the remains of six of the radio-tagged *malas*, with feral cat tracks all around them. The cat had gone for the throat—or in this case, the radio collar.

The commission enlisted Aborigines in cat control, but no one believes that cats can be exterminated from the area indefinitely. Making matters worse, the noncaptive *malas* soon began to range farther and farther from the site of their reintroduction, "chasing the storms" as the Aborigines themselves once did.

Don Langford has at times been disheartened, other times amused by such news. "With the sight of so much green on the horizon, so much good bush tucker somewhere else, there was no reason for those *malas* to stick around," he told me. Several have dispersed far beyond the reception distance of their radio transmitters and have never been heard of again.

Foxes. Cats. Fire-suppressed spinifex. Within six years of the release into the wild, only five radio-tagged *malas* remain of the twenty-five that were originally collared and booted out beyond the fence. This could mean that fewer than ten *malas* are still alive.

"It's hard to say," Don Langford conceded. "Some of their batteries have gone dead, but the animals may still be alive. But we're still having trouble from the cats. I'd reckon that there may be only eleven to fifteen *malas* left out beyond the fence. We're in a holding pattern now, simply trying to cut our losses, before deciding what steps to take next."

It's been hard for the biologists to accept the many setbacks. Still, they are proud of what they've tried, not only in biological conservation but in cultural restoration as well. The Aboriginal custodians of the Tanami Desert have not been passive bystanders in this process; they remain active participants. Not too long ago, the Conservation Commission received a letter from a government adviser stationed at an Aboriginal outstation just to the east of the *mala* reintroduction sites. He had been told by the local people that the biologists were the first government workers they had ever come to trust.

It's no wonder. Latz, Langford, Johnson, and others have kept in touch with the Warlpiri for two decades now. The biologists bring their own families out to stay at the Aboriginal camps near the study sites, and both adults and children have been affectionately given skin-names by the locals. Langford himself has taken in eight Aboriginal children over the years, helping them with schooling and medical needs. For all the racism and cultural polarization that I found nearly everywhere I traveled in the Australian outback, the *mala* collaboration seemed an island of mutual respect in the midst of a furious storm. Here, at least, affection and information were flowing in both directions.

As Langford led Dusty and me away from Killer's cage, my mind raced back and forth between two images. The first was that of Killer himself. Tense. Scared. An animal taken out of its wild context, now incapable of a healthy existence in a place where spinifex once stretched from horizon to horizon. Like many Aborigines, he had been robbed of his birthright. His ancient way of life was no longer possible.

But the other image that stuck in my mind was that of harewallaby tracks. They were hopping through time, as you can see them do on a petroglyph panel not far from Alice Springs. Wherever such sacred sites exist, hunters can visit them only if they leave their weapons behind, refraining from capturing animals anywhere near the Dreaming. In effect, their spiritual link to the land has created de facto wildlife refuges, where totem animals can regenerate free of human-induced pressures that might otherwise thin their numbers.

Both of these images flare up in my mind now whenever I see a feral cat or a government land where fire has been suppressed so long that it has created a tinderbox.

Not long ago, Aboriginal artist Alec Minutjukur recalled how his people formerly "hunted meat and gathered food...men danced in the traditional stamping step, and the people handed down stories to the children. This is how they were.... That culture then was as stable as a mountain range [but] they didn't see what was to happen.... They could not have seen beyond it."

Diabetes, Diet, and Native American Foraging Traditions

The consumption of "wild" foods has been interpreted as an adaptive strategy for periods of seasonal, other irregularly episodic, and long-term catastrophic shortages of cultigens. The very pursuit of wild foods generally can be construed as adaptive since, in that quest, individuals learn about new ecologies.

NINA L. ETKIN, *Eating on the Wild Side*

"It was this way, long time ago," explained the old Indian lady. She was a member of the binational Hia C-ed O'odham tribe that is scattered across Sonora and Arizona. A distant relative was translating her words for me: "The People were like a cultivated field producing after its kind, recognizing its kinship; the seeds remain and continue to produce. Today all the bad times have entered the People, and they [the O'odham] no longer recognize their way of life. The People separated from one another and became few in number. Today all the O'odham are vanishing."

Candelaria Orosco sat in a small clapboard house in the depressed mining town of Ajo, Arizona, recalling the native foods that she had hunted, gathered, and harvested before the turn of the century. Her leg hurt her, for the sores on it were taking a long time to heal because of the adult-onset diabetes that came to her late in life. Today this is a common affliction among her people, the O'odham, who suffer one of the highest incidences of diabetes of any ethnic population in the world. Orosco was trying hard to describe how her kin, the migratory Hia C-ed O'odham, had lived prior to such afflictions, when roughly five hundred of them had obtained their living from what outsiders consistently regard as a "hopeless desert." Around the time of Orosco's birth, a U.S. Indian agent had visited the O'odham and described their habitat in this way: "Place the same number of whites on a barren, sandy desert such as they live on, and tell them to subsist there; the probability is that in two years they would become extinct."

Yet Orosco was invoking a litany of plant and animal names in her native language, names referring to herbs and seeds and roots, birds and reptiles and mammals that had once formed the bulk of her diet. Even when English rather than O'odham words are used for these nutritional resources, the names of the native foods that once filled her larder still have an alluring ring. For meat, her family ate desert tortoises, pack rats, bighorn sheep, hornworm larvae, desert cottontails, pronghorn antelope, Gambel's quail, mule deer, whitewing doves, Colorado River squawfish, black-tailed jackrabbits, and occasional stray camels. Although the unpredictability of desert rains kept her people from harvesting crops on a regular basis in many places, they did successfully cultivate white tepary beans, Old Lady's Knees muskmelons, green-striped cushaw squash, sixty-day-flour corn, Spanish watermelons, white Sonora wheat, and Papago peas. They gathered a much greater variety of wild plant foods: broomrape stalks, screwbean mesquite pods, plantain seed, tansy mustard, amaranth, cholla cactus buds, honey mesquite, povertyweed, wolfberries, hog potato, lamb's-quarters, prickly pears, ironwood seed, wild chiles, chia, organ-pipe cactus fruit, old woman's cactus seed, and sandfood. When Orosco mentioned sandfood—an underground parasite that attaches to the roots of wind-beaten shrubs on otherwise barren dunes—my facial expression must have given me away.

"What's that?" she asked in O'odham.

I stammered, "Sandfood...are you saying that the old people knew how to find it, and they once told you how it tasted?" Few people alive today have ever seen this sandfood, let alone tasted it, for it is now endangered by habitat destruction.

"I said that I ate it. I wouldn't have told you that it had a good sweet taste if I hadn't eaten it myself. How could I explain to you what other people thought it tasted like or how to harvest it? Because it doesn't stick up above the ground like other plants, I had to learn to see where the little dried-up ones from the year before broke the surface. That's where I would dig."

She described how you can steam succulent plants in earthen pits, boil down cactus fruit into jam or syrup, roast meat over an open fire, and parch wild legume seeds to keep them for later use. Orosco spoke matter-of-factly of such work, the customary tasks of desert subsistence. There was no romanticism about the halcyon days of her youth, but it was clear that she felt some foods of value had been lost.

Her concerns about the loss of gathering and farming traditions were shared by her tribesman, the late Miguel Velasco, in an interview with Fillman Bell in 1979:

> We are from the sand, and known as Sand Indians, to find our way of life on the sand of the earth. That is why we go all over to seek our food to live as well. We cover a large portion of land in different harvest seasons to gather our food to store in time of winter season. Long time ago, this was our way of life. We did not buy food. We worked hard to gather foods. We never knew what coffee was until the White People came. We drank the desert fruit juices in harvest time. The desert food is meant for the Indians to eat. The reason so many Indians die young is because they don't eat their desert food anymore. They would not know how to survive if Anglos stopped selling them food. The old Indians lived well with their old way of life.

Oral accounts such as these are often regarded as "nostalgia for the old ways," even by eminent ethnobotanists such as Peter Raven, who used this phrase to dismiss my exploration of the value of Native American subsistence strategies, *Enduring Seeds*. If by "nostalgia" we mean a longing for experiences, things, or acquaintances belonging to the past, we may indeed include under its rubric some of the statements made by Indian elders. Consider, for instance, this commentary by Chona, recorded by Ruth Underhill in *The Autobiography of a Papago Woman* during the early thirties:

> We always kept gruel in our house. It was in a big clay pot that my mother had made. She ground up seeds into flour. Not wheat flour— we had no wheat. But all the wild seeds, the good pigweed and the wild grasses...Oh, how good that gruel was! I have never tasted anything like it. Wheat flour makes me sick. I think it has no strength. But when I am weak, when I am tired, my grandchildren make me a gruel out of the wild seeds. *That* is food.

Chona was clearly referring to foodstuffs that had formed a greater proportion of her dietary intake in the past than they did at the time she spoke with Underhill. Yet these foods were not exclusively relegated to the past, because they retained their functional value when she was sick, providing her with nourishment that mainstream American foods could not. Moreover, in Chona's mind, the wild desert seeds had remained the quintessential foods, embodying her cultural definition of what food should be. Because she did not consider the value of her people's traditional diet to be obsolete, Chona's respect for that diet should not be relegated to the shelf holding antiquarian trivia.

This point was brought home to me again by Candelaria Orosco. After we spent several hours looking at pressed herbs, museum collections of seeds, and historic photos of plants that I had presumed to be formerly part of her culture's daily subsistence, she brought out several of her own collections. She rolled out from under her bed two green-striped cushaw squashes that she had grown in her postage-stamp-sized garden. Then she reached under her stove and showed me caches of cholla cactus buds and some wild tansy mustard seeds she had gathered. These foodstuffs were not simply for "old times' sake"; they had been the fruits of her efforts toward self-reliance for more than ninety years.

Cynics or self-described "realists" might still dismiss the relict consumption of native foods by Chona or Candelaria Orosco as nostalgic and trivial, and they might dismiss my interest in Candelaria and Chona as a misguided attempt to elevate these women to the status of "ecologically noble savages." Because the plants and animals these women mentioned now make up such a small portion of the diet of contemporary Indians, few contemporary anthropologists even study them, claiming that such traditional foods now play no significant functional role in Native American nutrition or culture. If a Navajo man eats more Kentucky Fried Chicken than he does the mutton of Navajo-Churro sheep, is it not true that ecologically and nutritionally speaking, he is more like an urban Kentuckian than he is like his Diné ancestors? If an O'odham woman eats more fry bread than cholla cactus buds, is she not more pan-Indian than she is a part of her own tribe's historic trajectory?

The answer may be a qualified yes. I interpret many of the O'odham elders' statements as warnings to their descendants that the younger generations are abandoning what it means to be culturally and ecologically O'odham. This concern is explicit in the following statement by the late great O'odham orator Venito García:

> The way life is today, what will happen if the Anglos discontinued their money system? What will happen to our children? They will not want to eat the mountain turtle, because they have never eaten any. Maybe they will eat it if they get hungry enough. I think of all the desert plants we used to eat, the desert spinach we cooked with chile.... If we continue to practice eating our survival food, we may save our money we do receive sometimes.... The Chinese, they still practice their old eating habits. They save all their money. The Anglos don't like this. They [the Chinese] like to eat their ant eggs [rice]. They even use their long sticks to eat with, picking the ant eggs up with their long sticks and pinning it to their mouths. This is their way of life.

To be Chinese is to be one who eats rice with chopsticks, according to García's view as an outsider; likewise, an outsider should be able to recognize the desert-dwelling O'odham by their consumption of cactus, amaranth greens, or mesquite. Although such dietary definitions are too restrictive for ethnographers to take seriously, traditional peoples often use culinary customs as primary indicators of a particular culture.

O'odham elders relate their culinary traditions to their health and survival. The elders not only recall "survival foods" used during times of drought and political disruption but they also remember the curative quality of the native foods that were a customary component of their diets. These presumed curative qualities are now being scientifically investigated, for, in a real sense, native foods may be the best medicine available to the O'odham. The O'odham metabolism evolved for several thousand years under the influence of a particular set of native desert plant foods with peculiar characteristics that formerly protected the people from certain afflictions now common among them.

Through the 1930s, native desert foods contributed a significant portion of Pima, Desert Papago, and Sand Papago diets; mesquite, acorns, chia, tepary beans, cacti, and mescal were eaten as commonly as foods introduced by Europeans. At that time, the O'odham were generally regarded as lean, active people who worked hard at obtaining a subsistence from one of the most unpredictable but biologically diverse deserts in the world. Then government work projects and World War II came along, and rather than persisting with their own foraging traditions, the O'odham became cheap labor for extensive irrigated cotton farms in Anglo communities near their reservations. Others went off to the war and became accustomed to a cash economy and canned food.

When these people returned to their villages in the late forties, their gathering grounds and fields were overgrown or eroded due to lack of care, and off-reservation opportunities were still calling. Government advisers termed their ancient farming and foraging strategies risky and unproductive and offered no assistance in renovating the fields that for centuries had remained fertile under periodic cultivation. Instead, the tribal governments were encouraged either to develop their own large farms using the corporate model or to lease tribal lands to non-Indian farmers for them to do the same. Fewer than a tenth of the traditional farms of the O'odham survived these economic and social pressures. As the droughts of the fifties came and went, subsistence farming went by the wayside, while hunting and gathering remained activities for only a small percentage of them.

Before the war, diabetes had been no more common among the O'odham than it was among the population of the United States as a whole. Yet twenty-five years later, the O'odham had a prevalence of diabetes fifteen times that of the typical Anglo-American community. The average young O'odham man in the early 1970s weighed 44.1 pounds more than his 1940s counterpart and was considered overweight verging on obese. Since obesity is correlated with susceptibility to diabetes, pathologists at first concluded that the "escape" of the O'odham from their primitive, feast-or-famine cycle of subsistence had made calories more regularly available year-round; hence, they had gained weight and diabetes had set in.

The only flaw in this theory was that the modern wage-earning O'odham individual was not necessarily consuming any more calories than traditional O'odham or, for that matter, than the average Anglo. The difference, I believe, was not in the number of calories consumed but in the kinds of wild and cultivated plants with which the O'odham had coevolved.

A few years ago, I sent a number of desert foods traditionally prepared by the O'odham to a team of Australian nutritionists, who analyzed the foods for any effects they might have on blood-sugar and insulin levels following meals. High blood-sugar levels are of concern because they stress the capacity of the pancreas to keep pace with insulin production. If stressed repeatedly, the pancreas essentially becomes poisoned. Insulin metabolism becomes permanently damaged, and the dangerous dysfunctional syndrome known as diabetes develops. Yet when a person is fed acorns, mesquite pods, and tepary or lima beans, the soluble dietary fiber, tannins, and inulin in these foods reduce blood-sugar levels and prolong the period over which sugar is absorbed into the blood. Insulin production and sensitivity are also improved. In short, these native foods may protect Indian diabetics from suffering high blood-sugar levels following a meal. Mesquite pods and acorns are among the 10 percent most effective foods ever analyzed for their effects in controlling blood-sugar rises after a meal. Unlike domesticated plant foods, their fiber, tannins, or complex carbohydrates have not been genetically removed by crop breeders or milled away by industrial food technologists' machinery. Historically, the O'odham were consuming more than 120 grams of these "slow-release" soluble fibers a day; now they consume less than a third of that volume.

Recent studies suggest that many desert foods contain mucilaginous polysaccharide gums that are viscous enough to slow the digestion and absorption of sugary foods. Such slow-release gums have probably evolved in many desert plants to slow water loss from the seeds, seedlings, and succulent tissues of mature plants. The O'odham metabolism may, in turn, have adapted to such qualities after centuries of dependence on the foods containing these gums—foods such as prickly pear fruit and pads, cholla cactus buds, plantain seeds, chia seeds, mesquite pods, and tansy mustard seeds. All were former seasonal staples of the O'odham; all are nearly absent from their diet today. Together with Australian nutritionist Jennie Brand, I have advanced the hypothesis that these foods served to protect indigenous people from the diabetic syndrome to which they were genetically susceptible.

For O'odham families who remained on a traditional diet, their genetic predisposition to diabetes was not likely to be expressed. But diabetes-prone Indians on a fast-food diet of fried potatoes, soft drinks or beer, sweets, and corn chips find their insulin metabolism going haywire. Obtaining highly milled grains or finely processed root starches further aggravates the problem. At the Phoenix Indian Hospital, Boyd Swinburn compared the responses of twenty-two patients who changed from a traditional O'odham diet (which I reconstructed from historic accounts) to a fast-food diet consisting of virtually the same number of calories. When they switched to what we nicknamed the "mini-mart diet," their insulin sensitivity to glucose worsened, as did their glucose tolerance. Swinburn concluded, "The influence of Westernization on the prevalence of [adult-onset] diabetes may in part be due to changes in diet composition." For the O'odham and other indigenous peoples whose diets were recently Westernized to highly bred, industrially processed foods, a return to a diet similar to their traditional one is no nostalgic notion; it may, in fact, be a nutritional and cultural imperative.

Recently, I assisted nurse practitioners who were screening Seri neighbors of the O'odham for early warning indicators of diabetes. The Seri have persisted with a traditional diet far longer than the O'odham were able to. When a Seri tribal elder asked why we were recording the genealogies of those Seri women who did have high blood-sugar levels, I tried to explain the genetic component of diabetes to him—that among O'odham, diabetes is known to "run in families." The Seri elder, Alfredo Lopez Blanco, thought about this notion that we call "genetic predisposition" for a moment, and then rejected it as irrelevant.

"Look," he said, shaking his head, "their grandparents weren't overweight in the old days, and I don't think they had this sickness you call diabetes. They're sick now not because of their blood [inheritance] but because their diet has changed. They hardly eat mesquite or cactus or desert tortoise anymore. They eat white-bread sandwiches, Coke, sweets from the stores, and the pork rinds we call *chicharrones*. You don't need to know our family histories so much as you need to remind us to keep eating our desert foods!"

In desert villages where native food plants were formerly gathered, the majority of the O'odham are now classified as unemployed or underemployed. Because their income levels are so low, many Native American families are eligible for government surplus commodity foods, nearly all of which are nutritionally inferior to their native counterparts. At the same time, the hyperabundance of these federally donated foodstuffs serves as a disincentive for local food gathering. As one O'odham woman lamented, "why gather different kinds of beans when someone delivers big bags of pinto beans to our house every month?" The demise of local foraging, the indulgence in a welfare economy, and a worsening of health and self-esteem are linked. This syndrome is not restricted to the O'odham; because of their high Mexican and Indian population, by the year 2000 Arizonan and Sonoran health programs will spend at least two billion dollars annually on their four hundred thousand citizens suffering from diabetes.

Is it not ironic that at the same time, more than a half million agricultural acres in the Sonoran Desert have been left barren owing to excessive irrigation costs of producing water-consumptive, conventional crops? The sowing of native food plants, some of which require a third to a fifth as much water as conventional crops to obtain the same food yields, has not been given due consideration as a feasible option for the management of these lands. The society to which the food industry caters is simply not accustomed to the tastes, textures, and preparation techniques associated with these wild and semi-domesticated foods. And so the transplanted agriculture has damaged the health of the land, at the same time that it has diminished the land's capacity to produce the plant foods needed to sustain our own well-being.

I only wish that we had heeded the words of ethnobotanist Melvin Gilmore, who began his work among Native American farmers and gatherers seventy years ago, before the tide of diabetes and agricultural desolation had swamped them:

> We shall make the best and most economical use of our land when our population shall become adjusted in habit to the natural conditions. The country cannot be wholly made over and adjusted to a people of foreign habits and tastes. There are large tracts of land in America whose bounty is wasted because the plants that can be grown on them are not acceptable to our people. This is not because the plants are not useful and desirable but because their valuable qualities are not known.... The adjustment of American consumption to American conditions of production will bring about greater improvement in conditions of life than any other material agency.

FOUR

The Verdant Bridge:
Plant Domestication and the
Caring of the Garden

Historically, agriculture has increased diversity—
but more recently, modern farming strategies have
impoverished communities, habitats, and terrains.
Why? How?

Let Us Now Praise Native Crops

An American Cornucopia

Native gatherers, farmers, and crop breeders identified and developed the potential latent in the American flora, handing down to us a wealth of nutritious and pleasing plant foods.... The peoples, plants, animals, landscapes, languages, and traditions of the American hemisphere were strange enough to Europeans that...they regarded the place literally as a New World. French archaeologist François Bordes suggests...that a shock of equal magnitude is unlikely to occur unless intelligent life is found elsewhere in the universe.

NELSON FOSTER, *Chiles to Chocolate*

Let us now praise native crops—the fruits, tubers, grains, beans, and greens that have been cultivated in the New World since ancient pre-Columbian times. Some of these food crops have been nurturing cultures in the Americas for the last six to eight millennia. Seeds of these enduring native crop varieties have been passed from hand to hand through as many as one hundred generations of gardeners and farmers since the process of plant domestication began in the New World.

To appraise the genetic changes that have occurred in American plants as a result of this process, botanists seldom have more than a few carbonized seeds, some spikelet chaff, leaf fiber, or pollen grains with which to work. Nevertheless, we know with certainty that botanical changes of enormous magnitude have taken place. At the same time, agriculture and concomitant innovations in technology and social organization radically altered the trajectory of many American cultures.

By interpreting a handful of now-famous gourd rinds, minuscule corncobs, and spent bean pods so as to place these materials in their cultural contexts, archaeologists have provided some understanding of the changes that native crop domestication and diffusion have wrought on American civilizations. Yet much of the story remains to be told. Desiccated seeds, coprolite contents, and radiocarbon-dated charcoal must be reconstituted into images of people planting, selecting, harvesting, preparing, and eating their various crops. At the very least, this story includes thousands of pre-Columbian field and orchard crop varieties brought into American households to serve as the *materia prima* for hundreds of distinctive ethnic cuisines.

Perhaps the complexity of crop evolution makes us lose sight of the concurrent cultural evolution of culinary traditions: changes in grinding, roasting, brewing, baking, and fermenting techniques, not to mention customs of spicing and serving prepared foods. What comes to mind when we imagine pre-Columbian cuisines? Shattering our stereotypes of dreary mushes and charred meats, Teresa Castello Yturbide, Michel Zabe, and Ignacio Pina Lujan, in *Presencia de la Comida Prehispánica*, elegantly document the preparation of a variety of savory dishes that were first recorded in the early historic codices and that have persisted to the present in the indigenous communities of Mexico. *Tamales de rana*: Montezuma's frogs, spiced with *epazote* leaves, *chile pasilla* pods, and chopped prickly pear pads, wrapped together in a corn husk or the skin of an agave leaf and cooked over a hot *comal* made of clay. *Huautli*: the popped seeds of grain amaranth mixed with honey from native bees and sculpted into fantastic forms. *Casuela de iguana*: cleaned and quartered iguana meat stewed in a broth of *jitomate* and *chile costeño* thickened with a ball of maize mush that is mixed into the broth just before serving. *Huazoncle*: flower buds of grain chenopods (like quinoa or lamb's-quarters), stripped off the stalk while still tender, washed in a solution of baking soda, and then cooked in an omelette, perhaps using quail eggs.

To these Mesoamerican recipes we might add *mah-pi*: blue corn balls made by the Missouri River tribes from maize flour moistened with juneberries or blueberries and deer kidney tallow. Or *tarwi con saraphata* from the inter-Andean valley: freshly ground lupine seeds mixed with lime-treated hominy corn, stewed tomatoes, chopped onions, and greens, then boiled to a creamy consistency.

These particular pre-Columbian foods have survived and are still being prepared today by Native Americans, mestizos, or Ladinos in much the same manner as they were thousands of years ago. At most, lard or vegetable oils are added, wheat flour is sometimes substituted for cornmeal, and a wider range of herbs is used for seasonings. Many, many other indigenous foods, however, are no longer eaten on a routine basis, if at all. Their demise is part of a pattern of profound cultural change that has been correlated with several waves of native crop extirpation following the arrival of conquistadors, colonists, and diseases from the Old World.

Americans did gain valuable Old World crops through the Columbian Exchange, with remarkable "new foods" such as *mole poblano* arising out of the intermixing of ingredients and hybridization of cooking traditions from the two hemispheres, but the Old World crops introduced over the last five centuries have not compensated for the plant diversity lost in the Americas during the same period. The erosion of genetic diversity that began during the half century following Columbus's arrival has continued almost unabated down to the present. A biological treasure has been squandered; in a very real sense, it has been rendered inaccessible to all of humankind, not just to American cultures.

Since there was no "baseline" inventory of how much variation existed in American fields at the time of Columbus, we will never have a reliable estimate of how much crop diversity—how many genes, vegetable varieties, or plant species—has been lost over the past 500 years. (We hardly possess such an inventory for crops that exist today.) Yet fools rush in where archaeobotanists fear to tread. Seed conservationist John Carr hazarded the first guess more than a decade ago, estimating that 70 percent of the crop varieties grown in the Americas prior to Columbus are now extinct. In the U.S. Southwest, my own comparisons of native crop varieties cultivated by prehistoric farmers with those now grown by their descendants suggest that 55 to 65 percent of the region's diversity has been extirpated.

These losses are not just botanical statistics. To sense how the past five centuries of change have affected human families, their diets, and cultures, we must appreciate the way native crop diversity has functioned, the factors that have contributed to its development, and the pressures that have worn part of it away. We must imagine how these crops were a part of the immense fabric of American folklife, woven into a patchwork of fields in rural landscapes, planting ceremonies, and harvest celebrations.

If you walk through the small, terraced fields tended by Native Americans in the highlands of central Mexico today, you will see that their cornfields are not monocultural stands of maize. Instead, these *milpas* are a collage of greens, beet reds, violets, tans, stripes, and speckles. They are mosaics, with several maize varieties serving as dominant "overstory" crops and many other plants growing up their stalks or in their shadows: grain amaranths, squashes, beans, chile peppers, husk tomatoes or *miltomates*, *jaltomates*, and semicultivated greens such as *epazote*, *quintonil*, and *verdolagas*. Domestic turkeys may wander through these heterogeneous patches, picking grasshoppers and tomato hornworms off the plants. The terraced fields are often rimmed with hedges of prickly pear or century plants, and a nearby orchard may feature native *capulin* cherries and hawthorns along with Spanish-introduced fruits. These food, fiber, and spice crops offer products to be harvested through most of the year.

Discussions of American agricultural origins typically emphasize maize—its ancient domestication and primacy in a dietary triumvirate with beans and squash. To be sure, these three crops, each displaying great regional variation, were important in many ways. But American farmers have traditionally relied on a much wider range of crops, and that diversity has had ecological, economic, agronomic, culinary, and nutritional consequences. In summarizing the role that diversity plays in small-scale traditional agriculture, Daniela Soleri and David Cleveland point out that different varieties or species of greens may meet largely the same nutritional need but that their physiological and ecological differences increase the reliability of harvests and prolong the period during which greens may be available. (Of course, they also add a variety of tastes and textures to a family's diet.)

Particularly in unpredictable climates or marginal lands, diversity minimizes the risk of total crop failure, since different crops respond in different ways to droughts, early freezes, insects, and diseases. In heterogeneous fields, some susceptible crops simply escape being seen, smelled, or otherwise located by pests. Faced with a mixture of susceptible and resistant crops maturing at different times, an insect pest is impeded in its evolutionary ability to overcome the resistant gene found in just one of the crop varieties present. Fields that are structurally complex also abound with pest predators, since hedges, vines, upright annuals, and succulents provide nesting and perching sites for birds and other agents of biological control.

Matching specially adapted varieties to field sites with peculiar microclimates, soils, and water sources has the additional virtue of enabling farmers to utilize all the available space for production of one kind or another. Traditional mixed orchard gardens meet many needs besides those of nutrition. Soleri and Cleveland note, "Some [crops] may provide fruit or vegetables, medicine, building or craft materials, fuel and fodder. Others may be grown for the beauty of their flowers, and all may be grown for market."

Thus, though it is useful to profile single American crops and their culinary uses, it is crucial to keep in mind that each arose in a multidimensional ecological and cultural context. Evolutionary ecologists believe that certain Native American crops truly coevolved over hundreds of years of native intercropping. Likewise, cultures loosely coevolved with the sets of plants they domesticated or received from neighboring peoples and adapted for their own uses.

This process of coevolution began when early farmers started sowing, harvesting, and storing seeds through the winter. These simple actions worked to change the genetic structure of annual plant populations. Teosinte, wild beans, wild gourds, and a few other disturbance-adapted annuals became rapidly, perhaps catastrophically, domesticated. For instance, when beans were harvested and stored in the absence of selection pressures from seed-boring bruchid beetles, previous constraints on seed size, seed coat thickness, and seed coat chemistry were released. Under subsequent cultural selection, beans became larger and easier to germinate and lost certain bitter chemicals in the seed coat that had once served as feeding deterrents to the beetles. The storage vessels of farmers then had to offer the protection from pests that bitter chemicals once provided. And so the plants themselves became dependent upon human intervention.

While Native Americans continued to glean much of their subsistence from wildlands, the initial domestications encouraged many peoples to invest increasing effort in tending garden-sized plots of cultivated annuals. These annual crops were not broadcast—not sown by hand-scattering seeds—in the manner that Old World farmers planted wheat, barley, lentils, and oats, and this fact alone accounts for some of the varietal diversity in New World crops. Native American crops were usually planted in mounds or holes spaced several paces apart. They were probably gathered in a similar fashion—not collectively cut with sickles and then threshed but harvested one by one. These practices meant that Native American farmers had the opportunity to notice novel variants. Rather than mass breeding, as the Mediterranean wheat sower has done for millennia, the Mesoamerican chile pepper cultivator, the Andean potato farmer, and the Arido-American prickly pear propagator became experts at single-plant selection.

Some Mesoamerican *campesinos* continue this tradition today, sorting out each interesting variant, setting its seed aside, and planting that seed in a separate patch the next year to increase its kind. They are connoisseurs of subtle variation and readily take advantage of chance hybrids or somatic mutants that appear in their gardens or field patches. This sort of close cultural selection favors locally specialized ecotypes, farmer-specific flavor and color variants, and culture-specific ceremonial strains of crops.

The number of such folk varieties of crops probably increased dramatically in Mexico during the Late Preclassic and Classic Periods around A.D. 100–700, when domesticated annuals became major components of the Mesoamerican diet. As Lawrence and Lucille Kaplan point out, "this was a time of explosive population growth and the founding of new permanent villages and urban centers." A similar shift in agricultural intensification and diversification in arid lands that are now part of the U.S. Southwest began a few hundred years later, after communities there grew large enough to practice irrigated agriculture along the floodplains of desert rivers. Maize did not become a major dietary component in desert areas until the development of irrigation management by the Hohokam culture.

In South America, crop production in sedentary pottery-making villages began much earlier, perhaps 4,000 to 2,500 years ago. We may assume from studying the fields of their descendants that prehistoric Andean farmers grew more than just a few domesticated crops. They apparently encouraged or at least tolerated a variety of wild greens and semicultivated tubers in their fields, and sporadic outcrossing between wild and cultivated potatoes added to the genetic diversity found in that particular crop. By late prehistoric times there was perhaps a greater varietal diversity within Native American crops than in any era before or since.

Columbus, Cortez, and the Spanish conquistadors ushered in the first major decline in New World agricultural diversity. As Alfred Crosby has defined it, the Columbian Exchange included the dispersal to the Americas of dozens of Old World crops, hundreds of weeds, and some major animal pests. With the introduction of livestock, the dispersal of foreign and native plants alike was expedited, as their seeds were spread on the hair and muddy hooves and in the feces of cattle, horses, goats, and sheep. Within the first century following Cortez, certain regions of the Americas, such as the Valley of Mexico, were intentionally altered into habitats approximating European pastoral scenes, replete with forage grasses, grain fields, olive orchards, and the like. The inter-Andean valley was also rapidly overhauled, not merely as a visual landscape but also as a food-producing ecosystem.

At the same time, epidemics raged through the Americas, devastating the human population. If ethnohistorian Henry Dobyns's reconstructions are even remotely correct, diseases spread along well-established trade routes in advance of the Spaniards themselves, and they disrupted both local food production and extra-local exchanges of foodstuffs, medicines, and ceremonial goods. In less than a century, some regions lost three-quarters of their population, leaving in ruins large prehistoric irrigation works once maintained by collective labor.

In the southwestern United States, it appears that jack beans, century plants, and grain chenopods were among the crop casualties.

As European colonists began to till American soils, Old World crops were planted where native crops had flourished. In a few places, native crops and customs were officially suppressed by the Spanish. Between 1690 and 1750, such suppression led to scattered nativist resistance movements, some of which temporarily removed the Spanish from power. Whether these nativist movements included traditional crop and food revivals is a topic that invites further study.

As the Industrial Revolution developed and the population grew, the usurpation of native croplands accelerated. The Europeanization of the American landscape, along with its farms and crops, has continued well into this century, turning prairies into cereal monocultures, wooded parklands, and pastures as well as converting deserts into artificial (and surely ephemeral) Mediterranean oases. With the advent of farm mechanization and the coalescence of an international market economy, even European-style small farms became disadvantaged. The large industrial farms that took their place certainly have not nurtured diversity.

The tragic loss of mixed crops and livestock breeds during the twentieth century has been amply documented in economic and sociological analyses but perhaps never so poignantly conveyed as in *Leaving the Land*, a novel by Douglas Unger. Family farms with a mixture of crops, livestock, and poultry varieties were driven out of business by dovetailing economic and political forces that favored production zones focused on one commodity. As World War II began to affect the American heartland, Unger writes, "lives changed overnight, with crops, livestock, and machinery left in the care of wives, daughters [and older men like Ben Hogan].... The priorities of wartime farming gave Ben Hogan the choice of raising either sugar beets or turkeys." Unger explains the dilemma:

> There was supposed to be a corn shortage for the alcohol industry, alcohol necessary for the manufacture of explosives. But the USDA kept telling farmers that it was simply good sense for a man to raise either sugar beets or turkeys, since both could be processed right away, packed and made ready locally for immediate use. A man was free to raise just corn or wheat or beans, or other livestock animals than turkeys, free

to raise many different crops at once in diversified farming, he really was, there wasn't any law against it. He just wouldn't get much government subsidy money through the Farmers and Ranchers Stabilization Board for those crops, and there were also certain priorities at the Belle Fourche & Western Railroad shipping office.... So if a man in Wovoka County wanted to keep raising corn, wheat, beans, beef—diversified crops—just as he always had, he would have to wait several months or more before he could ship his harvest.

Farmers were also put under social and political pressure, told that "the boys overseas need beets and turkeys to win this war." Rural communities suffered further after the war as vertical monopolies forced many families off their land forever. In just a few decades the number of Americans living on farms plummeted from over 50 percent of the nation's population to less than 5 percent.

This trend is mirrored in statistics on Native American farmers in the United States, keepers of the native crops still extant north of Mexico. Between 1887 and 1934, 60 percent of all tribal trust and treaty lands—some eighty-four million acres—passed out of Native American hands as a result of the Dawes Act, a bill designed to promote the assimilation of Indians into the dominant society. Between 1910 and 1982 the number of Indians owning, running, or working on farms in the United States dropped from 48,500 to 7,150 despite an overall increase in the Indian population. And as native farmers were forced or lured off the land, centuries-old traditions of planting their families' heirloom seed stocks came to an end.

As if the tragedy at home did not cause enough damage to biodiversity and enough disruption of farming and culinary traditions, the United States began to export its new agricultural schemes to other countries. After World War II, industrial nations led by the United States launched well-intentioned programs to supply hybrid seeds, farm machines, fertilizers, and pesticides to developing nations. As early as 1941, crop geographer Carl Sauer warned policymakers about the impending loss of crop genetic resources and viable cultures, writing, "A good aggressive bunch of American agronomists and plant breeders could ruin the native resources for good by pushing their American commercial stocks.... Mexican agriculture cannot be pointed toward standardization on a few commercial types without upsetting native economy and culture hopelessly. The example of Iowa is about the most dangerous of all for Mexico."

Not long ago, I heard these same concerns voiced by an eighty-four-year-old Sonoran farmer who had been raising food for his family since 1910, when the Mexican Revolution erupted. "The hybrid corn has no taste," Casimiro Sanchez told me, "and when my neighbors save its seeds to regrow the following year, only small, irregular ears are produced. That's why I save the native seed, but the other people don't anymore.... [The community] has lost most of it already.

"If they don't start protecting the native seeds around here, local food production will eventually decline," he predicted, as we sat in his kitchen, looking at his recent harvest of open-pollinated corn. "The quality of the annual crops and even of the fruit trees will fall if we become dependent on introduced hybrids."

To our permanent disadvantage, the agricultural development foundations undertaking the Green Revolution turned a deaf ear to Sauer's warning and to native concerns, and they failed to study adequately and conserve valuable elements of traditional agro-ecosystems before beginning to change them. Thus their efforts temporarily resulted in higher crop yields per acre in many areas but also incurred great biological, environmental, and cultural costs. The question of whether the yield gains were worth more than the losses they caused has been the subject of a long and complex debate.

Now, another agricultural upheaval is at our door, superseding the Green Revolution. Called the Gene Revolution, this bag of biotechnological tricks will supposedly enable tropical fruits to be grown in more temperate climes by splicing freeze-resistant genes into their germ plasm, and they will turn maize and other nitrogen-consuming cereal crops into nitrogen-fixing plants by stitching into them genes from legumes. Although skepticism about such facile claims is mounting, the combined budget of all the crop genetic engineering firms in North America and Europe has already eclipsed the funds expended by the Green Revolution breeding centers at their peak.

Essential to the development of the biotechnology industry have been legislative and judicial acts enabling private firms to secure proprietary rights to plant genes, previously undescribed species, and novel breeding processes. An individual can now go to a remote farming tribe, collect a previously undescribed crop variety, and take out a patent or trademark on it. Such commercialization and rights usurpations have already become contentious issues with regard to blue corn, squashes, chile peppers, colored cotton, and amaranths.

Serious problems lie ahead as these crops pass from the hands of indigenous farmers to the cryogenic vaults of corporations that see them only as marketable commodities. For example, paddy-grown, fertilized, and pesticide-laden "wild rice" has created stiff economic competition for the Anishinabey, the Ojibway, and other Native American peoples of the Great Lakes region who harvest wild rice by hand and now manage many waterways in order to conserve this and other wild resources. For the Ojibway, the wild rice harvest has been a time for family cooperation, for singing, storytelling, and camping. One Ojibway youth explained to me that the harvest was more than an economic pursuit, that he "just loves the rhythm of the ricing."

As Thomas Vennum has recorded in *Wild Rice and the Ojibway People*, commercial paddy-grown rice is considered a desecration because the first fruits are no longer offered to the Great Spirit; the machine harvesters give the grain a dirty, oily taste; and greed, not sustainability, drives much of the current industry and its product marketing. So adamant are the Ojibway on this point that in 1982, Vennum reports, when a Saint Paul food store unwittingly donated paddy-grown rice for a Thanksgiving meal at the American Indian Center, "the Indians refused to take the free rice, even though it meant that their children might go hungry, because the paddy rice offended their cultural and religious sensibilities. Labeling the paddy rice as wild rice was analogous to misrepresenting non-kosher food as kosher."

The Gene Revolution makes fantastic promises to bring exotic foods to our dinner plates, but its ecological and cultural costs cannot be easily swept under the dining room rug. It is simply not enough anymore to claim that developing new markets for an underexploited crop is a "good" in and of itself. For decades, economic botanists have known of hundreds of good food plants unfamiliar to mainstream agriculture; the challenge before us is to ensure that these worthy old plants are utilized appropriately.

In the climatic zones to which they are adapted, many of the native crops offer commercial farmers lucrative yields with less reliance on irrigation water and chemicals than conventional crops require. This seems appropriate and good, especially when one also factors in other benefits, such as nutrition and taste. Nevertheless, hard questions must be asked, particularly about the appropriation and alteration of crops through the would-be Gene Revolution.

Who benefits? At whose expense? For how long? If blue corn, jicama, or *naranjilla* are marketed as novelty foods, what lasting benefit will there be? From my point of view, native crops deserve to persist as colorful and nutritious ingredients of truly American cuisines rather than going the way of most food fads. They need to become more than the trivial pursuit of gourmet consumers, instead providing new benefits for the farmers and gatherers, particularly for those Native Americans who have nurtured and been nurtured by these foodstuffs for centuries.

There *are* appropriate ways to revive these crops, but first we must guarantee their survival. This will take more than simply stashing seeds away in gene-bank freezers. Such a technical solution may preserve germ plasm, but it does not conserve the dynamic cultural context of the seed stocks, nor does it allow for their continued evolution and adaptation to changing conditions.

Dozens of groups, mostly small and community-haled, are now involved in the search for alternative, culturally supportive means of perpetuating genetic diversity in American crops. Of these, I am closest to Native Seeds/SEARCH, which is centered in Tucson; in the last decade this group has collected and redistributed seeds to more than two dozen tribes in the U.S. Southwest and northwestern Mexico. More than 1,200 folk varieties of fifteen pre-Columbian crops are kept in the gene bank at Native Seeds/SEARCH, but its primary goal is to see them conserved and used in the gardens and fields of the region to which they belong—and to which they are adapted. Often, Native American farmers have asked for help in relocating a variety they have lost, and the Native Seeds/SEARCH staff, encountering that particular variety in a remote village, has been able to return it to them. In several cases that we know of, these seed stocks, once reintroduced, have continued to grow, season after season, ever since.

In other cases, it takes more than a simple reintroduction to support native crop diversity and counteract the pressures working against this diversity. For several decades, applied anthropologists have helped rural development projects to direct Indian cultures away from their traditional ways of small-scale farming. Now it is time for the anthropology of resistance to be practiced in the service of native peoples who wish to retain or restore their agricultural heritage in the face of outside pressures to abandon it.

Today there are many nonprofit alliances, including the Traditional Native American Farmers Association, that actively assist native communities in maintaining their land-based way of life. By providing legal, social, and development services guided by the communities themselves, these organizations have offered timely assistance in thwarting deleterious development plans and have encouraged the emergence of leadership skills within the communities so that such aid will be unnecessary in the future.

Once such communities are relatively secure from immediate external threats and their basic set of indigenous resources is conserved, they may find several appropriate ways to revive their native crops. For example, participants in the Navajo Family Farms Project, based near Leupp, Arizona, have raised blue corn for consumption first at local schools and elderly programs, selling only their surplus corn off the reservation. Similarly, the Ikwé Marketing Collective of the Anishinabey Indians in Minnesota encourages its members to reserve as much of their hand-harvested wild rice as they want for themselves before selling their harvest to health-food stores. As Winona LaDuke explains, "by consuming our resources, we get a 'use value.' This value—whether from eating wild rice or berries—is critical to our poor community.... To feed our families, we might as well eat good native food instead of trying to get the money to buy 'white' food."

The persistence of agricultural and culinary traditions is of paramount concern to many Native Americans. It may not be possible to "reconstruct" the original context of native foods, nor would many Native Americans necessarily want to revive bygone diets. Nostalgia is not the driving sentiment in this movement, as some critics claim. Instead, it is powered by a sincere and sensible interest in retaining and renovating nutritional, aesthetic, cultural, and ecological values embedded in the native agricultural and culinary traditions.

For the rest of us, it also makes good sense to support a revival of traditional agriculture in the Americas. To gain access to traditional foods is an appealing reason but hardly the only one. Even if we ourselves are not growing or eating many of the ancient American crop varieties, they currently serve—and will continue to serve—as the primary resources for plant breeding programs seeking to increase the resistance of commercial crops to insects, disease, drought, and frost.

Globally, farmers face a changing climate, diminishing supplies of irrigation water and cheap chemical fertilizers, and the perennial problem of virulent new strains of pathogens. Old grain and bean varieties grown by native farmers are the backup force required to stave off famine should calamity strike the fields where major varieties are grown in monocultures over thousands of contiguous acres. Without the reservoir of traditional varieties to draw on, an epidemic, plague, or climatic shift might abruptly turn the breadbasket regions of the world into basket cases. For any future stability in the global food supply, diversity must be restored to all major food crops.

We also need to reform agricultural practices; here, too, native farming has much to teach us. In general, traditional Native American polycultures—several crops mixed in the same field—create greater habitat heterogeneity for field-dwelling animals and reduce the probability of a population explosion by any single pest. The majority of indigenous farmers still practice such intercropping, and non-Indians are now learning how heterogeneous agricultural "communities" can be managed with little or no petrochemicals, high-tech pest control, or intensive irrigation and cultivation. Even the so-called new ideas of alternative agriculture—Bill Mollison's permaculture and Wes Jackson's herbaceous perennial polycultures of prairie natives—build on intercropping concepts long practiced by indigenous farmers.

It is clear that both the crop genes and traditional knowledge still husbanded by Native American farmers have value to modern-day mainstream agriculture and will continue to have value in the future. But this information cannot simply be expropriated without causing certain losses; it is most complete and valuable when conserved in place. However stress-tolerant the plants may be in the field, however nutritious they may be in any diet, they have evolved to fit particular cultural and environmental contexts. Their beauty is derived from this fitness.

To praise appropriately the bean vines twining up stalks of maize or heirloom chile peppers outcrossing with wild chiltepines in nearby hedgerows, we must also praise the cultures that first observed them and then tolerated or intentionally nurtured them. Ultimately, the most potent way of conserving biological diversity may be to protect the diversity of the cultures that have stewarded the plant and animal communities on which our agriculture is based.

Harvest Time

Agricultural Change on the Northern Plains

*If heaven had given me a choice of my position and calling,
it should have been on a rich spot on earth, well watered, and
near a good market for the production of the garden. No
occupation is so delightful to me as the culture of the earth,
and no culture comparable to that of the garden.*

THOMAS JEFFERSON, 1811

Harvest weather: the sunrise was pouring mauve and burnt-orange light over the undulating land. Farmers' windbreaks, rising between grain fields and wheatgrass pastures, were stained with these same tones: burnt orange and mauve leaves were showering the ground. Only a sprinkle of rain mixed with this morning's wind, but rolling fog threatened to mask the terrain. The weather was pressing residents to gather what was still left standing in the fields, for soon all would change.

I had risen early to begin the drive from Bismarck and Mandan northeastward toward the geographic center of North America. Before reaching the continental midpoint, I veered westward from the Missouri River at Lake Sakakawea. Following the waters of the reservoir upstream I arrived at New Town, North Dakota, tribal headquarters of the Hidatsa, Arikara (Ree), and Mandan. Along the Upper Missouri, this time of year was once called "the moon of ripe maize." In weather so uncertain, the Indian farmers of the Missouri floodplain would work tirelessly to pull all the maize and squash out of the fields.

Those elegant fields of native maize deeply impressed botanist John Bradbury, who had encountered corn in the eastern United States and in tropical Latin America but none that could compare with the fields on the Upper Missouri in 1811: "I have not seen, even in the United States, any crop of Indian corn in finer order or better managed than the corn about the three villages. The women," he added, "are excellent cultivators."

Now these former fields lie beneath yards of water behind Garrison Dam. 155,000 acres of the Three Affiliated Tribes' holdings—including nearly all of their Class 1 and Class 2 farms on the fertile bottomlands—were drowned in the 1950s by the filling of Lake Sakakawea, a flood-control and irrigation development that serves a few non-Indians downstream. The "Village Indians" were forced to move their farmlands away from the river, onto short-grass prairies, mesas, and badlands that their ancestors had chosen not to cultivate.

Each of these three cultures has within its oral history the memory of being forced out of other regions before settling in the Upper Missouri Valley. Tradition recalls that the Mandan first crossed the Mississippi River at the Falls of Saint Anthony, and archaeologists set the date of Mandan arrival in Dakota country around 1100 A.D. Perhaps by 1300 A.D., the Archaic Mandan had become the first village agriculturists of the Upper Missouri. Around 1650, all the Mandan groups that had previously been scattered along the Missouri floodplain were pushed out of South Dakota and southern North Dakota by the Sioux and other emigrants. They then concentrated around the Heart River, a Missouri tributary. This is where the first European visitors to the area found them farming, roughly 250 years after Columbus.

The Arikara and Hidatsa have inhabited this stretch of the Missouri for a shorter period of time, but they too have become "native" to the region by profound adaptation to its environment. The proto-Arikara moved into the Upper Missouri after 1400, having been driven out of the central semiarid plains, perhaps by warfare or by an extended drought.

Hidatsa legend maintains that the tribe emerged into its present existence after climbing up a vine from beneath Devil's Lake in north-eastern North Dakota. Archaeologists speculate that linguistically related groups pushed their way up from northern Illinois into the Red River Valley around 1500 but did not become the unified Hidatsa tribe within North Dakota lands until about 1700. Others suggest that the proto-Hidatsa were a subtribe of the Crow, splitting away from the parent tribe around 1650. Sometime before 1700, they obtained corn and other seed from the Mandans and "relearned" or adapted their agricultural knowledge to fit their new homeland. Smallpox epidemics beginning in the 1780s and, later, threats from the Sioux encouraged these three tribes to cooperate with one another.

I knew that hard times had hit these tribes often, despite their history of sharing resources. Given the severity of disruptions that they have suffered since 1790—smallpox, droughts, land grabs, grasshopper infestations, and inundations—it is amazing that they have survived to reside in "New Town" at all.

When the earlier towns of Van Hook and Sanish were being evacuated as the waters behind the dam rose in the 1950s, the tribes had a contest to decide what they should name their newly combined, relocated community. One poignant suggestion—turned down in favor of the more upbeat name of New Town—was that the names of the two forsaken villages should also be combined, so that the community could be known as "Vanish."

The three tribes have not vanished, despite the inundation of their river-bottom farmlands for the past thirty years. Now I wondered if their seeds and agricultural customs had vanished despite the persistence of the people themselves. I wanted to hear what they had to say about any agrarian traditions that might remain. What was left of the nineteen maize variants that had been described at their villages by various visitors between 1830 and 1920? Did the women still sow any of the kinds of squash that many American gardeners grew in the early decades of this century? And what became of their handful of bean varieties, among them the progenitor of the Great Northern, at one time the most popular soup bean in America?

Good farming depends just as much on the survival of appropriate agricultural practices as on seed selection. Did any families continue to save and select seed stocks, using the sophisticated techniques that their forebears had developed? Did the women still cook foods based on these native plants, and had such ethnic specialties reinforced their sense of cultural identity? Had their ways of farming changed when they moved up to the exposed prairie mesas and plains?

I had brought along some seeds, long ago collected from these tribes, seeds that deserved to grow in this watershed again, among these people. I had small red Hidatsa beans, glossy and lovely in the palm of my hand. And the puffy, pale, oval seeds of Arikara winter squash; an early Hubbard type, the mature plant has blue-green stripes on salmon skin. These seeds had been given to me by heirloom seed saver Glenn Drowns. I also carried seeds of a Mandan yellow pumpkin, last grown by Dan Zwiener, and similar in seed size and shape to the early *Cucurbita pepo* gourds raised in the Mississippi watershed thousands of years ago. And I had the fine-tasting Arikara "yellow" beans, long and kidney-shaped, ranging in color from beige to yellow-orange.

These seeds had been freely donated by Drowns and Zwiener, who are members of the Seed Savers Exchange. They were progeny of seeds collected at Fort Berthold on the Upper Missouri almost a century ago. The varieties I had with me were mentioned in Oscar H. Will & Co. seed catalogs at least as far back as 1913, and that seed house continued to feature them until the late 1950s. Sometime along the way, they had gotten into the hands of an heirloom seed collector intent on seeing them survive even if they were never presented in a commercial catalog again. And so they had been passed on, from season to season, and hand to hand, until they had landed in my luggage, bound once more for their homeland.

I needed to find gardens in order to find gardeners, but in New Town and other reservation settlements, there were few to be seen. Gardens were not common in the other large communities on the reservation, either. On the drive in toward New Town, I had cruised White Shield on the eastern Arikara side of the reservation to ask about a family that had once farmed quite a bit. One of the men of this White Shield family talked with me at their modern tract house, miles away from where their fields had been. His response was polite, perfunctory, and the same that I heard elsewhere over the next two days.

"No, we don't garden anymore," he said in an oddly cheerful tone. "Since we moved from out there in the country, we don't grow any corn anymore. It's been years since we moved away from it all."

I searched for gardens and fields of mixed crops as I passed homesteads that still remained "out in the country," but the few that I did see belonged to non-Indian families. About half of the remaining agricultural lands on the Fort Berthold Reservation are either owned or leased by whites, who now plow large tracts of the short-grass prairie for barley, wheat, oilseed, sunflower, and safflower. The gardens they keep are mostly filled with zucchinis, hybrid sweet corn, and short-season tomatoes. In contrast, members of the three tribes have never become accustomed to tilling the upland soil in their new backyards for similar fields or gardens. They point to marauding gangs of dogs, children, and yard-loving birds that do considerable damage. Women repeatedly told me, "You just can't garden in town."

I had read that two-thirds of the families had successful gardens in 1948, when they were still in the bottomlands. And every year, the same women who tended those gardens with the help of their children canned or dried 23,000 quarts of wild fruit, gathered mostly from the floodplain and the wooded draws below the mesa tops. Wild plums, juneberries, chokecherries, and a type of ground bean proliferated along riverbanks or on moist slopes above side streams.

Was this tradition lost? After roaming a while, I came upon the gardens of the Lone Fight brothers and sisters, where I learned that the tradition was still alive indeed. They clustered around the old country house of their aunt, Mary White Body, on the edge of New Sanish, overlooking the lake. A couple of frolicking boys chased each other through the three small gardens and over to where my car was parked. "My aunt—she's not home. We'll go get my mother." The boys scurried indoors.

When they bolted back out the door, followed by their mother, their cheeks were full, and they were chewing on a sugary brown chunk of homemade sweet.

"Corn balls!" I exclaimed to myself, thinking of traveler Henry the Younger's first taste of them in 1806. He had been presented with "a dish containing several balls, about the size of a hen's egg, made of pears [juneberries], dried meat, and parched corn, beaten together in a mortar.... Boiled for a short time," he reported, "we found them most wholesome."

"Slow down on those corn balls, you boys!" Donna Lone Fight sighed. "Save some for later on!" After introductions, Donna and I wandered over to a garden planted by her twin brother, Donald. There, beets, watermelons, sweet corn, carrots, and honeydew plants were coming to the end of their season. They had produced amply. Donna pointed across the grass to a blue corn crop another brother had planted, and in a different direction to a third plot. I felt some relief— at least there was one native crop maturing in the garden.

"Did your family plant more before?" I asked.

"They did, but it all came to a stop around 1952 or 1953. They were from Old Sanish, and it's all underwater now. Trees, fields, school-house, home. They say you can see a lot of it, standing there beneath the water. So many of them moved to New Town then," and, she explained, they haven't grown any of the old things over there. As another community member said when he saw the kinds of seeds I gave Donna, "there is so much that we forgot to take with us before the flood."

The boys ran past, still taking bites out of their corn balls. Donna made them go get me one.

"That's an old kind of food here. Not many people make it any-more. An Indian woman over in Parshall comes around selling them now and then. Maybe she grows a lot of corn, or knows someone who does. She must use an awful lot of it."

I thanked Donna and the kids, gave them some seeds to try for the following year, and headed over to Parshall, fifteen miles away.

Vera Bracklin sat on a living room chair, exhausted, holding her grand-daughter in her lap. She had just fed ten families who were all mourn-ing loved ones. No doubt Vera was used to such large-scale cooking. Sometimes in one batch she would cook up thirty quarts of flour corn, juneberries or blueberries, kidney tallow, and sugar into 120 to 140 corn balls.

"What we call it...in Hidatsa is *mah-pi*. For corn balls, you need soft corn, flour corn, to make it. Mine is corn from my mother-in-law. I can't raise it here, but there's a white lady who gives me room to plant out at her place." Vera Bracklin processed as much corn as she could get her hands on; the door-to-door sales of corn balls helped to keep her family afloat.

It was the kind of work women in her family had done for a long time. She remembered the effort her grandmother made to thresh cleanly all their Great Northern beans: "My grandmother used to raise a lot of beans. On a windy day, she'd put a tarp down. She'd take a panful of uncleaned beans, and let the wind blow the leaves away."

Vera glanced down and looked tired again. "But then we lost everything," she recalled. "It seems like they lost the Indian way of living when the dam forced their relocation."

Indian elder Austin Engel had expressed similar sentiments immediately after the reservoir had flooded out the villages. The tribes had been paid a sum of five million dollars to relocate nine-tenths of their people, rebuild houses and roads, and develop new lands. Yet village communities became dispersed in a way that made Engel feel that their "traditional source of stability is gone."

"Farming became more difficult," Engel explained. "We were far from the neighbors with whom we used to exchange work. The big farmer was taking over the West, and we didn't know how to compete, except to lease our land to him."

I recalled that earlier, others too had feared that the native ways might end, particularly after the smallpox epidemic of 1837. There had been epidemics prior to 1804, when Lewis and Clark wintered among these people, but the tribes had recovered in the years that followed. By the 1830s—when such notables as German prince Alexander Philip Maximilian, Carl Bodmer, and George Catlin stayed with these tribes and recorded their customs—the tribespeople had become prosperous farmers, hunters, gatherers, and traders.

Catlin described the extent and density of the crops: "We trudged back to the little village of earth-covered lodges, which were hemmed in, and almost obscured to the eye, by the fields of corn and luxuriant growth of wild sunflowers, and other vegetable productions of the soil." Prince Maximilian noted that the tribes "cultivate...without ever manuring the ground, but their fields are on the low banks of the river...where the soil is particularly fruitful.... They have extremely fine maize of different species." He was so impressed by their maize, beans, gourds, sunflowers, and tobacco that he took seeds of these crops back to botanical gardens in Europe, where they flowered and presumably set seed. The transatlantic introduction of New World crops such as these did much to enrich Europe's royal gardens and peasant fields.

The Mandan tribal population had grown to 1,600 by 1837. Then smallpox hit them like a tidal wave. A total of 15,000 people, native and immigrant, were killed by the disease on the Upper Missouri that year. Only 150 Mandans survived. The Hidatsas were reduced to 500.

When John James Audubon came through their villages in 1843, the survivors' lives were in ruins. They were so distraught and weakened that their once orderly villages had fallen into disrepair, and the stench of garbage and rotting carcasses was everywhere. Low mounds of dirt, under which smallpox victims were buried, dominated the surroundings instead of the fields of corn that Catlin had seen. After five or six years, these mounds were still barren of all vegetation. Audubon's traveling companion Edward Harris wrote that "the mortality was too great for them to give the usual burial rites of their people by elevating the bodies on a scaffold as described by Catlin." Overall, Audubon could hardly believe that these were the same places that Catlin had portrayed as active ceremonial centers, with lovely earthen lodges laid out in regular rows. He wrote that "the sights daily seen will not bear recording; they have dispelled all the romance of Indian life I ever had."

The remnants of the two Sioux-speaking tribes, the Mandan and Hidatsa, abandoned their disease-torn villages to move together to a new location in 1845. There, they began to build another life at Like-a-Fishhook, a bend in the Missouri where Fort Berthold was soon established. The Arikara families joined them in 1862, and considerable intertribal marriage began, perhaps out of necessity because of their decimated populations. Nevertheless, the Arikara tongue, a Caddoan—not a Sioux—language, has persisted to this day amid the numerically dominant Mandan and Hidatsa.

The agricultural practices of these people were not intensively studied until a half century later, yet their ancient folk sciences of bottomland cultivation and seed selection had remained intact. Horticulturist-anthropologist George Will Sr. wrote in 1930 that "through the terrible catastrophes of the 1830s…[and] continual harassing by the Sioux, the three tribes, the Mandan, Arikara, and Hidatsa, preserved their agricultural crops and varieties and carried them down even to the present."

Will's farming ethnographies were complemented by those of ethnobotanist Melvin Gilmore and oral historian Gilbert Wilson. Among the three of them, they documented many aspects of the remarkable folk science that still guided the agriculture of the three tribes after the turn of the century. In some ways, Wilson's record of the farming knowledge shared by Buffalobird-Woman is the greatest testament to the intelligence of a single native farmer that we have from this continent.

Buffalobird-Woman, also known as Maxidiwiac, told Gilbert Wilson how Hidatsa families began to develop new fields on bottomland soils, how they fallowed old ones, and why they chose not to plow up the sod on the short-grass prairie ground in the hills to farm as the government wanted them to do: "The prairie fields get dry easily and the soil is harder and more difficult to work. Then I think our old way of raising corn is better than the new way taught to us by white men." To prove her point, the seventy-three-year-old woman referred to the quality of maize that she had raised in this manner. "Last year, 1911, our agent held an agricultural fair on this reservation. The corn which I sent to the fair took first prize…. I cultivated the corn exactly as in old times, with a hoe."

Maxidiwiac was aware that "corn could travel" and that strains planted within "traveling distance" of one another could be contaminated. To keep each of them pure, she planted different maize varieties some distance apart from each other, perhaps farther apart than corn pollen would normally travel. This was important, "for varieties had not all the same uses with us." Some were used for grinding; others, as green corn; still others, for stews. Indiscriminate varietal intermixing would have been costly. At the same time, "we Hidatsas knew that slightly different varieties could be produced by planting seeds that varied somewhat from the main stock." Her people selected these variants not only for color but for other qualities as well.

In view of their sophisticated practices of seed selection and isola-
tion, is it any wonder that George Will gathered from the three tribes
six kinds of flint corns, nine to ten kinds of flour corns, and a sweet
corn? These maize variants differed in color, taste, texture, ear size,
number of days to maturing, and bushiness of the foliage. Most of
these strains were exceptionally hardy, for they could survive the
harshness of Dakota weather. They were also, for the most part, short,
heavily suckering plants, with ears developing at or near ground level,
within a protective cover of foliage and heavy husks that shielded
developing ears from frosts and hailstorms. The seeds could "sprout
in spring weather that would rot most varieties of corn," Will claimed,
and could produce harvestable ears after "about sixty days in a favorable year...rarely more than seventy days."

Such adaptations paid off not only for the three tribes but for thousands of white settlers on the Northern Plains who later adopted these
native corns and beans. Before Will and others passed the three tribes'
native strains on to the Montana Agricultural Experiment Station for
evaluation, the European-American farmers in that state hardly grew
any corn—fewer than 10,000 acres in 1909. The dent corns accessible through catalogs from the East and Midwest simply did not have
sufficient tolerance for the growing conditions found in the semiarid
West.

The three tribes' corns gained regional acceptance following widely
publicized experiments by Atkinson and M. L. Wilson at the Montana station, which demonstrated the superiority of the northern
flints. Will devoted a decade to promoting them through his family's
mail-order seed business and through his own writings. By 1924,
Montana's corn acreage had increased to 420,000 acres. In fifteen years'
time, the three tribes' flint corns had allowed nearly a fifty-fold
increase in Montana maize production.

These native corn varieties have made a tremendous contribution to
Northern Plains agriculture. But I had yet to see even a single mature
plant of native maize on the Fort Berthold Reservation. And while
Vera Bracklin had some corn planted in the garden of a non-Indian
friend, she deferred to an older, more knowledgeable woman on the

other side of the reservoir. "You should go see Cora Baker near Man-daree," she suggested. The Bakers, she explained, not only grew a variety of crops but kept other traditions alive as well.

So, on a rainy Sunday morning, I drove out from Mandaree through the rolling hills that spilled into Bear Den Creek. Fields are fewer on this far western side of the reservation, which gradually climbs into the badlands. The area had once been dismissed as "good country for rattlesnakes and horned toads," but that did not keep some families from the old Lucky Mound village from finding solace there after relo-cation. Bear Den Creek is perhaps more sinuous and wooded than the now-flooded Lucky Mound Creek, yet it may have been enough like it to have attracted the exiles from the lake floor.

As I came into the Baker homestead from the dirt road that ends at their driveway, I could see their garden. I walked to their door, hearing cornstalks rustling in the wind. Cora, a soft-spoken, atten-tive woman with neatly pulled-back gray hair, welcomed me in.

"Some people I've met around here the last few days thought that you would be one who might like to have some of these old seeds," I offered. "They say that you still grow others like these."

"Old seeds?" Cora asked, showing a mild interest. "Could I see what you mean?"

I pulled out my now-crumpled envelopes from the Seed Savers Exchange and poured Hidatsa red beans into Cora's hand. She just looked at them, saying nothing, as if seeing an old friend for the first time in years. She sat down, then looked at the other kinds of seed, identifying them and commenting on how they were used.

"May I keep them? May I grow these? Here, put some in envelopes for me. I'll go get you some of our family's Indian corn to try."

Cora came back with two ears of flour corn from her garden and a gallon jar full of seeds from her sister's field. She filled a small bag with seeds from the jar and gave them, along with the two ears, to me.

"Keep them separate," she warned me, "because corn can travel." She said that she was trying to sort the blue out of some of her white corn that had become mixed. By recurrent selection and roguing, she was working toward her goal, much as Buffalobird-Woman would have done seventy-five years ago, and much as George Catlin's companions would have done 150 years ago, during the final harvest prior to the smallpox epidemic.

The continuity was there: Cora's daughter Mary joined us to express her desire not to let these seeds escape again. "We had so much going for us down at Lucky Mound, it's hard to believe that we could have lost everything."

But not everything has been lost, for Cora's family's seeds and the skills her family passed on to her remain. Cora told me how her family separated out the seed corn from the corn they would eat and braided the husks of the seed ears together, in an arc an arm's length in size.

While Mary and Cora spoke about their Hidatsa agricultural customs, I could also hear the falling leaves rustling against the windows and roof, reminding me of George Will's words about the harvest season of 1947: "The season of the year when the Indians of our Northern Plains used to harvest their main crop is here. The soft, hazy autumn days with hot noons and cool nights heralded the full ripening of the crops in the Indian fields.... All was bustle and confusion as the women and girls hastened to breakfast early from the always simmering pot of boiled corn, beans and meat which...hung over the fire.... As the women sat about the pile of corn for husking, the wise old grandmother kept her eyes open for plump, large and straight-rowed ears of pure color. These she took and put aside...for braiding."

Sitting in Cora Baker's kitchen, I knew it was the time for braiding seed stocks together again.

Tequila Hangovers and
the Mescal Monoculture Blues

*During the several thousand years that man and agave lived
together, agave has been a renewable resource for food, drink, and
artifact.... As civilization and religion increased, the nurturing
agave became a symbol, until with its stimulating juice man made
it into a god. The religion and god have gone, but agave still
stands as a donor species of the first water.*
HOWARD SCOTT GENTRY, "The Man-Agave Symbiosis"

I heard an aplomado falcon scream once above me. But mostly I heard
the sound of semitrailer trucks groaning through their gears. Loaded
with century plants, they were downshifting as they ran the switchbacks into the barranca below. Near a train stop called Cuervo in the
Mexican state of Jalisco, I was ambling along a volcanic ridge; the
ridge was covered with row after row of the century plants known as
tequila azul. Their swordlike leaves had been cropped back, but they
retained enough spiny teeth to slow the pace of my journey. The
armored plants were both numerous and massive enough to cast a
blue-green hue across the land where I was hiking.

I trampled wild marigolds, barnyard grass, and amaranths coming
up between the tightly cropped rosettes of *tequila azul* but could
hardly penetrate the rows of the century plants themselves—and these
were not just any century plants but the blue-blooded king of all

mescals, the highly bred species called *Agave tequilana*. While the pruned tequilas sat only hiphigh, the uncropped ones at the lip of each terrace swung their swords up to my shoulders.

I looked up from the rows immediately before me and realized just how blue this world was. The next ridge over was also tinted with *tequila azul,* as was the ridge beyond that. Far beyond was a minor outlying cordillera of the Sierra Madre Occidental. It too was blue with evergreen oaks and madrone seen at a distance. It was as if the local *mescaleros* had intentionally selected the *tequila azul* out of the grayer or greener patches of agaves so that their plantations would match the color of the mountains on the farthest horizon. So they cut back the forest, replacing its many-hued cover with a powdery blue, opting for a color-coordinated world of their own making.

I turned around. Below me, a solitary *mescalero* was using a machete to thin the weeds overwhelming his agave patch. On the ridge above me, a dozen campesinos contracted by Tequila Sauza were armed with *coas de jima*, oval-shaped hoes with long handles. Each of these men would attack between 90 and 120 ripened agaves today, cutting back most of the leaves that had been produced over the past decade. They would manicure the thorny masses into blue-and-white pineapples, each *piña* weighing fifty to a hundred pounds. The men would then transform themselves into mules—their grim nickname for themselves—hauling *piñas* over to the semitrailer destined for the town of Tequila, where tons of agaves would be converted into gallons of alcohol. I was surrounded by blue-tinged ridges managed exclusively for the purposes of inebriating my fellow Americans.

I suppose I mean "my fellow Americans" in a way different than that with which LBJ began each of his speeches. I suppose I mean "all of my potential drinking buddies in the Americas at large." While a third of all tequila produced is shot down the throats of Mexicans, nine out of ten of the remaining swallows are destined for the bellies of gringos—U.S. and Canadian citizens in North America. Tequila has been a global commodity since 1970, when its sales spread to more than forty countries. It has become more than that in North America, the destination of much of the forty-seven million liters exported from Mexico; it borders on serving as some strange liquid currency between the psyches of the Mexicano and the gringo. As I was soon to learn, it has grown into what every American and Mexican business partnership dreams that its products will become. Certainly it is the dream of NAFTA, poured into a salt-rimmed glass and chased with a lime.

A pickup truck rolled up to the Cuervo station, with Ana Guadalupe Valenzuela Zapata barely visible above the wheel. What she lacks in height, Ana makes up for in other ways. She is a dark-haired, rosy-cheeked agronomist with unforgettable green eyes. We became fast friends when, on a whim, I volunteered to be her translator at the first U.S.-Mexico exchange of agave researchers hosted by our mutual mentor, Dr. Howard Gentry, about a dozen years ago. Since then, we have periodically rendezvoused to talk about the ups and downs of our personal and professional lives, always using the rise and fall of agave cultivation as the metaphor for what is happening in our respective worlds.

This time, as she drove me back from Cuervo station to the Sauza distilleries on the edge of Tequila, I asked Ana about the cross-cultural nuances embedded in the tequila trade. She laughed at my question and tried to shrug it off, but when she finally answered, her remarks sparkled with insight. "Remember that Don Cenóbio Sauza—the one who consolidated the cottage industries of tequila making into a commercial agro-industry—was married to a North American woman," she said. "It was their collaboration that brought this provincial product into the United States in the 1870s. Now look at it: there are only about thirty companies legitimately distilling tequila in Mexico, but somehow their products are variously packaged into more than 400 brands of tequila sold in the United States. Figure that out!"

When I first came to Tequila in 1977, the Sauza company was still using steam-heated rubble-brick ovens to roast the pineapple-like heads of agaves. Now, as Ana pointed out to me, Sauza exclusively uses autoclaves enclosed in thirty-foot tall stainless steel vats. The other companies are converting to autoclaves as well, which are perhaps a more efficient way of cooking agaves to extract their sugars. But this technique requires considerable capital investment. Such capital flowed into Tequila only after the meteoric rise of the margarita cocktail, which has fueled the doubling of U.S. consumption of tequila since 1970.

"The tequila extracted from autoclaves...Ana, does it have the same taste as that coming from steam ovens?" I asked as I gawked at the giant vats of fermented mescal brew towering above me.

"It's hard to say, but we feel there's some loss of the smoky flavor. Maybe it's a taste that comes when a few of the *piñas* have been somewhat scorched in the steam-roasting. I've heard that autoclaved sugars never have the slightly bitter aftertaste found in the liquor expressed from roasted agaves fermented the old way....Without a doubt, you can detect differences in taste between the traditionally processed mescal and the newer tequilas."

Until the late nineteenth century, the making of tequila was much like the making of other mescals. In fact, the distilled beverage made in Tequila's rustic backyard stills was not even called *tequila* until 1875. Before that, it was simply one of many drinks known as *vino-mescal*. But Tequila's entrepreneurs helped this home-brewed hooch achieve the status of a specialty mescal, just as unblended scotch is no longer considered some mere run-of-the-mill whiskey—and the rest, they say as they tilt their glasses, is *pura historia*. The *vino-mescal* of Tequila, Jalisco, became known world over as *tequila* proper, the hottest of all firewaters.

It was not until a century after tequila achieved this name recognition that Don Cenóbio Sauza and his competitor Don Jesús Flores began to modernize the distillation process, using technologies imported from the United States and Europe. Around that time, they also abandoned the underground conical pits that had been used since pre-Columbian times to roast mescal for food and for mildly fermented beverages. Those old conical pits were heated with many loads of oak gathered from neighboring woodlands. But once the extra-local demand for tequila began to grow, the distilleries sought out huge quantities of firewood, impoverishing the forest cover surrounding the pueblos of northern Jalisco.

The nineteenth-century deforestation of Tequila's valleys and ridges made the expansion of agave cultivation that much easier. The Sauza, Cuervo, and Orendain families encouraged thousands of *campesinos* to plant the blue agave instead of other mescals for food and fiber; many of these same farmers abandoned their *milpas* of maize and beans to work full time for the tequila industry.

It was then that an unprecedented tragedy struck their farmsteads. Social historian Rogelio Luna Zamora has chronicled how an epidemic devastated field after field. It was a plague that the *mescaleros* called the "gangrene of the *tequila azul*." This was the first time that a plague of such proportions had appeared among agaves anywhere in Mexico. The culprit blamed for bringing a booming industry to its knees? The worm at the bottom of the bottle. It was a larva that burrowed into the heart of the plant, moving along (destroying agave tissues) until it had ravished its host.

This was just the first of many plagues to hit Jalisco, fed by the way in which the crop had expanded throughout the northern part of the region in less than a century. The larvae proliferated most rapidly where agave monoculture was most intense.

Perhaps the Mexican mescal plague was not as severe as the Irish potato famine, but it was an early warning against too rapid an expansion of a monocultural crop. This warning signal, says Ana, went unheeded: "José Antonio Gómez Cuervo, governor of Jalisco at the time, is said to have offered a prize of 500 pesos of gold to the person who could discover an effective remedy for curing the agaves and liberating them from the plague. Yet the plague was stimulated by the very expansion and dominance of the blue agave cropping that his own family had promoted. At last, the plague subsided a bit as *campesinos* learned to trim back infected leaves and destroy the larvae in them."

Ana sighed, as if dizzy with the larval feeding frenzy that had gone on in her imagination. "I'm afraid the agricultural industry somehow forgot the message of that plague. Sadly, it is happening all over again, but this time, the *mescaleros* say that the agave plants have AIDS, not merely gangrene."

As far as scientists like Ana can tell, the blue agave plantations have been suffering from an outbreak of multiple maladies since 1988. At least two bacteria and one fungus are running rampant in the agave plantations, causing stems to rot and leaves to dry up and wither. The plantation workers collectively call these problems *el anillo rojo*—the red ring disease—because they turn the leaves from slate blue to yellow with rust-toned bands encircling them. As the plants begin to wither and die, a puslike goo oozes from the leaf tips. But the plantings are also infested with weeds that harbor insects—the very insects that carry diseases from one agave to the next. The weeds also compete with the agaves for sunlight and water, further adding to their stress and, ultimately, to their susceptibility.

Before Ana and I had left the fields near Cuervo station, we had rolled over one after another of the recently cut *piñas*; they were rotten to the core. Many of the untrimmed plants still standing showed the telltale signs of larvae boring through their leaves. Most of the *piñas* cut from the fields through which I'd hiked would soon be rejected at the distillery, for they had too little uninfected tissue to cook and ferment. The fields casting their delicate blue over the volcanic landscape of northern Jalisco were degenerating into a muddy brown, spoiling from the inside out.

Ana's hunch is that this multiple-malady plague has been driven by rapid overexpansion in the planting of just one vulnerable variety, the *tequila azul*. In less than a decade, the land covered by this single, vegetatively propagated clone of tequila expanded from 40,000 acres to nearly 120,000 acres. About the time these plantings began to reach maturity, prices dropped precipitously, for overproduction had led to a buyer's market. Plantation owners could no longer afford to invest more money in tending their plantings. Their fields became infested with weeds or even abandoned altogether.

The bacterial diseases first caught hold around 1988 in the higher elevations. They did not appear in significant numbers in the lower terraces and valleys until 1994. Now, the *"SIDA del Agave tequilero"*—the AIDS epidemic of the blue-blooded century plants—is reported at every elevation, in well-managed fields as well as in abandoned ones.

The way *tequila azul* plantations have been managed undoubtedly served as the environmental trigger to this plague, but there is also a genetic vulnerability in this narrowly selected variety of agaves. Today, vegetatively propagated clones of *tequila azul* make up more than 99 percent of the 150 million agaves growing in Jalisco. If there ever was an easy target for any infestation, tequila monoculture is it.

As late as 1977, varieties of four species of century plant were regularly mixed and roasted together to make the mescal that the rest of the world called tequila. The *tequila azul* variety was already dominant but not ubiquitous. When an elderly *mescalero* named Juan Gonzalez Enciso took me through the fields and holding areas of mescal harvests destined for the Cuervo distilleries, he pointed out many representative plants of the other varieties, ones that are rarely found in commercial operations today.

Old Juan waxed eloquent about these other heirloom mescal varieties: *sigüín*, the only race still with an indigenous name, known for its small, roundish form and early ripening; *chato*, or *saguayo*, a large squat mescal with a thick flower stalk and fibrous leaves; *bermejo*, a tall mescal with many leaves; *moraleño*, a shiny-leafed plant with showy qualities; and *criollo*, a wild-looking plant similar to those growing in the barrancas. Ana has learned of other varieties as well, some of which have resistance to the insects and diseases attacking the *tequila azul*, among them *mano largo*, "the large hand"; *zopilote*, "the vulture"; *pata de mula*, "mule foot"; *azul listado*, "blue listed"; and *mescal chino*, "Chinese mescal."

Today, outside the gardens that Ana herself has planted for conservation purposes, it is difficult to find a full row of any one of these other varieties. Official norms of the Mexican government regulating the tequila industry have put pressures on growers to plant *tequila azul* and nothing else, even though the presence of these other varieties slowed the spread of diseases in the past. After each tightening of government regulations—first in 1972, then in 1978, and finally in 1993—the factory purchasers of ripened agaves became more and more reluctant to let the other varieties slip into the heap. The ten or so other heirloom varieties native to the Tequila vicinity no longer account for even one in a thousand plants there; when they are kept at all, they are usually grown for hedge, fiber, or ornament.

Ana, who is accustomed to swimming upstream against the current—first as a female agronomist in male-dominated terrain, then as a conservationist in a domain framed by short-term profits—is fighting to change the reliance on only one genetic strain of agave. Her dream is of another Jalisco, one not so blue. It would hold in place a more diverse range of agaves than she sees around her now.

And so Ana has gone back to school, hoping to gain a few skills that will help change minds, not merely farming practices. She is out to get a second master's degree, this one in business administration, to help her with a most peculiar kind of business. Her thesis is devoted to the planning of a museum and botanical garden aimed at conserving agave diversity and preserving traditional knowledge about mescal cultivation and use. She envisions a botanical garden full of all the folk varieties of agaves remaining in Jaliscan plantations, hedgerows, and house yards, as well as all the wild species of the Sierra Madre. She is collaborating with her sister, a young architect, on blueprints for a museum that will chronicle the cultural significance of agave diversity from pre-Hispanic times to the present, replete with archives of historic documents, exhibits, and demonstrations of traditional processing techniques. And the two sisters imagine a "museum without walls" with meeting rooms and an auditorium where *mescaleros* can come and tell their own stories.

In the meantime, she has not forsaken her science. All last summer, she was busy measuring and recording the diagnostic characters of the remaining folk varieties from plantlets she propagated more than a decade ago. These dozen surviving folk varieties of cultivated agaves are not the only family members in danger. Another forty-eight wild species in the agave family are imperiled in Mexico; several more are threatened in the United States and Guatemala. In most of these cases, the destinies of the century plants are linked to those of indigenous cultures whose foraging and horticultural practices have nurtured them for centuries. Few agave species grow in habitats completely untouched by humankind; most have been the subject of cultural as well as natural selection. They have, over the centuries, adapted to the burning, tending, and terracing of the indigenous drinkers, weavers, and landscapers who have shaped the Mesoamerican terrain.

Will Ana's efforts make a difference in the tequila industry? It is more likely that some of the biggest tequila makers will instead invest in planting thousands of clones, tissue-cultured in laboratories where they have been genetically engineered for resistance to the prevailing pest or diseases of the moment. The cloning of tequila plants, unfortunately, will never raise the ethical eyebrows that the cloning of sheep has raised. On the other hand, such cloning will never give the tequila industry as much security as would heterogeneous fields where several species of agaves grow in close proximity to one another. Ana's vision of agave genetic diversity depends on buyers at the distilleries caring whether or not the farmers with whom they work are buffered from wildly varying yields and prices.

Not long before this visit with Ana in Tequila, I had had the horrific experience of being stranded in Los Angeles traffic for hours against my will. At the time, I was so weary that I couldn't figure out how to escape this metropolis in which I knew no place to rest.

It was much like a story from Kafka: as my car inched forward, I doubted that I would ever get free of all the asphalt, concrete-reinforced bridges, barricades, overhead lights, and glowing metal signs. I saw no vegetation, no animals, no handmade objects. There were few signs that "life" actually existed, other than the thousands of cars moving through the twilight. I could see humans only through their windshields darkly.

We all seemed to be going down the same chute as rapidly as we could, but I could not for the life of me fathom where we were going. All the exit names seemed vaguely familiar; they were the names of towns or suburbs found all across America: Glendale, Ontario, Riverside, Inglewood, Lakewood, Garden Grove, and South Gate. I could have been anywhere in the United States. The sameness made me sick to my stomach, sick and enraged in my head, sick and sad at heart.

That same sense of sickness came over me as I looked at all those rotting heads of *tequila azul*, pineapples spoiled by their own monotony. Yet I did not think of the plants themselves as sickening; I felt that they were a symptom of some larger disease of contemporary societies, especially those that promote or even accept just *sameness*.

Fortunately, that nightmare had a counterpoint in my imagination—a dream that Howard Scott Gentry had passed on to Ana and me. Dr. Gentry, who spent forty years of his life collecting and studying agaves, acted as mentor to Ana and me at a time when we felt like nothing but strays. We both needed to come under some elder's wing. Gentry not only encouraged us in our field studies but also offered us inspiration through the stories he would tell. Many of those stories emerged over shots of mescal during our late-afternoon get-togethers in his garden.

For all the adaptability he had developed while traveling as a plant explorer, Dr. Gentry never learned to sleep in the city. A dream or nightmare would often wake him in the middle of the night, and he would remain awake, pondering its significance for hours. Fortunately for us, he wrote one of those dreams down. In it, he had been told by his U.S. government employer that his agricultural duty station had been transferred. Instead of basing his work as a plant explorer out of USDA headquarters, he was to move to Mexico in order to establish a genetic conservatory for all the agaves in the world. It would be located at Tepoztlán, an awesome montane landscape south of Mexico City. There he was charged with designing a means to keep all the various forms of mescal alive in one place.

When he arrived in Tepoztlán, he could not believe his eyes. The Mexicans had fashioned a huge elevator to move agave plants up and down the cliff face above the village. This elevator moved not only vertically but horizontally as well. It allowed Gentry and his colleagues the mobility to place each agave species in the micro environment to which it was best suited. By matching up agave species from all over Mexico with niches on the cliff face or within the barranca below it, Gentry's team was able to tend the full gamut of century plant diversity from tropical jungles to coniferous forests, all in one locality.

Gentry never saw his vision bear fruit. "It was," he would say, taking one last swig of bootleg mescal, "just a dream."

But I'm sure that he wanted it to happen. Ana's plans would have made him deeply happy. Who knows whether the tequila industry will ever share such a dream, but I am sure there will be others who will help Ana keep it alive.

Before we left Tequila, Ana drove me around the town in search of a statue I had once seen. This statue—of Mayaguel, the goddess of agaves—was an icon that had enchanted Dr. Gentry, Ana, and me one afternoon as we leafed through a book of Aztec codices. The last time I had seen the statue, someone had stolen the copper-blue agave out of Mayaguel's hand; she had looked forlorn, nearly desperate, left without her very reason for being. A goddess with no flame to keep. Now, with another plant placed within her grasp, Mayaguel seemed once again full of purpose. I hope that when I visit her again one day, I will find her in the midst of a place no longer painted with monotonous blue but resplendent with a full palette of colors.

FIVE

Conserving Relationships

Ancient stories can guide us in our efforts to
preserve natural and cultural heritage during
an era in which much is at stake.

Hornworm's Home Ground

Conserving Interactions

*The character of the individual fruit tree simply cannot be
understood without reference to others of its species,
to the insects that fertilize it and to the animals
that consume its fruit and disperse its seeds.*
DAVID ABRAM, *The Spell of the Sensuous*

Have you ever imagined a hornworm procession: tens of thousands of
pinstriped, multicolored larvae gathering together for a desert prom-
enade? I had been dreaming of them for weeks but had hardly seen a
"worm" all summer. The spring drought had been so prolonged that
not a single green-and-yellow larva had flashed before my eyes, nor
had I spotted any of their metamorphosed white-lined sphinx moths.
I longed to see even one moth hover before a blossom of the rare plants
I had been monitoring since early May. Such night-flying hawkmoths
are needed to pollinate certain desert flowers if these floras are to form
plump, seed-rich fruit. The absence of hawkmoths meant that nearly
all the flowers had withered and aborted, leaving little hope for the
ripened fruit this year.

Week after week, my Desert Alert work crews had meandered up
and down desert slopes, searching for moths, their eggs, or their larvae, but we had had no success in finding them through late July. It
looked as though some of the rarest plants in Arizona would not be

pollinated sufficiently to produce any progeny at all this season. There were a few more flower buds that could still develop into blooms, but I doubted that a hawkmoth would arrive in time even if they were to blossom.

Night after night, I had been entirely preoccupied by the fate of these flowers. I was sorely in need of a time-out to clear my mind or at least to muddle over something different. I decided to drive out to see some old O'odham Indian friends living in the heart of the desert fifty miles west of my home.

I was hardly five miles from my front door when I noticed something wriggling across the road. I dismissed it at first. No hornworm in its right mind would venture onto burning black asphalt on a midsummer's desert day. The pavement would be wavering around 160 degrees, which was hot enough to fry any low-riding pilgrim.

Then I caught sight of a second wriggler. It looked like nothing more than a greenish noodle when seen at sixty miles an hour, but I tried to steer away from hitting it nonetheless; I would feel awful if my tires flattened one of the few hornworms seen all summer.

Fortunately, I spotted another. And another. I must have splattered the green guts of the fourth sitting on the pavement in the path of my front right tire, despite another valiant attempt to swerve in time to miss it. I began to count every one that I passed on my way to Hot Fields Village. By the time I slowed to a stop in front of the Cruz family adobe, I had tallied 463 hornworms on the march, enough to share with friends

"I brought you something for dinner," I hollered to Margie Cruz, who groaned when she opened the cardboard box I had filled with hornworms.

"Ohhhh!" she grimaced in mock horror, peering down into the box, shaking her head. "I thought we told you already that we don't eat no worms anymooooore. The kids especially—they won't eat them."

"But can't you fix them up so the kids wouldn't know what we're having?" I pleaded. Then, I whispered, "Just hide them under some spaghetti sauce and no one will notice until they crawl on top of a meatball...."

"You got to squeeze out their entrails before you cook them up," her husband Remedio interjected. "We don't treat them like noodles, we roast them in lard in a frying pan so that they taste like popcorn. Or sometimes we put them on a stick over a campfire, then string the cooked ones up like a necklace. Old ladies used to wear strings of them around their necks and snack on them like candy."

Marge and Remedio were still amusing themselves by peering into the box and groaning when their grandchildren ran into the kitchen. They peeked over Marge's shoulder and saw that my take-out food was alive and squirming. They all shrieked in unison and tore back out of the kitchen toward the TV room. There, they turned up the volume of some monster film, as if to blast away any memory of the creepy-crawlies close to home.

"*Makkum,*" Remedio repeated over and over, like a murmur. "*Makkum.*" This is the O'odham name for this kind of larvae, a widespread sphingid species called *Hyles lineata* by scientists.

"Where do they come from, Mr. Cruz? I've been waiting for them all summer long, but I hadn't seen any until today."

Remedio Cruz glanced up at me, then back down at the floor. "I don't know for suu-ure," he sighed, as he always did just before making an astute observation, "but I think they came out with that rain about two weeks ago."

I realized that he was probably right—the larvae looked as though they were in the third or fourth larval stage, maybe as much as the fifth. They could have hatched from eggs soon after the one modest rain we had received, for it had probably been wet enough to send them on their way toward metamorphosis into moth-hood.

"But all of a sudden they're crawling around out there in the desert," I said. Remedio blinked his eyes; I wasn't sure if his hearing had begun to fail him or if he was still trying to figure out what I was talking about. I scratched my head, then tried tentatively to phrase my observation in his native tongue: "*Hegam mamakkum o oimed gnhu g tohono jewed-c-ed.*"

Remedio smiled knowingly. He had seen the hornworm emigrations many times over his seventy-some years of living in the desert. He sometimes forgot that I had only been a desert dweller for two decades and that what was commonplace to him was often some special event to me.

"They come from the *makkum ha-jewed*," Remedio explained to me, referring to the name of a summer wildflower that he had once shown me in his fields. It was a sticky-leafed, low-growing herb that I had identified as *Boerhaavia coccinea*, one of several related plants collectively called "spiderlings" in English. But *makkum ha-jewed* referred to only two of the stickier species of local spiderlings. This O'odham name means "the hornworm's home ground," although in another Piman dialect the same plant is called "the hornworm's mother."

These native names cryptically encode the notion of a plant that moths require for their early life stages. Lepidopterists have encoded the same notion in their technical jargon, using the term "larval host plant." Both *makkum ha-jewed* and *larval host plant* speak to a pattern of relationships between a particular moth species and the flora that nurtures it.

"Once those worms eat all the leaves on the *makkum ha-jewed*, they all start to wander around just like you said. They must be looking for something special, because sometimes they don't stop to eat other plants. They all come marching out of my backyard one morning, going over there toward the fields." He nodded toward the old fields for which the village was named. "Then they crawl onto my devil's claw plants or onto the chiles and tomatoes I've been hand-watering, and they eat them all up. Then they wander back through the yard before the sun goes down. I never have figured out where they go to sleep. Sometimes if it rains real hard at night, though, it will knock them out. A lot of them will drown."

"I wish I could figure out when they will be turning into *hohoki-mal*," I said, referring to the moths that had yet to be found visiting the now-withered flowers in my field plots. I wondered whether there would be time for any moths to metamorphose before the last floral buds broke open that summer.

"I think that maybe there's a chance you could be seeing some of those night butterflies soon," predicted Remedio, failing to remember the English word *moth*. I couldn't be sure that he knew which moths the green-and-yellow larvae turned into. He did, however, know when the moths would begin a sequence of events with which he was intimately familiar: "About this time after a good summer rain, those little night butterflies start to swarm around our porch lights."

I had gone out to Hot Fields to get my mind off moths and plants, but they had shown up anyway. Within a week, the larval densities in the desert began to soar just as Remedio had suggested they might. They continued to do so for another month. I watched the march of larvae day after day for a fortnight.

Finally, on the last flowering night of the season for the rarest of plants I was tracking, white-lined sphinx moths arrived to hover before the blossoms, reaching their tongues into the deep, sweet nectar pools and getting their faces and wings plastered with pollen. The next morning, the delicate scales of moth wings had been left like calling cards in a few of the blossoms, and pollen had been sprinkled onto their receptive stigmas. Where some of these blossoms had been, bulbous red fruit would emerge, and they would be chock full of shiny black seeds.

If the moths had not arrived in time, the rare plants would not have reproduced at all, even though they were "protected" within a couple of national parks and wildlife refuges near my home. All the legal protection in the world would not ensure their survival if the moths failed to arrive to bless them and transfer their pollen from one blossom to the next. When and where this might happen, I realized, was something that grade school–educated Remedio Cruz could predict far better than I. Despite my Ph.D. studies in desert ecology, I was a novice in observing the life histories of local moths—species that Remedio and Marge had lived among all of their lives.

I had been learning native plant and animal names from Remedio for nearly twenty years when I finally realized that he also had considerable knowledge of the ecological interactions among particular plants and animals. I had hardly ever stopped to ask him about nature's relationships, for I presumed they were unnamed and therefore unknown. I was not the first conservation biologist to have downplayed the importance of such knowledge in being a good steward of the natural world. Ecologist John Thompson has recently commented, "The diversity of life has resulted from the diversification of both species and the interactions among them.... Nevertheless, the focus of studies on the conservation of biodiversity has often been primarily on species rather than interactions."

Many desert ecologists and conservation biologists remain unaware of the rich oral commentaries on ancient relationships between plants and their coevolved animal dispersers, foragers, and pollinators. A few years ago, a graduate student studying the history of ecology mentioned to me that he had read of a curious "discovery" made by biologists at the University of Texas three decades before. Vern and Karen Grant described how hawkmoths visiting sacred datura blossoms often exhibited "intoxicated behavior" for a while after having drunk nectar from this hallucinogenic plant. Floral chemists have described a complex chemical brew in sacred datura nectar, including aromatics, amino acids, fatty acids, and terpenoids. But no one had verified that the psychotropic alkaloids atropine and scopolamine found in datura seeds and leaves were also present in the nectar, especially in quantities sufficient to induce intoxication. Nevertheless, the Grants hypothesized, something was making the nocturnal *Manduca* moths get dizzy and trip the night fantastic. They inferred that sacred datura nectar provided enough psychotropic rewards to these moths to lure them away from other flowers that were blooming simultaneously.

Around that time, I stumbled on an ancient datura "hunting song" recorded by Pima Indian José Luis Brennan from an elderly neighbor, Virsak Vali, around 1900. It was a prayer to ensure the successful capture of deer, but it was also used to cure the psychosomatic "staying sicknesses" from which Pima individuals who had broken taboos occasionally suffered. I could tell from reading the Piman text that a clumsy translation had obscured a rich ecological message. While the text was certainly alluding to nocturnal hawkmoths visiting sacred datura flowers, Brennan's collaborator Frank Russell had used the English term *butterfly*, and the ceremonial plant had been reduced to being "a weed." After hours of consulting Piman-speaking friends and O'odham language texts, I worked up a new translation, which I hoped would be closer in spirit and biological precision to the native text:

> Stopping for a while in the white of dawn,
> stopping for a while in the white of dawn,
> rising to move through the valley
> where the blue evening flies away,
> rising to move through the valley.

Sacred datura leaves, sacred datura leaves,
eating your greens intoxicates me,
making me stagger, dizzily leap.
Datura blossoms, datura blossoms,
drinking your nectar intoxicates me,
making me stagger, dizzily leap.

Leaving the ground, the winged one overtakes me,
his bow looms large as he shoots to wound me;
my horns are severed, strewn hither and yon.
Leaving the ground, the winged one overtakes me,
his arrows loom large as he shoots to wound me,
my foldings, shot open, strewn hither and yon.

As flying insects, insects aflight, we are crazily set ablaze,
we drop to the ground, drop off to sleep as our wings flap still,
our last gasp, our last chance to fly back from way over there.
As drunken hawkmoths, hawkmoths drinking, we are set ablaze,
wings pressing shut, then spreading again,
fluttering, fluttering, way over there.

It is clear from this song that the same kind of psychotropic "trips" that medicine men associate with ingesting datura are attributed to both the leaf-feeding hornworm larvae and the nectar-drinking nocturnal moths. Decades before the Grants' scientific "discovery," the oral tradition of indigenous desert people evocatively celebrated the same alkaloid-mediated relationship between animal and plant.

Indigenous desert dwellers do not name the entire spectrum of insects found within their home territories, nor are they necessarily aware of most interactions between the plants and animals there. But they do know about interactions between animals and the major food plants that fill their larders, even when these interactions might seem obscure to the outsider.

One such interaction seems especially obscure to most desert dwellers today. Mesquite pods were, up until this century, the most important food in the Sonoran Desert region. But these pods were easily infested with minuscule bruchid beetles if they were left to sit under a mesquite tree after they fell. Female bruchids would lay eggs in the seeds, and the hatchlings would bore their way out by eating enough of the seeds to make them inviable. Remedio Cruz and his O'odham kin call these tiny beetles *kui kai mamad*, "mesquite bean babies." Once they have infested a bunch of mesquite pods, its value as food plummets.

The Seri Indian neighbors of the O'odham had an unusual way of finding pods that had been removed from the bruchid-dense desert floor beneath mesquite trees. Long after most mesquite pods had fallen from the trees, the Seri would search for piles of them in pack-rat middens. I once went out into the desert with Angelita Torres, who used a long stick to pry open the messy mounds of desert plant matter collected by these furry desert archivists. Angelita said that she could recover several pounds of edible mesquite pods in a matter of minutes. She was, in a sense, short-circuiting the food chain. Rather than gaining one-tenth of the food value of pods by eating the pack rat— as she occasionally did—she and her family ingested all of the nutritional value that the pack rats would have consumed.

The Seri were particularly observant of such interactions between native plants and animals, perhaps because their families depended on such knowledge in order to survive times of famine and drought. One out of every ten of their names for plants refers in some way to an animal, and at least half of those names accurately encode knowledge about native plant-animal interactions.

As important as it was for the Seri to understand such ecological associations in order to feed themselves, some of the interactions they describe had little utilitarian value. Why, for instance, would Seri hunters pay particular attention to the kinds of wildflowers that desert tortoises eat, when the wildflowers themselves are not considered edible by the Seri nor are they the best indicators of where to look for *ziij hehet coquij*, "the live thing that hides in bushes"? What do they "gain" by giving three very different-looking plants (from different families) the same name, *hap oacajam*, simply because mule deer stags scrape the velvet of their new antlers off on the branches of widely scattered individuals of these plants? While such information may have helped Seri men decide where to hunt, I have noticed that the Seri also delight in being sensually and intellectually aware of these ecological relationships for "knowledge's sake" alone.

While sitting on a beach talking to Seri turtle hunter Jesús Rojo

about his people's names that allude to plants and their animal associates, I could see that the terms were more than mere words; they
were also prompts to images that were like scenes out of a story. We
were talking, for instance, about a red algae found on the backs of sea
turtles, and Jesús reminded me that only one kind of sea turtle is
adorned by *moosni yazj*, "the green sea turtle's covering." It is found
only on a rare population of green sea turtles that does not emigrate
away from the Seri's coastal waters in the wintertime but instead goes
dormant, sleeping on bottoms of shoals that are laden with red algae
and that lie between the Sonoran coast and Tiburon Island. Jesús and
other Seri men who formerly made their living as turtle hunters treat
this rare population as though it were its own species; in fact, biologists have speculated that it may indeed be a distinctive breeding pool
of sea turtles.

   As Jesús talked of this sea turtle and its algae, he began to sing a
song about them, and as he sang the song, he motioned with his hands
how the sea turtle would rise from the channel bottom and come up
for air. Then he sang another song about an equally distinctive population of sea turtles, and he mimed the act of harpooning one of them.
Each name gave rise to an image, the image to a song, and the song
to a larger drama, enacted with gesture, voice, and eye movements.
Each was an ancient story, one in which turtle, alga, and harpooner
danced to the same music.

   Only now are we beginning to see the conservation value of such
local knowledge—now that these sea turtles and other rare critters
have been decimated through the spread of modern hunting technologies. Although most Seri alive today have never seen even a single Sonoran pronghorn antelope—an endangered subspecies now
limited to fewer than 500 individuals—they still remember a winter
herb that it once ate. The Seri name for a wild mitten-leaved bean is
haamoja ihaap, "the pronghorn's bean food;" the name comes from a
now-moribund dialect spoken by a band of Seri that once wandered
into the southern reaches of the pronghorn's range. Even in the core
of its range 200 miles to the north of the Seri, the pronghorn has been
exceedingly rare for nearly a century, as a result of being gunned down
by the first recreational trophy hunters to venture into the region.
Haamoja is such an archaic word that contemporary Seri had coined

another, more descriptive term to describe this animal when they are shown pictures or photos of it by biologists. Yet many of them still use its ancient name as part of the term for the lentil-like bean that grows on the silty flats that the pronghorn frequented. The plant had escaped the notice of wildlife biologists charged with inventorying the remaining pronghorn population's diet, but once the biologists heard of the Seri "lore" about this plant, they conceded that it deserved to be added to the roster of potential nutritional resources required to sustain this endangered animal.

Is such linguistically encoded knowledge about ecological relationships disappearing? Among the Seri, the younger generation can still name 70 percent of the native animals in photographs we provided, but their elders have an average score of 90 percent. Janice Rosenberg, who interviewed more than fifty Seri individuals about traditional ecological knowledge, found that the children were unaware of many local interactions involving insects and reptiles in particular—ecological relationships that their grandparents could discuss in detail. Seri youth were even less familiar with the traditional songs and rituals about floral and faunal relationships that their elders still held dear.

Ethnobotanist Kay Fowler has already witnessed dramatic changes in both cultures and environments over three decades of research in the Great Basin. But as she has conceded, "even by the time we started collecting traditional knowledge about plants and the animals associated with them, we were...getting less than half of the traditional knowledge [that] once existed." She had the good fortune to be out with traditional foragers when *Pandanus* moth larvae appeared in abundance one year, and the Owens Valley Paiute had a field day collecting them off desert plants to eat. But such harvests are few and far between these days.

In other regions, the survival of indigenous knowledge of plant-animal interactions may be in even greater doubt. Nancy Turner reports that the Salish people of the coastal rain forests of Washington have used banana slugs as a poultice for cuts and wounds because these slugs consume a certain set of plants that collectively have medicinal value. But there are fewer than ten Salish speakers left in this world; the details of which medicinal plants the slugs love are passing out of local knowledge. Richard Ford reports that the same is true in the Rio Grande pueblos, communities where, twenty years ago, speakers of the Tewa language distinguished dozens of kinds of trees and wildflowers from one another; today, young children use the old word for "firewood" for most trees and the old word for "weed" for most herbaceous plants. Should such a collapse of all names for flowering herbs into one catchall term come to the Seri, their community might lose track of which wild bean the endangered pronghorn antelope ate or which bush the desert tortoise hid under. And if that happens, what will become of the images, the gestures, songs, and stories once conjured up by native names?

It has been more than two decades since I first heard the ominous warning given by field ecologist Daniel Janzen, that "what escapes the eye is the most insidious kind of extinction—the extinction of interactions." That prophetic phrase—and the sound of Jesús Rojo singing his sea turtle songs—echoed through my head as I drove back through the night from the hornworm's home ground. My hope is that I can keep the images of that home ground alive in my mind's eye and eventually learn the songs that keep it vibrant.

The Parable of the Poppy and the Bee

I want to find our cousin
somewhere in the dawn, sporting
the pungent gleam of dew and sun,
our secret cousin Glimmer of honey,
our crazy cousin Wild bee's delight.
Some call the wild bees gone, their hymns
extinct. Some call the glade still and cold.
Yet I call her and call her back.
I call our cousin's many names,
who sang the psalms that saved us.
KIM STAFFORD, *Oregon Reunion of the Rare*

We wandered for several hours in the desert heat, up and down faint trails on gypsum-laced bluffs, before we saw it. At times, I sensed we might not see it at all. The landscape looked barren, torn up by years of off-road vehicle racing and overgrazing by livestock. Few flowers, insects, or even lizards were active during the dry spell of early summer. I was easily convinced that "it" was indeed rare in this valley near the Nevada-Utah border.

The "it" that brought me to the Virgin River basin was not the Joshua tree, not the crimson canyon, not the casinos, the health spas, or the white-water raft trips. I was after a rare wildflower, a small poppy called the dwarf bearclaw poppy, which was federally listed as an endangered species in 1979. Although legally protected, it had suffered from a five-year drought, during which nearly every elderly bearclaw had died off, and only a few new seedlings had sprouted to replace them. But drought had not merely affected the bearclaw poppies; it affected the other native organisms interacting with them as well.

I walked the trails and gazed out over the desert shimmering in the heat. Steve Buchmann, my bee-minded counterpart, was seeing more than midday mirages. Apparently spotting the first poppy, he whistled for me to come over to the bluff where he knelt a few hundred yards away. I did just that.

"I haven't found any yet," he said, sighing and gazing down at a patch of feathery, blue-gray poppy plants.

"Yes, you have," I replied. "That's *Arctomecon humilis* right at your feet." They looked like little cabbages set against the chalky soils of the gypsum outcrops. Seeing just one of the plant's velvety white blossoms, I was sure it was a poppy. I wondered if the heat had gotten to Steve, who ordinarily would have known a poppy when he saw one.

"The bees, I mean—I haven't yet seen any native bees. I've seen several open flowers, but none of the new species of bee, *Perdita meconis*, that Vince and Terry have been working with here in the Virgin."

Steve seemed to notice every open white flower in sight. While I had come to this place to see a rare plant, Steve had come to see an even rarer bee. Each of us had our biases, mine botanical, his more entomological. Both of us had come to see "it," but "it" had a blossom in my mind, while Steve's "it" had wings. We were witnessing an endangered ecological interaction of considerable antiquity. Few of us fathom how vital this pollination process may be to the reproduction and survival of rare plants, let alone to our own survival.

The poppy-loving bee had been described by scientists only in recent years, even though the poppy it loved had been known by botanists for more than a century. Fortunately, the bee had finally received the attention it deserved from Steve's colleagues in Logan, Utah, entomologists Terry Griswold and Vince Tepedino. When Terry identified *Perdita meconis* as a new species, specimens had been collected only from the area in which we stood and from the Kelso Dunes, 200 miles to the west. Vince and his students had carefully determined that in each of these localities, this bee pollinates only one kind of plant: a prickly poppy in the Kelso Dunes and the endangered bearclaw poppy here in the Virgin.

Meanwhile, I was thrilled at this glimpse of the poppy so thoroughly studied by one of my botanical heroes, Kim Harper. Dr. Harper and his Brigham Young University students had organized counts of all known bearclaw poppies year in and year out. They had determined that the small patches of poppies were already quite genetically uniform, perhaps because inbreeding had been going on for generations. At last I could see such patches of poppies "in the flesh."

Steve, I soon realized, was less than satisfied with the mere sighting of the poppy. After several hours of searching, he was frustrated that he would have little news to pass on to Terry and Vince, for the poppies bore no bees on this particular day in June.

Or at least they bore no native bees this late in the flowering season. Steve pointed out to me a feral (nonnative) honey bee that approached a dwarf bearclaw poppy, then zoomed away to a flowering buckwheat nearby. This type of bee may casually visit the poppies, but it did not do so this day. A single far-ranging bee can serve as an effective pollinator for the poppies earlier in the season, but we were too late for that. Even though these poppy plants are not exclusively dependent on *Perdita meconis* for producing their fruits and seeds, we noticed that the number of full black seeds within each fruit among the hundred some poppies was still low. Despite the presence of honey bees—as well as earlier visitations by poppy-loving and other solitary bees—the poppies were not filling all of their fruits with seed.

Scientists once believed that the only plants that could be threatened by low pollination rates were ones dependent on a single insect partner to spread their pollen around—the yucca with its yucca moth, for instance, or the fig with its fig wasp. We now know that the majority of flowering plant species can suffer low seed set when pollinators are scarce—even if they have a wide variety of pollinators under ideal conditions. In less than ideal conditions, most of these animals will make fewer and fewer visits to a rare plant population when it becomes too small to provide them with sufficient rewards.

In the case of the bearclaw poppy, its habitat is protected but its most dedicated pollinator is not. When I called on Vince Tepedino in Logan to ask him about the vulnerability of the poppy-loving bee, his answer was immediate: "This bee should perhaps be listed as an endangered species just as the poppy is, since it is known from so few places"—fewer localities, in fact, than the poppy itself.

It is unlikely that Dr. Tepedino's concerns for protecting the bee will be heeded in the near future. When he spoke with me, there was a moratorium on listing *any* more species as federally endangered. Given the current antienvironmentalist climate in some states, the mere thought of championing "some spineless little critter" like a bee would give some politicians a headache. The flower-loving fly of the Delhi Dunes of California, which is federally listed as an endangered species, is an example of a pollinator that has already suffered the ridicule of the "Wise Use Movement" and the sarcasm of commentators on the six o'clock news. And yet, fewer than 500 of these flies persist anywhere in the world, and they need only a few football fields of sand to survive.

Rare invertebrate species have become fall guys for the antienvironmental movement, which has argued that the government should only concern itself with bona fide "wildlife"—in other words, game animals—and leave the fates of plants or bugs to chance. During the summer 1995 debates about the reauthorization of the Endangered Species Act, lobbyists kept quoting a segment of a book called *Noah's Choice*, which pitted a little-known beetle against a highway project that would have provided rural dwellers with better access to a hospital. The take-home message was that the survival of beetles and other creepy-crawlies in their habitats could not possibly contribute to the well-being of humans. Bugs only get in the way of our economic endeavors.

If you are a bee, fly, or a beetle, this has not been your best time: more rollbacks of environmental legislation have been proposed during the past decade than ever before in U.S. history. Is it any wonder that the few spineless critters I've watched in the past few months were all ducking underground, frantically trying to get out of the way of the antienvironmental bulldozer? That bulldozer pretends that all bees and beetles are replaceable by others and that none of them has special habitat needs.

As Buchmann and I drove back from the Virgin basin toward Saint

George, Utah, I naively asked him a question that many pollination ecologists have been asked by resource managers: "If an endangered plant can be pollinated by introduced honey bees just as well as by native bees, why not move a few hives into each rare-plant habitat and solve the problem that way?"

"Gary," he groaned, feigning shock, "you should know better than to fall for quick fixes! A mobile beehive for every rare plant might have been a reliable stopgap solution a few years ago, but today, honey bees are dropping like flies. Over the long haul, it's never wise to put all your eggs—or pollen grains—in one basket. By investing exclusively in honey bee pollination, you're making things risky both for the rare plants and for the native bees that have coevolved with them."

With two decades of research under his belt at the USDA Carl Hayden Bee Research Laboratory, Steve could recite on a moment's notice the grim statistics regarding honey bee declines. Since 1990, nearly half of the managed honey bee colonies in the United States have been lost to diseases, parasites, pesticide poisonings, or infestations by fierce Africanized bees. In one part of the Southwest, 85 percent of all feral bee colonies in rock shelters, caves, and tree trunks have succumbed to mites over the past five years. Other states are reporting a near-total loss of their feral honey bees.

There are now fewer honey bees in North America than at any time since before World War II. More than two-thirds of the remaining hives are infested with pests and diseases that are not easily controlled; in fact, some of the mites are developing resistance to formerly lethal miticides. And Africanized bees, which first arrived in the United States in 1990, have now spread to more than a hundred counties. Because so many people now fear these so-called killer bees," beekeepers in heavily-populated areas are having to abandon their businesses under the threat of lawsuits from neighbors.

These trends are a painful reminder that without sufficient honey bees to provide the pollination services essential to U.S. crop production, we will have to rely increasingly on wild pollinators or face food shortages. Already, dozens of native bees pollinate as many flowers of alfalfa, cranberries, blueberries, and sunflowers as does the European-introduced honeybee. Should honeybees continue to disappear from the southern half of the United States, wild pollinators will have to take up the slack in pollinating other crops. It is estimated that within a few years, pollinators other than managed honey bees will need to provide four to six billion dollars of annual crop pollination services to American farmers.

Yet many of the native bees that pollinate our food crops are also vulnerable to a variety of threats. Like the poppy-loving bee, they are finicky about which flowers they visit and where they nest. Almost all pollinators have nesting requirements that scientists have not yet learned to simulate or artificially duplicate. Their habitats must also be kept pesticide-free, for most native bees are smaller and more sensitive to chemical poisoning than honey bees are.

While nearly 200 kinds of bird and mammal pollinators of plants are known to be globally at risk, no one knows how many insect pollinators are vulnerable to extinction. The recent *Global Biodiversity Assessment* lists fewer than 3,000 insects as endangered, but that number is low due to lack of data. The world's more than 100,000 invertebrate pollinator species are as affected by deforestation, contamination, and habitat fragmentation as any organisms can be, but definitive listings of threatened species have been published only for European butterflies. Hardly any reliable information exists with regard to the numbers of bees, wasps, flies, or moths that may be on the brink of extinction.

Yet paying exclusive attention to the extinction of species may divert us from recognizing other kinds of losses—the extirpation of pollinator populations, the disruption of the "traplines" they follow from one flowering plant to the next, the depletion of nest-building materials, the compaction of nest holes by trampling or plowing, and the fragmentation of migratory corridors. In autumn of 1996, I encouraged the Arizona-Sonora Desert Museum to convene a task force of eighteen conservation scientists and resource managers to consider what to do about the extinction of plant-pollinator interactions. Authorities from four countries, from the Xerces Society for invertebrate conservation, Bat Conservation International, government agencies, and numerous universities drafted an international policy proposal for protecting pollinators. They suggested that such extinctions will be averted only by setting aside sizable tracts of pesticide-free habitat and by restoring the "nectar corridors" of flowering plants required by migratory pollinators.

Such pollinator conservation measures will not merely help bear-claw poppies in Utah; they will also aid Hawaiian silverswords, the evening primrose of California's Antioch dunes, the night-blooming cacti of the Arizona-Mexico border, and a primrose now languishing without seed set in the suburbs of Tokyo, Japan. The parable of the bearclaw poppy and the poppy-loving bee can remind us that plants may be vulnerable without coevolved pollinators, and vice versa.

Native pollinators have consistently provided our croplands and wildlands with the kind of support that has kept our country fruitful. Let us remember them every time we smell a poppy or take a bite into a delicious, succulent fruit, honoring our collective debt to them. Hopi maidens mark the autumn with the Butterfly Dance; the Yaqui Deer Dancers spin and rattle their way through their ceremonial cycle wearing silk-moth cocoons around their calves; and the Hindi of peninsular Malaysia devote hundreds of hours each year to rituals that placate, charm, and sing poetry to the giant Asian bee, *Apis dorsata*. We should emulate the wisdom of these native peoples and celebrate, respect, and support our native pollinators. In doing so, we will clearly be expanding our sense of community, acknowledging at last the presence of other members who have been in service to us all along.

Waiting for the first visitor, I begin to recite the names of threatened pollinators from around the world. I recite this litany not sim-
ply as a way to stay awake; it is also for the pleasure of the images
they evoke: Mahogany Gliders, Honey Possums, Dibblers, Mariana's
Flying-Foxes, Little Flying Cows, Moss-forest Blossom Bats, Crowned
Lemurs, Golden-mantled Saddle-backed Tamarins, Little Woodstars,
Purple-backed Sunbeams, Turquoise-throated Pufflegs, Marvelous
Spatulatails, Yellow-footed Honey Guides, Four-colored Flower-
peckers, Apricot-breasted Sunbirds, Bishop's O-os, Regent Honey
Eaters, and Duvaucel's Geckos.

As I mull over the music of their names, I shudder with the recognition that those sounds may be all I will ever get to know of such
animals. Many of these pollinators are known by just a few diligent
zoologists, who have had the fleeting luck to be in the right place at
the right time. Such times are becoming less and less frequent. On
this "Red Book" list of threatened pollinators are some 82 mammal
species, 103 birds, and one reptile. Many of the species have dwin-
dled down to fewer than a thousand individuals. Others, such as the
Mexican long-tongued bat and lesser long-nosed bat, which have been
infrequently seen in the Baboquivari range, are so poorly known that
population estimates have varied wildly over the years.

Like the endangered wildflower, little is known of these pollinators' life histories: their frequency of reproduction under favorable
conditions, their longevity, their responsiveness to rainy years or to
years of drought like this one. They are almost gone, yet all we can
say about their way of life is that they have been attracted to flowers
for millennia. We presume that they were effective in pollinating certain loosely coevolved blossoms, yet some might merely have been
casual floral visitors that drink nectar without moving pollen from
one bloom to the next. Often all we know is that one individual in
one species in their genus was once observed ducking its head into
the blossoms of a certain flowering plant. What range of native flowers they visited before invasive weeds arrived in their homeland, we
don't know. All we have left are clues. The shape of a beak, muzzle,
or tongue relative to the shape of a flower. A dietary need for a certain mix of sugars and amino acids that incidentally match the nectar composition of a local plant. A hovering behavior that suggests

this bat or moth or bird might be a "legitimate" pollinator. ("Legitimate," in this sense, distinguishes the pollinator from the "casual visitor," an animal that can feed on the same plant's nectar or pollen without aiding in the plant's cross-pollination.)

Three nights ago, suffering insomnia and a fever due either to flu or to biophilia, I stayed up through the twilight hours counting how many of the vertebrate wildlife species in the 1994 *IUCN Red List of Threatened Animals* were likely to be pollinators. I tallied 186 vertebrate species, but they are mere needles in the haystack compared to the total number of pollinators on this planet—some 100,000 invertebrate species have been caught pollinating the 240,000 species of plants that depend on animals to carry pollen among their flowers. It will be decades before anyone can be sure what percentage of these 100,000 invertebrate pollinators are imperiled, so little is known about the "spineless" creatures today. For now, I must focus on the 186 distinct species of pollinating vertebrates that are at risk. They belong to "genera," or kinship groups of animals, containing somewhere between 1,030 and 1,220 species, most of which are presumed to lap up nectar and carry pollen. By my late-night calculations, 15 to 18 percent of those potential pollinators are already of conservation concern. That is to say, they are listed by the World Conservation Union (IUCN) as rare, threatened, endangered, or possibly extinct. At least 100 of the 165 vertebrate genera of floral visitors now include threatened species. In other words, at least 60 percent of all genera or "kinds" of pollinating animals include one or more species at risk of extinction.

Tonight, I am not laboring over the numbers in superficial global surveys of threatened species. Instead, I am camped in their midst, perched high in the mountains within a national wildlife refuge on the line between the United States and Mexico. I have been watching poorwills diving after hawkmoths, bats darting across the canyon, and micromoths landing on the flowers of the rare Kearney's blue star, a plant that appears over a few square miles in the world. My insect net is by my side, as are my notebook, pen, flashlight, and a mason jar filled with mothballs.

As I reach to clamp the "kill jar" over an insect crawling on the blue star's inflorescence, I hear a scream echoing off the canyon walls above me. Somewhere on the higher ridges behind my back, a female mountain lion is caterwauling—*yowling her heart out*—while I clumsily screw the lid back on a glass jar filled with nectar-feeding insects. "Forty-five seconds of screaming, presumably puma," I write in my field journal at 8:54 P.M., in case I end up in the kill jar of *Felis concolor* later on tonight.

An insight flashes into my adrenaline-inundated mind: while the relative rarity of carnivores such as cougars is well recognized by scientist and layperson alike, the increasing scarcity of pollinators has remained beyond the reach of our society's antennae. I can affirm, "This is the first cougar I've heard caterwauling in my quarter century of living in the Southwest." I can recall, "I've lived in puma country for twenty years, but only once, on the other side of these mountains, did I ever even catch a glimpse of one in the wild."

But who on this earth (other than a few batty zoologists) has a real awareness of pollinator scarcity? When ecologist Martin Burd recently sorted through hundreds of case studies of low seed set in flowering plants, he attributed 62 percent of these reproductive shortfalls to pollinator scarcity. An offhand comment by Burd may be even more telling: the very showiness of flowers might be an indication that good pollinators are naturally hard to come by, and even harder to find under not-soo-natural conditions.

Big, fierce carnivores have also been found to be scarce even under the most natural conditions we find today. If we consider that the bulk of their habitats have been degraded, fragmented, or invaded by weeds, it should not surprise us that sixty-five species in the order Carnivora are globally threatened, endangered, or otherwise at risk because of human pressures that exacerbate their natural rarity. As Steve Harrison has recently written in the *Global Biodiversity Assessment*, "large predators are likely to become [even more] scarce or disappear from fragmented ecosystems. . . . Losing lions or cheetahs from fragmented African savannas may have enormous impacts on the vegetation and fire regimes, for example—effects that will be played out over the next several decades or centuries."

Of course, carnivorous mammals are not the only keystone predators in biotic communities. Predatory snails, squid, octopus, crabs, crocodiles, rattlesnakes, harriers, and aplomado falcons play pivotal roles in their respective communities, marine or terrestrial. Pull out the keystone from the arch of life, and the entire structure of a community may collapse.

The past century's declines in nectar-feeding vertebrates may be ushering in ecological changes as severe as those associated with the decline of meateaters. A roost site in the Philippines once housed hundreds of thousands of flying foxes; today you can witness a few hundred on the best of nights. The Panay Giant Fruit Bat is altogether gone from the Philippines. The Okinawa Flying Fox is extinct; so are the ones from Palau and Reunion. The Solomon Islands have lost their endemic Tube-nosed Fruit Bat, while Puerto Rico has lost its Flower Bat. Cuba has lost its Red Macaw. No one is sure whether Turquoise-throated Pufflegs occur in Colombia or Ecuador anymore. When was the last time any birder you know spotted a Robust White-eye? Or an Oahu O-o? A Kloea? A Koha Grosbeak? A Black Mamo? *Ula-ai-hawane?* Birds and mammals are not the only floral visitors that are vanishing. Of the two reptiles that have been documented as legitimate pollinators of flowering plants, one is already red-listed: Duvaucel's gecko, on a small island off New Zealand.

The loss of such pollinators may dramatically affect how much fruit is available to both wildlife and humans in certain habitats. In peninsular Malaysia, for instance, dawn bats apparently serve as the sole pollinators of the luscious tropical fruit known as the durian, but the bats must have more than durian nectar as a food source—they rely on the continual flowering of coastal mangroves as their primary nutritional resource. In their flights from roost site to mangrove forest, they pollinate durians "almost as a dietary afterthought," according to Charles Peters's observations for the World Wildlife Fund. Unfortunately, mangrove habitats are considered foul-smelling "swamps" in Malaysia, as elsewhere in the world, where they are often dredged or bulldozed away by developers of coastal resorts and marinas. Janet Abramovitz has prophesied in *State of the World 1997* that "without this year-round mangrove resource, the bats are unlikely to survive." In their absence, the highly valued durian crop is likely to decline precipitously.

While rare carnivores and scarce nectar feeders may differ in their *salience*—that is, their intrinsic perceptibility to humans—they are similar in their importance to the integrity of their habitats. Both groups of vertebrates demonstrate the *connectivity* between species essential to the healthy functioning and cohesive structure of biotic communities. If pollinator guilds are defaunated, animal-pollinated plants that formerly dominated a mature community are likely to decline, while weedy wind-pollinated plants are likely to find open niches. If carnivore guilds are defaunated, then the populations of grazers and browsers may explode. Herbaceous understories may be eliminated or the recruitment of woody canopy plants may falter. In both cases, the natural functioning of a biotic community may be irreparably damaged by the demise of ecological relationships that have evolved over millennia.

While the pollination relationship is between flowering plants and their animal mutualists, the predation relationship is between very different kinds of animals: carnivorous animals and their prey. In both cases, however, *connectivity* is the unifying principle. Just as most carnivores rely on a relatively modest set of prey items, most pollinators depend on a rather narrow range of flowering plants that feature certain fragrances, positioning along stems, floral tube shapes, or scheduling of nectar secretions. Coyotes and honeybees may be extreme generalists, but the majority of carnivores and nectar feeders are quite limited in what they can find to feed on. In fact, pollinators may generally be more restricted than carnivores in their diets—and thus potentially more vulnerable. Even though few pollinators form exclusive allegiances with just one kind of flower, they are limited in the range of flowers they can work. In contrast, bears, mountain lions, and wolves are much more prone to open-ended opportunism—even an occasional human may hit the spot.

Some cultures give special recognition to predators with whom we share prey, explicitly acknowledging that the carnivores are needed if prey populations are to remain healthy. Richard Nelson, the Alaskan ethnozoologist and essayist, has thought about this relationship while hunting with Koyukon Athabaskan families in Alaska:

> The Koyukon honor a kindred relationship between people and wolves as fellow predators. When they come upon animals which wolves have killed but don't immediately touch [to eat], they say that the wolves have left this meat for people. Conversely, the Koyukon will kill an

animal and while caching its meat, they will cut some fat off and leave
it off to the side for the wolves. They do this so that the wolves need
not bother the cache in order to feed themselves.

An elderly O'odham Indian once told me that he always left out a
container of saguaro cactus syrup for the owls inhabiting the giant
saguaros near his home, before he took the rest of the syrup to make
wine for his people's rain-bringing ceremonies in the summer. The
owls he ritually fed were most likely the elf owl or now-endangered
ferruginous pygmy owl, both inhabitants of saguaro nest holes in
southern Arizona. The latter predator is a dusky bird whose black
nape spots look as though it has eyes in the back of its head. The old
O'odham winemaker told me that he fed the owl first because he knew
that the owl would be watching him as he prepared the cactus syrup
for the wine feast; if he did anything awkwardly, perhaps the owl
might forgive him for it.

In the Yucatán Peninsula, Mayan keepers of five native species of
stingless bees believe that "the actual work with the bees cannot be
separated from the rituals which accompany it." Should they fail to
enact annually their rain-bringing ceremonies, not only do the rains
refrain from coming but the bees become weak, honey production
declines, and their crops fail to produce fruit. To avert these tragedies,
the Mayans perform a rite that lasts twenty-four hours called the *Hanli
Kol*, which requires that honey from the native bee, *xunan kab*, be left
out in their fields as a thanksgiving. The ceremony, which allows the
regeneration of the stingless bees, was traditionally enacted every four
years under the revolving patronage of various beekeepers in the
Mayan villages. Today, there are only 500 Mayan families who still
keep stingless *Melipona* and *Trigona* bees, but this ancient art is being
revived. The bees do more than produce a dark, musky honey; they
effectively pollinate sixteen crops in Mayan dooryard gardens, as well
as an unknown number of rain-forest trees in the wildlands surrounding Mayan villages.

These deep-seated cultural relationships with predators and pollinators contrast sharply with the manner in which North American
and European urbanites relate to the same animals in zoos and museums. To begin with, 87 percent of all American zoo-goers admit that
they would never have the opportunity to see wild predators and pol-

linators if it weren't for zoos and safari parks. According to Roper Starch Worldwide public opinion pollsters, 85 percent of Americans have an abiding faith that such artificial animal facilities "help the environment" by raising endangered wildlife to help prevent their extinction. This widespread belief is ironic, since fewer and fewer zoo professionals feel that caging a few individuals of an endangered species does much to keep that species from extinction. And even when zoos do exhibit endangered predators, they seldom allow them to practice *predation*, the ecological process that makes carnivores what they are. Only a few zoos, such as one in Singapore, allow visitors to see lions and tigers eating dead sheep or goats. In Great Britain, there has even been a law enacted to shelter zoo visitors from the uncouth sight of mammals being fed other mammals.

"It's like sausage," quipped David Hancocks, when he directed the Arizona-Sonora Desert Museum, "you may like it, but you don't want to see how they make it."

Even if they were to let carnivores prey on other animals, most zoos aren't well suited to sheltering wide-ranging predators anyway. The animals don't have sufficient space to leap or lunge, they lack the environmental heterogeneity to stalk prey successfully, and they do not have the challenge to hunt. Before they were released, captive-bred condors in California were fed by puppets so as not to imprint on humans, but puppets could not teach them to hunt in a characteristic condor manner. Yet if their human trainers had taught them to hunt in the open, it would increase the possibility that condor hatchlings would end up congregating around human settlements waiting for handouts rather than hunting for themselves.

The most innovative of zoos simply cannot ensure that female mountain lions will receive the stimuli needed to inspire them to caterwaul, to be good hunters, to be what they have been for many millennia. The ecological interaction that set mountain lions on their evolutionary trajectory—*predation*—has no real way to take place in zoos. But what about that other ecological interaction, *pollination*? Can it be demonstrated in zoos, botanical gardens, and living museums in ways that remind visitors that there is more at risk than isolated species, for age-old relationships between wild species are truly imperiled as well?

To date, few zoos and museums have more than postage stamp-sized exhibits on pollination. The highly touted "Pollinarium" at the National Zoo in Washington, D.C., is hardly larger than an Airstream mobile home—a mere 1,250 square feet under glass. It contains one species of hummingbird (Anna's) and a few butterflies (heliconids, long-wings, and orange Julias), each of which is limited to a few showy floral partners such as orchids, passionflowers, and lantanas. Tourists pass before these contrived encounters like voyeurs watching forced sexual acts on a stage. Like many indoor pollination exhibits within museums across the United States, the Pollinarium gives credence to the mistaken belief that the domestic honeybee is an ecological sensation, rather than revealing it to be the worst competitor that a diversity of wild pollinators has ever faced.

I remember my disappointment about the National Zoo's portrayal of pollination as I sit in the darkness next to Kearney's blue stars. I remembered that zoos and botanical gardens have an even poorer track record for conserving imperiled partners in plant-animal interactions over the long haul. I recall what had happened when I worked at the Desert Botanical Garden with some of the first seeds from Kearney's blue stars that had made it out of the wild into horticultural greenhouses of endangered species recovery programs. The seeds germinated well, the seedlings grew fast in plastic pots filled with enriched soil, and the plants flowered profusely, but they produced no seed on their own for lack of appropriate pollinators. Although horticulturists later learned to use cat's whiskers to trip the flowers so that pollen could be transferred to receptive stigmatic surfaces, the Botanical Garden population of blue stars never attracted sufficient numbers or the right kinds of pollinators to do the trick. It was as if the blue stars' bodies were there, but their spirits had flown away.

As the dawn light begins to seep into the canyon shadows, I turn my attention back to the pale blossoms before me. This time I have not been selected as a puma prey item. Costa's and broad-billed hummingbirds arrive to hover before the blooming scapes of the Kearney's blue star. So do bee flies and skippers. Not every visitor is an effective pollinator; not every live hunk of meat to visit this canyon gets to sacrifice itself as cougar food. Some interactions between species are more probable—and more fruitful—than others.

Why Chiles Are Hot

Seed Dispersal and Plant Survival

Unless they have chiles, they think they're not eating.
BARTOLOMÉ DE LAS CASAS, 1552

We tried not to talk in hyperboles, but after all, it was high noon on summer solstice during the hottest week on record in the Sonoran Desert. Mexican ecologist Humberto Suzan was helping me measure the microenvironmental conditions at the driest and northernmost edge of the range of one of the hottest chiles in the world. Whenever one of us ripped our flesh on the omnipresent barbed wire, cactus spines, or the needle-like thorns of desert shrubs, we would attempt to respond with a superlative curse, in Spanish or English. *"¡Sananabichi!"* I would yell. *"¡Chile chingón!"* Humberto would cry as blood spurted through his torn jeans. We had only two and a half hours in the merciless sun on this cloudless day to find out how hot chile plants actually got; and despite all obstacles, we had to keep moving from plant to plant, taking measurements whenever we could.

Humberto and I were attempting to determine the extent to which shady microenvironments beneath desert shrubs protected wild chile plants from the damaging solar radiation of such a hellishly torrid day. We were already aware that air temperatures at nearby weather stations had exceeded 110 degrees for seven days running. As planned, we were doing this work during the period of the year when high moisture deficits and excessive radiation often damage or kill both the seedlings and the mature shrubs of other tropically derived plants. As we measured the ambient light reaching the chile leaves hidden below the canopies of desert shrubs, we realized that they were often ten to fifteen degrees cooler than the ambient temperatures outside the canopies. Beneath one particular shrub—the desert hackberry—only one-fourth of the ambient light trickled through the shrub canopy to reach the tender chile. While I cursed to Humberto that the sun was frying my brains to a crisp, he hunkered over the computerized data logger, dazzled by our results: the chiles weren't fried at all!

It hardly amazed us that the desert could be so hot, but we were awed that so many chiles could be found growing where it was at least a little cooler. At the edge of the Sonoran Desert in southern Arizona, such buffered microenvironments are few and far between. Even nearby canyon bottoms where vegetation is lush, the canopies of desert hackberries still cover only 15 percent of the ground; on drier slopes, the amount of ground covered by any vegetation at all may drop to 5 percent. Nevertheless, nearly 60 percent of the wild chiles we located were found under this one "nurse plant," the hackberry—a percentage that is many times higher than would be predicted if chiles were randomly dispersed. Humberto and I confirmed that the distribution of chiles is indeed not random, for they are highly associated with the meager cover of hackberries, wolfberries, and graythorns.

How do they arrive at these "safe sites"? We wondered about this as we made our way up the slope above Rock Corral Canyon. Back at our four-wheel-drive vehicle, we put our monitoring equipment away, then paused in the shade of a mesquite tree, sharing a canteen of water and a light lunch. For me, a picnic lunch is never complete without some dried wild chiles as dessert, so I popped a few in my mouth while Humberto reviewed the data we had gathered. That was when the notion hit me—that the very piquancy that made chile peppers notorious among humankind might be like the "guide" on a guided missile! For some reason, the "pepper" genus *Capsicum* had given up the nasty arsenal of chemicals shared by most other members of the nightshade family—poisonous glycoalkaloids—in favor of the odorless, colorless chemicals called capsaicinoids. Could it be that this latter set of secondary compounds help chile seeds reach "safe sites" to which they would not otherwise be dispersed if they lacked these metabolites?

To answer such a question, I had to learn what creatures did and did not disperse chile seeds. This homework was not as easily accomplished as I had originally hoped, for there were virtually no published observations of animal feeding behavior on chile bushes in the wild. I therefore turned to indigenous American folklore for clues; there I learned that wild chiles were called the equivalent of "bird peppers" in many languages. A Pima Indian man in Sonora, Mexico, claimed that the local *chiltepines* were eaten and dispersed by red-feathered birds such as cardinals, pyrrhuloxias, and finches. On hearing this claim, a mutual friend of ours—an ornithologist—suggested that male finches might keep their plumage brilliant enough to attract females by seeking out and metabolizing the beta-carotene in chiles. But this did little to explain the very piquancy of chiles. Moreover, I soon learned that birds of other feathers also disperse wild chiles— red plumage is not a requisite.

In fact, other indigenous peoples of tropical America also associate wild chiles with a particular set of birds, although these associations differ from the one made in Sonora. The Huastec Mayans refer to wild chile fruit as *taa' ts'itsin its*, "the chile excreted by birds," and the Chontal Mayan nickname for wild *amashito* chiles means much the same: *aj tso yup*, "Mr. Shit-Out Fruit." Both Mayan groups are aware that tyrannid flycatchers, chachalacas, thrashers, and mockingbirds can disperse chiles, but their traditional stories underscore the importance of one bird in particular: the great kiskadee. They claim that this highly loquacious frugivore constantly signs the name of chiles in their language; in fact, they say they originally learned their name for chiles from the great kiskadee. It is considered by the Maya to be the "planter" of wild chiles in the thornscrub emerging from recently abandoned slash-and-burn fields. When I met ethnobiologist Marco Antonio Vasquez, who had been studying among the Chontales for a decade, he suggested that the great kiskadee and the Maya have participated in a system of "proto-cooperation" that has kept wild chiles abundant in their habitat. The Maya would open up patches of the forest for planting, and the kiskadees would effectively disperse this highly valuable medicinal culinary herb to those sites.

Just when I was getting frustrated with the changing roster of birds I had to take into account as potential dispersers, I received some much-needed help. Out of the blue, a laid-back Louisianan—one who had grown up ingesting Red Devil hot sauces—showed up in southern Arizona to suggest the solution to my problem. Don Norman was an itinerant avian ecologist with two keen interests: zydeco music and the ways in which birds respond to secondary chemical compounds such as capsaicinoids. Within a few weeks during wild-chile fruiting time at Rock Corral Canyon, Don determined that while cardinals sampled the red and green *chiltepínes* only infrequently, thrashers and mockingbirds were much more active in dispersing the fiery fruits.

Back in graduate school during the "off season" for chile addicts, Don made some even more remarkable discoveries in the laboratory. When Don and his colleagues fed house finches and cedar waxwings meals containing 1,000 parts per million capsaicinoids—about the average concentration in a quarter-inch-round *chiltepín*—the birds exhibited no behavioral problems or weight loss as a result of eating these "hot dishes." In contrast, three small mammal species found the same meals repulsive. In other laboratory experiments, researchers worldwide have observed that all mammals (other than humans) either develop an aversion to chile-laced foods or are killed by forced doses of capsaicinoids. The birds tested to date, on the other hand, not only tolerate chiles but pass chile seeds through their digestive tracts without significantly lowering their germination rates compared to seeds left untreated. The same cannot be said for chile seeds passed more slowly through mammalian guts, for they emerge either badly damaged or altogether unviable—that is, unable to germinate.

Don and I surmised from these bits of evidence that capsaicinoids are far more selective than glycoalkaloids in deterring seed consumption by vertebrate animals. Whereas nearly all animals were discouraged from feeding on glycoalkaloid-rich nightshades, only those animals that inevitably damaged chile seeds—or inefficiently dispersed them—were discouraged by the capsaicinoids.

We realized that several other pieces of the puzzle were still missing. Capsaicinoids did not deter birds from feeding on chiles, but did they "guide" birds to ripened chile fruits that were ready for dispersal? The answer is not straightforward. On the one hand, since capsaicinoids are not colorful or fragrant, they do not *attract* birds to chile fruits. Instead, ripened chiles produce pleasant-scented pyrazines, the same chemicals that provide cultivated bell peppers with their characteristic aroma. Could it be that once birds experience the piquancy of wild chiles, they acquire a certain predilection for them? We hypothesized that birds may learn to associate red colors and pyrazine-imbued fragrances with the presence of piquant peppers.

Another piece of the puzzle was tougher to find. Did those birds known to feed on wild chiles have a higher probability of dispersing their seeds to the "safe sites" under hackberries or other "nurse" plants? Don's field observations were not sufficient to help me here, because frugivorous birds are seldom caught in the act of dispersing minuscule seeds from their mother plant to other safe sites. Most frugivorous birds of the deserts and tropics forage for only thirty seconds to a minute in any canopy laden with small fruits, and they may sample only two to three fruits before they fly away again. It is the lucky ornithologist who catches an identifiable seed dripped down the bib of a bird or passed through its guts!

Nevertheless, it became clear to us that cardinals, mockingbirds, and thrashers spent far more time foraging on the abundant hackberries, wolfberries, and graythorn fruits around Rock Corral Canyon than they did on the relatively scarce *chiltepines*. In Arizona, chile plants are seldom found in densities of more than twenty per acre, and these produce several hundred to a few thousand fruits. These fruits do not necessarily ripen at the same time. In contrast, hackberry and wolfberry bushes at the same density present tens of thousands of fruits in flushes during any single week, offering frugivorous birds far better reasons to take up residence in a desert canyon than a chile patch ever could.

Fortunately, two other insightful field biologists showed up to intern with me. Josh Tewksbury and John Tuxill realized that wild chiles were "piggy backing" on the abundance of these other red-berried fruits. Perhaps the birds were initially attracted to canyons with many hackberries and wolfberries. Then, we reckoned, once they were down foraging in the canopies of these shrubs, they might sense the pyrazines wafting up from the cool understory chiles below.

When Josh and John compared wild chiles to all other desert fruits with respect to their shape, size, sheen, color, and seasonality, the chiles clustered most closely with hackberries, then with wolfberries. It is as though the wild chiles have been selected to mimic the fruits that birds are likely to encounter in greater abundance. Just how the birds ultimately discern chiles from the other fruits is a mystery that Josh has begun to solve on his own, employing a suite of innovative experiments in the lab, on the museum grounds, and in the field.

Chile fruit may get dispersed from one berry-fruited shrub canopy to the next by being inadvertently picked up by resident frugivores that spend most of their time foraging and defecating in the canopies of hackberries and wolfberries. Chile seeds are most likely to be dispersed to the canopies of the shrubs whose fruits provide the most stable or abundant resources for resident frugivorous birds. It is unlikely that small mammals would cache their fruits in the same nonrandom pattern, even if they were to leave chile fruits uninjured.

We realized that our story had looped back on itself. When we compared the "light extinction profiles" of hackberries against the four most dominant trees and shrubs on our chile sites, we found that they provided one of the densest canopies—one where chiles had a better chance of surviving damaging radiation. They could also survive killing frosts under hackberries, for a dense canopy buffers understory plants from the cold by reducing reradiation and temperature loss. This too is a critical factor for the survival of a plant at the northern edge of its range—although this did not seem so obvious on that blazing summer-solstice day when Humberto and I anxiously wrestled our light sensors beneath thorny shrubs and popped chiles to cool ourselves down.

Humberto has moved back to Tamaulipas, where wild chiles are regularly sold on the highway between his home and the U.S.-Mexico border. Josh has dispersed to Montana, Don back to Louisiana, and John to Panama. The fiery little suckers we studied are harder to find north of the Mexican border, where they are sometimes sold to aficionados for as much as thirty-five dollars a pound. We have recently realized that Rock Corral Canyon is one of only a half dozen or so sites where wild chiles grow in Arizona, and an ideal one for demonstrating how habitat-based conservation management of crop relatives can be accomplished. As such, Jim Donovan and I have nominated the Rock Corral Canyon area for the special U.S. Forest Service designation of zoological and botanical area, to be set aside to conserve not only chiles but eighteen other relatives of crop plants as well. Wild cotton, carrots, beans, grapes, gourds, onions, walnuts, and agaves are among them. For resource managers, it has become clear that wild chile populations cannot continue to reproduce or evolve in place unless the nurse plants and their bird dispersers are also protected. Rock Corral Canyon holds more than chiles; it is a place where the kind of ecological interactions persist that have been essential to the evolution of most New World crops.

I am looking forward to the day when Humberto, Jim, Josh, John, Don, and I can take our children to Rock Corral Canyon to show them the treacherous slope where their fathers braved the heat to investigate these interconnections. And when one of them asks one of us, "Papa, why are chiles so hot?," we will look at one another and reply with a rhyme much sweeter than our earlier curses: "So birds will disperse them to nurses, while other creatures will not!"

Where Creatures and Cultures
Know No Boundaries

*We figure and find stories, which can be thought of as maps or
paradigms in which we see our purposes defined; then the world
drifts and our maps don't work anymore, our paradigms and
stories fail, and we have to reinvent our understandings, our
reasons for doing things.... What we need most urgently, in
both the West and all over America, is a fresh dream of
who we are, which can tell us how we should act.... They
will be stories in which our home is sacred, stories about
making sense of a place without ruining it.... Wreck it
and we will have lost ourselves, and that is craziness.*
WILLIAM KITTREDGE, *Who Owns the West?*

Whenever I take refuge, hike, or run through this arid country, so
barren, bald, and desolate to the unaccustomed eye, I close my eyes
and listen to the voices. I am not inclined to aural illusions, nor do I
have a particularly good ear. But sound waves travel in the desert air,
bouncing off sand dunes, volcanic crater walls ornamented with pet-
roglyphs, or desert pavements shaped into intaglios by prehistoric
pilgrims. Sound waves also travel across boundaries, boundaries like
the ephemeral lines that separate nations.

I close my eyes now and listen for the voices I have heard in the

Gran Desierto de Sonora, from the Sea of Cortez coast and Colorado River delta eastward through lava, sand, and silt flats. I remember how once, when crawling deep inside a lava tube high up on the flanks of the Sierra Pinacate, far beyond where any light could penetrate, I was surrounded by a low, pulsating hum. Near the Colorado River delta—at the Cucupa village of El Mayor, Baja California—I offered an elderly woman a handful of a cereal grain now extinct from the area, Sonoran panic grass. She moved her thumb across the grains, sifting seed from chaff, and whispering, "*Shimcha, shimcha,*" as flood-waters lapped up against the pilings that kept her ramshackle wooden hut from being washed to sea.

Voices. Voices rising from a well on a bedrock bench above the Rio Sonoyta—wailing voices of children reputedly sacrificed so that the well wouldn't fill up with ocean water and then overflow and flood the world. Whoever sacrificed those children so long ago got their just deserts—most of the region now receives less than four inches of rainfall per year, and certain spots have gone thirty-six straight months without a drop falling.

Tunes trailing through the air, still following behind pilgrims who trekked to the "Big Waters"—the Sea of Cortez—to receive both salt and songs laden with Ocean Power. I remember camping one time at Lopez Collada, the railroad camp in the dunes where, decades before, seventeen gandy dancers had died in a sandstorm later dubbed the "white night of death." I had ridden a boxcar down there in the dark, then crawled off into the lee side of a dune as another storm came up, one with a chilling, relentless wind. I had finally fallen asleep thinking I had heard banshee voices. Shivering in my sleeping bag, I forgot where I was until a half hour before dawn, when a train thundered by on the tracks fifty yards away, and I sat straight up. In the faint light, I could see that Pinacate Peak was covered with snow for the first time in years.

I will never forget flying over "Old Man's Cactus" mountain—in the Sierra Suvuk of Sonora—and hearing the octogenarian archaeologist Julian Hayden wheeze above the roar of engine and propeller, "Look, boys, down there, it's one of the ancient intaglio drawings scraped out on the desert pavement: a sixty-foot-tall male figure with a forty-foot pecker!" Or the time I heard the Sand Papago loner Francisco "Chulpo" Suni speaking passionately in his native O'odham tongue as we strolled around Quitobaquito Springs with a lovely O'odham woman twenty years his junior who had offered to translate Chulpo's words for me.

"I didn't follow all he was saying," I commented to the young woman when Chulpo went off in the bushes for a few minutes.

"It's probably good that you didn't," she replied, amused but blushing ever so slightly.

"Why? What was that he was saying when he gestured toward the pond and the mesquite trees?"

"'Marry me and we'll move here,'" she said, trying to imitate his voice. She giggled and waved her arms toward the springs and the mesquite *bosquet* just as Chulpo had done a few minutes before. "'This place has all we need—plenty of water, lots of firewood, and all the roadkills we can eat lying there on the highway across the fence line in Mexico.... I can cook you *carne asada* over the campfire every night, and we can sleep under the stars.'"

The voices are not all human. The long-billed curlew's *Cur-leee* as it takes flight on the mudflats before me just below the Colorado River delta in the Upper Sea of Cortez. Or the common poorwill, the smallest of our nightjars, calling its name as it sits, blending in, on a rocky slope of volcanic tuff. The long-billed curlew and poorwill are but two of the 400 birds found in the desert and at sea here; 75 percent of all avian species that migrate between the United States and Mexico are found within this stretch of coastal desert.

Yet diverse as the bird life is, the birds do not dominate the voices heard here. During the heat of summer, cicadas thrum with a metallic cadence that approaches a migraine headache in intensity. Within a herd of javelina, individuals will snort to one another as, after raiding a cornfield on one side of the border, they scuffle beneath a barbed-wire fence to seek sanctuary in the national park on the other side. And as an Indian elder once told me, you can even hear the cries of mating desert tortoises. While mounting, males of this seldom-heard reptile species will wail loud enough for their voices to be heard reverberating off canyon walls hundreds of yards from where they caress their partner's carapace.

———

These are voices of cultures and creatures that recognize no political boundaries, yet they have sometimes had their lives torn apart by them. Endangered Sonoran pronghorn antelope—now numbering fewer than 500 individuals—are periodically hit by trucks passing along Highway 2, the Mexican thoroughfare that parallels the U.S.-Mexico border. U.S. border patrol and customs officials regularly stop and harass O'odham and Cucupa citizens of Mexico as they attempt to visit their relatives in the United States, and the Mexican *aduana* makes it just as difficult for American Indians to participate in ceremonies and fiestas south of the border. Highway right-of-ways along the international boundary allow the rapid spread of weeds like buffelgrass introduced from South Africa and Saharan mustards escaped from the Mediterranean. These weeds fuel wildfires that kill natives along a quarter-mile strip on either side of the fence. The desert border becomes more than a no-man's-land under the pressures of drug trafficking and military surveillance; it also becomes a land of diminished culture, wildlife, and vegetative cover. Ancient voices are drowned out beneath the rumble of trucks hauling semitrailers of post-NAFTA products from one nation's market to the next.

But wherever there are such cultural or political boundaries on this earth, the conservation movement may be open to strange and unfamiliar voices, and the participatory process may take sudden and unanticipated turns. Consider the turns I've witnessed over the past decade of working in these Sonoran Desert borderlands, a region divided into near-equal halves by the governments of the United States and Mexico more than 140 years ago. In 1853, the aboriginal homelands of the Tohono O'odham (Desert Papago), the Hia C-ed O'odham (Sand Papago), the Paipai, and Cucupa (a Yuman-speaking tribe) were fragmented among the states of Arizona, Sonora, and Baja California. We are still reckoning the effects of this political fragmentation.

Prior to the Gadsden Purchase of Mexican lands, indigenous peoples south of the Gila River lived in low population densities, perhaps only 250 to 500 of them supported by the rock tanks and seeps in the riverless stretches between the Gila and the Sea of Cortez. Following the California gold rush and the Civil War, cattlemen came into this country and forced native hunters and foragers away from aboriginal water holes. Later, the remaining O'odham and Cucupa who had not been relocated were blocked from access to parts of their former territories by fences and immigration officials. They could no longer drift with the seasons back and forth between hunting and gathering camps, so they were forced to abandon places their ancestors had used for centuries. No wonder the country became known as the *Gran Despoblado*, the "Big Empty," to newcomers who could hardly fathom its history or hear the voices still echoing within it.

Much of this arid terrain had indeed become *despoblado*, for it was gradually being emptied of the cultural traditions that had nurtured it. By the mid 1990s, Chulpo, the lone Hia C-ed O'odham living at a former farming village in the middle of a wildlife refuge, had become known as a "hermit"; in truth, he was a remnant, a relict of a community that had once included ten to twelve families. Now he too hears voices and hardly thinks of his former neighbors as being gone.

Others ignore these voices. From the 1930s through the 1970s, as conservationists or military strategists looked around for spectacular "wilderness" landscapes in which to place national parks, wildlife refuges, proving grounds, or biosphere reserves, the western Sonoran Desert borderlands attracted their attention. Organ Pipe Cactus National Monument was established in the late 1930s, and Cabeza Prieta National Wildlife Refuge soon followed. Luke Air Force Base blocked access by ground and by air to a large domain now known as the Goldwater range. Designations of "critical environmental concern" and "biosphere reserve" status were overlain on these areas decades later. Finally, Mexico followed suit, recognizing the value of two landscapes of unprecedented immensity that are now known as the Sierra Pinacate y Gran Desierto de Altar reserve and the Alto Golfo y Delta del Rio Colorado reserve.

When these reserves were being planned in October 1988, something peculiar happened at a binational meeting sponsored by the Governors' Commission of Arizona and Sonora. Advertised as a review of scientific research on the Sierra Pinacate—the austere volcanic shield just south of the Arizona-Sonora border—the meeting's hidden agenda was to rally support for linking Mexican biosphere reserves to Organ Pipe Cactus National Monument, Arizona's desert biosphere reserve. Conservationists felt that Organ Pipe, which had received

UNESCO biosphere reserve status in 1978, needed a "sister park" across the border in Sonora.

Meeting organizers anticipated that cross-cultural communication would be an issue at the October meeting, but they were surprised when two dozen O'odham leaders from both sides of the border arrived, requesting a slot on the schedule for the first morning of the conference.

That first morning, after the meeting was formally inaugurated, the O'odham leaders were invited to speak to the assembly regarding the cultural history of the area. Instead of a single leader coming to the podium, eighteen native participants came to the front of the room to speak on behalf of their communities; no single individual felt that he or she alone could express the native people's depth of concern. While they voiced their hope that the Pinacate could be protected from development, they affirmed that it remained a sacred mountain for them, where they continued to take pilgrimages to honor their place of emergence.

Some scientists scoffed at the notion that the O'odham still had any attachment to the Pinacate and doubted that they went there at all anymore. I later remembered that I had once seen a bandanna stuffed with ceremonial tobacco that had been slung high up into a saguaro cactus on the slopes of their sacred mountain. They did not commemorate their pilgrimages with T-shirts that announced, "I've done the Pinacate," but offered subtle gestures toward the land instead.

The government resource managers grew wary when the O'odham bitterly recited how their historic homesteads had been bulldozed at Organ Pipe Cactus National Monument after a sole member of their tribe was paid to waive their collective rights to the place in 1957. They requested that their traditional historical sites in the Pinacate be better protected than those in Organ Pipe had been. Further, they argued that they should be involved not only in cultural resource protection but in natural resource management of these areas as well, since their subsistence traditions had given them familiarity with the plants and animals that live in the Pinacate.

On hearing the O'odham claims and requests, the Sonoran state

secretary of ecology walked out of the meeting, refusing to acknowledge that the O'odham had any rights in Mexico at all. Perhaps he,
like some of the American conservationists, feared that recognizing
aboriginal land rights in the region would disrupt conservation plans.
At the same time, the O'odham participants at the meeting were concerned that they might be left out of any long-term land management plan and that their own cultural legacy in the area would be
further obscured. Cucupa fishermen in the Colorado River delta vicinity had suffered similar doubts when they were told after the fact that
their homeland had been decreed a Mexican biosphere reserve and
that all fishing might be suspended. At times, the tension between
the bureaucrats and tribal leaders was palpable; bridging their positions seemed irresolvable.

But in the years following the conference, a remarkable transfor-
mation has occurred: O'odham and Cucupa community members are
now regular participants in dialogues regarding the three biosphere
reserves along the Arizona-Sonora border. The transition began when
environmentalists helped the O'odham fight mines that threatened
to deplete the aquifer feeding some of their sacred springs. Then the
Sonoran O'odham and the Mexican government signed an agreement
to collaborate on the protection of natural and cultural resources in
the region, acknowledging the Sierra Pinacate as the aboriginal homeland of the O'odham. Most significantly, a Hia C-ed O'odham leader,
Lorraine Eiler, became the first chairperson of the International Sonoran Desert Alliance, a grassroots group with board members from five
distinct cultures that regularly meets with state and federal land management agencies in the region. The Cucupa soon became involved
as well, holding meetings with Mexican officials to rectify the earlier
problems regarding fishing rights. The International Sonoran Desert
Alliance became the forum in which natives and newcomers, government agencies and community groups, scientists and traditional-
ists, could all come together at the same table.

"Having grown up in the middle of the desert and looking back
on all the things that have been done to this place, I did feel we needed
to get involved," Eiler recently told an assembly in Hermosillo,
Sonora. She and other O'odham leaders candidly spoke to government
and nongovernmental organization representatives gathered to join

formally the protected areas and communities of the region into a single Sonoran Desert Ecosystem Council. This council will be the formal body responsible for coordinating activities among agencies on both sides of the border and for ensuring that community programs move in synchrony with government initiatives.

At this same meeting, an O'odham leader from the Mexican side of the border, Felix Antone, spoke of continuing pressures on the flora of the borderlands, providing a rationale for cross-cultural collaboration as a crucial strategy for protection of vulnerable resources. Describing how ancient mesquite and ironwood forests are still being clandestinely cut down within O'odham homelands—even those within nominally protected areas—Antone was passionate: "Trees are being cut down in my homeland to make charcoal and to fire adobe bricks. With them, other plants are disappearing. All plants on Mother Earth are our medicines. It seems like the laws are not enough to protect these trees. So this [idea of cooperative vigilance] has always been in my heart: to give it to [the collective effort] of all of you to protect this earth, this water, these plants, this air.... It gives me great pleasure to be here."

The terrain of which Antone spoke covers more than 4.6 million acres, making it the largest network of contiguous protected areas anywhere within the world's deserts. The water to which he refers includes the Colorado River delta and the Upper Sea of Cortez, where the *vaquita*, an endangered cetacean, survives as an endemic population of fewer than 500 individuals. At least 750 plant species have been collected from the area. Richard Felger, Anita Alvarez, and I have annotated the region's flora with hundreds of O'odham, Cucupa, Spanish, and English common names, so that the botanical knowledge of all resident cultures can be honored.

Although the level of plant diversity in this coastal desert region is not especially high, it is complemented by the cultural diversity of the region; this means that plant uses and management traditions are quite varied. "I feel that [the Alliance] is a very unique group because it is taking into account the cultural traditions as well as the biological richness of this region," acknowledged Dr. Maria Elena Barajas, who served as Sonora's state director of ecology. She has been one of many participants who have tirelessly devoted themselves to the process of cross-cultural communications. She added that "no one among us [the ecosystem council founders] is interested in taking land out of the hands of local peoples. But as far as stronger coordination goes, President Zedillo has already said in a speech in Nogales that this is something he is willing to do."

Mexican Environment Secretary Carabias and U.S. Interior Secretary Babbitt expressed their support for this remarkable coalition for biological and cultural conservation during the spring of 1997. On May 5, 1997 the secretaries formally signed a letter of intent for joint work in natural protected areas along the border. As the highest ranking environmental officials for their countries, they agreed that the protected areas of the western Sonoran Desert borderlands should serve as a prime model for transboundary cooperation in natural and cultural resource management. At the state-to-state level, Barajas worked with the Sonoran Institute in Tucson to get the binational network of protected areas endorsed by the governors of Arizona and Sonora. Another dozen nongovernmental organizations devoted to conservation and cultural preservation have endorsed these initiatives.

Most rewarding has been the sense from rural communities—especially the indigenous ones—that their involvement is no longer token. Community workshops have been held, new local products from renewable plant resources are being developed as sources of income for residents, and an annual conference brings together teachers, folklorists, craftspeople, storytellers, and musicians from both sides of the border.

Carlos Yruretagoyena, chairperson of the International Sonoran Desert Alliance, feigns a grimace, then smiles when he recalls how many meetings he's attended over the past couple of years to ensure that community members are heard. He is optimistic that they are truly helping to shape the destiny of the region's protected areas.

"We're an open forum," he reminds us, open not only to people in power within government agencies and large conservation organizations but to local farmers, ranchers, basket makers, fisherfolk, and herbalists as well. "We're a totally open forum," he repeats, "and that has been the magical thing."

Is that "magic" something that can be found in other regions, too? Perhaps other places in North America do not have as many indigenous communities in or near protected areas, but there are other kinds of cultural heterogeneity to consider. Whether it be remnant Algonquian Indians, Mennonites, and Amish around the Great Lakes, or Florida Crackers, Seminoles, and Haitian and Cuban refugees in the Everglades, each region's peculiar mix of ethnic communities contributes to the multicultural heritage of the land. Even where one European immigrant culture has dominated communities for several centuries, its farmers, commercial fishermen, ranchers, and loggers all have valuable insights regarding the land and often maintain rich oral histories.

The International Sonoran Desert Alliance has brought together peoples from various walks of life and diverse ethnic backgrounds who *care* about the fate of the land and value its cultural history. Perhaps this collaboration would not have worked if it had been controlled by government bureaucrats, by one or two local businesspeople out for a quick buck, or by off-road vehicle clubs that view the desert merely as "open space." Participants have had to talk out problems, and the few individuals inclined toward platitudes and posturing have usually ended up letting down these defenses.

True parity among participants from different cultures or nations is difficult to achieve when each has vastly different economic resources, traditional knowledge bases, and technical information at its disposal. While the International Sonoran Desert Alliance cannot instantly solve all local land issues, it has already demonstrated that for some issues, the complementarity of perspectives from participating cultural communities forges solutions that have a chance to endure.

By its very presence, the alliance challenges the widely held but erroneous notion that only scientifically educated Anglos care about and can contribute to conservation. A recent national opinion poll by Beldon and Russonello reveals that while only 23 percent of Anglos felt that the extinction of plants and animals is a serious problem, 30 percent of African Americans, and 41 percent of Hispanic Americans were very concerned about these extinctions. Ironically, the same survey showed that concern over extinctions *decreased* with higher income and education levels; we cannot rely on the good judgment of the "elite" if plants, animals, and cultural history are to be conserved.

Biodiversity conservation plans that ignore other cultures' ties to the land are doomed to failure and will inevitably fall short of their ultimate goals of protecting natural and cultural resources. Unless conservationists acknowledge that diverse "cultures of habitat" have played key roles in safeguarding biodiversity, they will undermine the very processes that have served to sustain native flora and fauna.

A half century ago, when Aldo Leopold roughed out his "land ethic," he hardly considered the future involvement of diverse cultures in protecting fish and fowl, wetlands and mountains. When I worked as an intern at the first Earth Day's headquarters more than twenty-five years ago, the links between biological and cultural diversity were little understood, let alone heralded as a source of hope. But by 1993, when hundreds of Native American, African-American, and Hispanic-American environmentalists had joined together with other people of all colors to set an international agenda for environmental justice, it was clear that a major shift had taken place in the conservation movement. It is a shift toward inclusiveness and away from the heroic actions of a select few. It asks us to listen to the many voices associated with the land—to learn from them, to celebrate them...and to safeguard their legacy.

Showdown in the Rain Forest

Will our suffering in Guatemala never end? In a world in which globalization moves forward...little do the things matter to which our people attribute real value: life itself, our trees, our customs, the smell of the forest, the medicinal plants it contains.

THE BIO-ITZA COMMITTEE, San Jose, Peten

The pueblo of Flores—the village of Flowers—covers every square inch of an island in the midst of Lake Peten Itza, a shallow, limestone basin surrounded by one of the largest remaining lowland rain forests in the Americas. Flores is the capital of Guatemala's *departamento* of the Peten, which occupies one-third of the country but contains less than 2 percent of its population. Much of it is impenetrable, and nearly half of the Peten remains covered by rainforest canopy rich in allspice and *chicozapotes* left by the Maya.

The Flores settlement is occasionally threatened by rising water levels, which can submerge the gravel causeway connecting it to the mainland. You can reach some of its clapboard lodges and cafés only by "walking the plank"—passing over flooded streets on narrow floating bridges—or by hitching a ride in a dugout canoe. Something about Flores reminds me of a teetering Noah's ark: filled to the brim, barely keeping its deck above the water.

The Peten itself is also under threat—Guatemala may lose one-third of its remaining primary forest by the year 2000. During my time in the Peten, the pressures on protected areas became brutally evident. I walked into the rain forest the very day some of its strongest Guatemalan advocates walked out, after having been beaten and threatened with death by loggers and soldiers in cahoots with one another. What occurred during the following days convinced me that there has been a war going on in the rain forest that is no more subtle than the wars in Bosnia, Zaire, or the Persian Gulf. Wherever powerful economic interests can convince local entrepreneurs that conservation plans are working to exclude them from using nearby local resources, a battle is bound to erupt.

How conservationists communicate their goals to local communities has become *the* critical issue that makes or breaks the best-conceived plans to shelter the forest's diversity from the storm of assaults on it. Fortunately, the Peten is also home to some of the most intensive efforts to create rather than destroy jobs for the campesinos—in this case, the Ladino and Mayan forest dwellers. While no one can claim that such innovative conservation efforts have already secured a safe future for the Mayan rain forest, they were already far enough along to attract my family and me to the *Selva Maya* in December of 1992.

We arrived in Flores in time to see a new sort of flowering in the Peten—a fresh splash of color along streets where washed-out pastels dominate the stuccoed walls and tarnished grays or rusty browns tint the laminated tin roofs. All of a sudden, Flores had become a scene enriched with the cherry reds of miniature poinsettias sculpted from the gum of the chicle tree; with the flowery orange and purple designs of Mayan embroidery; and with the hot pinks, fiery yellows, and magentas of T-shirts painted with the images of orchids, humming-birds, leopards, howler monkeys, macaws, and toucans. Overnight, Flores had been set ablaze with wild tropical scenes created by dozens of artists—not only local Peteñeros but visitors from Mexico's Yucatán peninsula and Costa Rica's Monte Verde as well.

These tropical arts and crafts had blossomed at the *Primera Feria Eco-Artesanal de la Selva Maya* (the First Festival of Eco-crafts of the Mayan Forest). It included a week's worth of workshops, demonstrations, and exhibitions of tropical products handmade by master crafts-people. The event was cosponsored by Conservation International's

Pro-Peten and the Mexican Association for Art and Popular Culture (AMACUP), a nonprofit group that uses traditional crafts as a basis for sustainable development. Even in its first year, the fair attracted visitors from more than a dozen countries. A stronger indicator of its success was the extent to which it engaged local Peteñeros, many of whom stayed to apprentice with visiting artisans, designers, and marketers for several days. The spirit of the event was contagious. Out of its momentum, new income has been generated for hundreds of people now working with chicle, *xate* palm, allspice, and potpourris. People were not simply *talking* about making a variety of sustainably harvested rain-forest products; they were *doing* it.

"It's always gratifying to be part of an innovative movement," said AMACUP's Marta Turok, looking back at the eco-crafts fair. "But the challenges are not to be underestimated. The presence of lowland Mayans, highland Mayans, and non-Indians, together with national and international organizations as well as private corporations, reflects the complex tapestry of interests. Our purpose in bringing together the artisans of Guatemala, Mexico, and Belize is to show that it is possible to fashion something larger from small, self-sustaining economic alternatives sensitive to the environment and to cultures."

On the final day of the event, however, the festive feeling was suddenly quashed. The day after the fair had begun, some local conservationists had been reported missing. Soon rumors of their fate began to ripple through the gathering. Despite the optimism that had been engendered by the festival, there was no escaping the reality that the Peten was under siege—100 to 150 square miles of the Peten continues to be deforested each year. The festival's participants did not doubt that many products and artistic creations could be derived from the jungle, but they began to wonder aloud whether these offerings would be enough to save the *Selva Maya* from certain destruction or its protectors from the wrath of its spoilers. As if the usual signs of cartloads of firewood and smoke-filled skies were not enough, we began to hear the sordid details of a drama that chilled us all.

The drama was set before the backdrop of a sudden change in Guatemalan government policy on woodcutting in the protected areas of the Peten. In particular, the change addressed the Mayan Biosphere Reserve, a belt of biological diversity stretching from the Sierra Lacandóna on the Mexican border clear to the Belize. Just a couple of weeks prior to the festival in Flores, some well-connected "wise use" lumber entrepreneurs had convinced the Guatemalan congress to pass Decree 72-92. It commanded the National Council on Protected Areas (CONAP) to open up its reserves for the removal of all previously felled or abandoned wood. In effect, it tacitly sanctioned renewed logging in the nominally protected areas of the Peten, where there were unfortunately too few wardens to monitor whether trees were being newly felled or simply removed. The decree went into effect over the objections of CONAP officials and the Peten's governor, Carlos Asturias Paz. It also undermined the pledge of increased forest conservation made by Guatemalan president Serrano at the Earth Summit in Rio just five months earlier.

Governor Asturias quietly encouraged some young activists to reveal how logging interests had begun to deforest the Mayan Biosphere Reserve the minute their political cronies had pushed through the decree. With the governor's blessing, state police were assigned to accompany conservation officials from CONAP and from the National Institute of Anthropology and History, as well as a journalist from Guatemala City, as they investigated the Peten logging. Leaving in two unmarked vehicles on Wednesday morning, December 2, they headed eastward from Flores toward the town of El Naranjo, where the Mayan Biosphere Reserve adjoins the Sierra Lacandóna National Park. There they were to confirm reports of degradation not only of the forest but of Mayan ruins as well.

They did not return that night or the next day. By late on that second day their colleagues in Flores realized that something was terribly wrong. It was an inquietude that many Guatemalans have felt over the past thirty-five years, during which 140,000 of their countrymen have been left dead or missing.

The group was spearheaded by activist reporter Omar Cano Herrera, who worked for *Siglo Veintiuno*, "The Twenty-first Century," a fine national newspaper. He had agreed to photograph any contraband logging encountered en route, on behalf of his traveling companions, who included Spencer Dempsey Ortiz-Kreis, the twenty-four-year-old coordinator of the Mayan Biosphere Reserve, and his CONAP supervisor, Alberto Luna Franco, also twenty-four.

They went upriver from El Naranjo by boat to Paso Caballos and back, documenting dozens of boats hauling illegally cut logs. When they got back on land just after dark, they decided that the group would temporarily split up. One truckload of them decided to drive down the road to buy some food while the other was to stay in camp, working on written documentation. That's when the trouble erupted.

Reporter Cano turned to CONAP's Alberto Luna and gasped, "Luna, kill the engine—I think I see an angry mob there in front of us by the river." As soldiers and wildcat loggers descended on the truck containing Ortiz and the others, Cano and Luna fled on foot in the dark and dove into the waters of the Rio San Pedro, hiding out until the next morning. The loggers and several armed soldiers tied up the other five, dragging them and beating them. The state police guards—the Guardia de Hacienda officers accompanying the conservationists—were threatened with grenades, then disarmed. All five captives were dragged by rope to the local military base where they were left out overnight in a thunderstorm, then beaten again in the morning.

Unsure of what had happened to their companions, Luna and Cano cautiously descended to the road when they heard the sound of a truck Thursday morning. It was not the CONAP truck that they expected but the mob of soldiers and loggers patrolling for them again. The sixty vigilantes tied Cano and Luna up, whipped them, and threatened them with hanging. "We were at the point of being massacred," Ortiz later recalled.

It seemed that someone knew of Cano's mission to report the illegal logging to his Guatemala City paper. He was forced to eat mud, then beaten with his cameras before the film was removed and thrown into the jungle. Only one of the cameras has been recovered, but other newspapers have since taken and printed aerial photos of the illegal felling of trees within the protected area. The bludgeoning continued for hours, leaving Luna with a concussion and Cano with a broken nose as well as dozens of lacerations.

Several hours later, the local posse left the conservationists beaten, bloodied, and half-naked at the mercy of the soldiers, who had not moved a finger to assist the government officials who were held captive. One of the contraband loggers signaled to the armed guards and said, "Soldiers, please tell your commander that we've fulfilled our order."

After being taken into custody by the military, the prisoners were further interrogated and brutalized at the army base. It was clear that neither the military nor the vigilantes from El Naranjo cared whether Luna and Ortiz were vested with the authority to protect and manage the Mayan Biosphere Reserve, where the incident occurred. As one gun-toting soldier sneered at Spencer Dempsey Ortiz—who was officially *in charge* of the land where they stood—"as far as we're concerned, you're all subversives."

Because the loggers had set up a roadblock on roads going into the area, word got back to the governor. He called the vice president of Guatemala, demanding that a helicopter be sent to get the captives out of El Naranjo. The captives were finally allowed by the military to be flown out to a hospital. The soldiers releasing them claimed that the confrontation would not have happened if Ortiz and Luna had been in uniform and if the group had not told locals that "they were only tourists, looking at Mayan ruins." Within hours, military spokesmen were denying that the incident had happened at all.

Vigilantes and their military accomplices no doubt assumed that the young men had been taught a lesson and would be too timid to report their harassment for fear of future retaliation. But as Alberto Luna later related, Cano had made up his mind to name names and cite details to an extent unprecedented in Central American environmental reporting. "If we leave here alive," Cano confided to Luna, "I'm going to make a full exposé by Sunday."

By Saturday, December 5, as the festival was winding up, *Siglo Veintiuno* printed five full pages of firsthand accounts from the captives as well as graphic photos of their lacerations. Paperboys in Flores sold an unprecedented number of copies of this issue, in part because there were still so many conservationists milling around the Peten. But the issue also riveted the attention of Flores residents, many of whom worried that Cano and his companions had too boldly blown the whistle on the military, which operated one of its largest bases right on the shores of Lake Peten Itza.

But fear of retaliation did not keep others from moving quickly to rally support for Cano and the conservation officials. Governor

Asturias made a brief appearance at the crafts festival and promised to bring to trial not only the *contrabandistas* but any collaborators in government service as well. The few fax machines in Flores sent notice of the conflict to advocates of human rights, freedom of speech, and wildlife protection around the world.

By Monday, December 7, nearly every newspaper in Guatemala City had begun to run a series of front-page stories and scathing editorials protesting the treatment of the press and the conservationists. One week before, many of the same journalists who wrote these stories had been expelled from the national palace when they pushed the president's secretary of public relations on the issue of freedom of the press. Now, they were not alone in the fight. Expressions of solidarity poured in from the International Committee for the Protection of Journalists, the Foreign Press Club, and the Affiliated Labor Unions of Guatemala, as well as Guatemala's archbishop of the Catholic Church and the national government's human rights advocate. Conservation organizations everywhere voiced their outrage that managers had been tortured by the military while trying to carry out their duties. The Committee for the Defense of the Natural and Cultural Patrimony of the Peten, Greenpeace, the Defenders of Nature Foundation, and the Center for Studies of Mayan Culture were among the dozen organizations that condemned the aggression against Luna, Ortiz, Cano, and the others in their group, calling for full disclosure of any subsequent investigations made by government officials.

The storm of support for the released captives made the military backpedal on its excuse for what happened—that guerrillas in stolen uniforms must have been involved, for its men would never take part in such an incident. Within days, military spokesmen were declaring that "they, more than anyone else, were interested in the truth" and were authorizing their own investigation. By the end of one week, seven alleged captors and torturers had been arrested and one commanding officer in the Peten was implicated in directing the torture. The newspapers reported that organization after organization was urging the congress to repeal Decree 72-92 and to rid the *Selva Maya* of quasi-legal deforestation for good.

Later in December, in a surprise move—one clearly responding to national and international indignation—Guatemala's Supreme Court ruled that Decree 72-92 was unconstitutional and that CONAP's protected areas and parks should be considered inviolate. A battle had been won on paper, but CONAP's dedicated conservation officials did not receive any more authority or operational resources for carrying out this renewed mandate for protection.

Conservationists expect to have continuing difficulties in protecting the forests of the Peten. Even if the clandestine logging operation at El Naranjo were to be shut down, others could crop up and work for months, unnoticed by the government officials who are currently incapable of doing much about them. Many locals still wonder whether protectionists will always support Peteñeros in their efforts to make a decent living off local resources. Because many Peten residents feel they have few economic options, any conservation scheme that is accused of endangering existing sources of revenue is sure to be met with anxiety, frustration, and at times, violence of the kind suffered by Cano, Ortiz, and Luna. Logging interests—backed by the military—still have the power to undermine CONAP's efforts, claiming that conservationists are the real threats to the Peten's economic future.

Under such pressures, it is not surprising that Conservation International's Pro-Peten Project has emphasized to local people its goal to create rather than to destroy sources of income. Of course, the Peteñeros are not the first rain-forest people to hear this; "sustainability" and "ecodevelopment" have become merely more buzzwords for the likes of the World Bank and the U.S. Agency for International Development. As social critic Scott Atran has acerbically noted, "there are more nongovernmental organizations per square foot of the Peten than anywhere else in the world. Altogether more than fifty groups are spending tens of millions of dollars there, but they have hardly changed the rate of deforestation."

One participant confided that the true success of the eco-crafts fair was that it forced so many of the nongovernmental organizations (NGOs) to row in the same direction; it was the first time that so many had agreed to come together under the same roof. Robert Heinzman, past director of Pro-Peten for Conservation International, conceded that the project's goals and methods would seem strange to most mainstream conservationists in the United States. "As a non-profit, nongovernmental organization, we are gearing up to generate dozens of small for-profit businesses in the area. It's about time someone offered these people tangible alternatives to seeing the entire forest cut down."

When I spoke with him, Heinzman was near exhaustion from having worked a string of twelve-hour days for several weeks in a row. He was attempting to weave together three different strategies that would all have to be successful if Pro-Peten's plans for the region were to work. First, he was collaborating with Guatemalan foresters on how to manage better the high-quality products that can be selectively harvested from the *Selva Maya* without destroying the forest canopy and its diverse wildlife. Critics doubt the efficacy of this strategy; Scott Atran, for one, remains concerned that selective cutting and transport of high-value hardwoods is still causing deforestation. At the same time, Conservation International's staff has been trying to identify the kinds of ecological tourism that will bring in foreigners to appreciate and support the preservation of the Peten's archaeological and natural wonders while allowing local Guatemalans to garner a great share of the resulting revenues. For Mayans, who did not have a general word for "nature" or "environment" until recently, these borrowed terms have come to mean "what tourists come to see."

The third strategy—and the one highlighted at the *Feria Eco-artesanal*—hinges on the success of the other two. If the forest canopy can remain intact and if tourism brings new potential consumers into the region, what nontimber products can be marketed to them without depleting the resources of protected areas? In the past few years, Pro-Peten has decided to speed up the development of a variety of rain-forest products that can be manufactured through local cottage industries.

Take chicle, for example. Few Americans know that all of our chewing gum once came from this tropical tree, for the products in our gum machines and groceries now use a dozen ingredients other than those derived from the time-tried chicle. Nevertheless, another chicle tradition has persisted in a few patches of Mesoamerica—the shaping of miniature figurines, much like those made famous by Mexico City marzipan confectioners and plaster-of-paris sculptors. Tiny figures of flowers, fruits, and fauna, of sinners and saints, can be shaped of pure chicle and tinted to approximate natural colors. Although chicle is abundant in the Peten, it had not recently been used there in crafts until AMACUP brought in a chicle artist from Puerto Vallarta, Mexico, to teach the shaping process to locals. By the end of the week, they were selling batches of chicle as decorations to restaurants and were turning down dozens of offers for each of their prototypes. Over the long haul, however, chicle sculptures appear to be more tedious to prepare than other potential products.

But chicle was not the only rain-forest resource that caught the eye of local artisans. They scanned other demonstrations of product development using local vines, herbs, hardwoods, resins, *jicara* gourds, gums, palm leaves, and oils. It was clear from their enthusiasm that they could see how nontimber forest products could become as lucrative as lumber.

These experiments with tropical hardwoods, gums, gourds, and flowers are part of an "Artisans and Ecology" project created by Marta Turok of AMACUP and Chip Morris, another authority on handmade Indian crafts. Chip, a MacArthur Fellow and, like Marta, a Mayan textile expert, has written straightforwardly of their philosophy for "ecological" development: "Artisans use a minimum of resources and apply a maximum of skill and labor to produce works that reflect both people and place." If former loggers can become artisans who can sell their wares to tourists, Chip believes that "ecotourism will become a source of income rather than a burdensome intrusion on them. If the people who live in and around protected areas find that they can benefit from rather than be restricted by biological reserves...then they will become guardians and promoters of the reserves for their own good."

Well aware that the proof is in the pudding, Chip invited us to go with him to the village of El Remate, on the edge of the Cerro Cahui Biotopo, a wildlife sanctuary recently set aside to protect the ocellated turkey.

El Remate is a half hour's drive from Flores, not far past the military base where Cano was moved after his rescue. On a stretch of shoreline along Lake Peten Itza, eighty local artisans now make their living selling wood, stone, and bone sculptures to tourists en route to the Mayan ruins at Tikal, a World Heritage site. Several years ago, before Chip Morris, Carlos Augusta Soto, and friends held a carving workshop in the area, such a cottage industry was only a dream; it has since employed more than 300 carvers scattered through five municipalities, not just those in El Remate.

I talked with Carlos as he worked a block of wood held in a vise beneath a palm-thatched hut on the lakeshore. Not long ago, he had still been trying to farm the poor, limey soils of this karstic landscape, but as he recently admitted, "the land itself wasn't adapted to cropping with maize and beans year after year." He picked up carving from family members who participated in the training workshop and has helped spread the skills to others in his community. At first, he used just one or two woods. Now, he told me, he enjoys the different qualities of a variety of local hardwoods. He rattled off a litany of tropical trees as familiar to him as if they were cousins: *"chiricote, ramón colorado, morz, pije, rosul, jobillo, chicozapote, puntero...."* He carves toucans, lizards, bivalves, and Mayan gods, as many as eight a week.

After talking with Carlos, Chip and I went up the hill to see an area where an indigenous Mayan-style limestone-based architecture has been revived. The buildings were as lovely as sculpture, yet functional as well. Chip mused over the difference between fine art and mass-produced crafts: "Each carver down there, at one point or another, desperately needs to be recognized as an artist and will spend an enormous amount of time perfecting a new design. It may not end up being what keeps his family fed, but he'll make time for it anyway, for himself and for recognition from other carvers.... They'll try a diversity of materials and carving styles too, from bone and jade, to wood turning. Most guys I know get tired of doing just one thing over and over."

After my daughter and wife purchased a toucan and set of salad serving spoons from Carlos, we took a motorized launch across Lake Peten Itza to the Cerro Cahui sanctuary to look for the turkeys considered threatened in the Peten and the Yucatán Peninsula. The wildlife sanctuary stretches along a ridge above the lake in the shape of a gigantic alligator. Once we began to hike along the rustic trails of the *biotopo*, we realized that we were walking beneath the massive canopies of the very hardwood trees that Carlos uses for his carvings. *Chicozapote, jobillo,* and *ramón* rose above us like giants: at eye level were the buttresses of their trunks.

We rounded a corner to a point where we could see the lake. My partner, Caroline, pointed something out to my daughter that nearly made Laura's eyes pop out. There, in the lukewarm drizzle, two keel-billed toucans frolicked in the kapok canopy above us. The landscape may have been muted by the ground-level clouds and constant rain, but those toucans stood out. Their yellows, greens, reds, and velvety blacks were as brilliant as the colors we'd seen in the arts and crafts back in Flores.

When we returned to our hotel on the island, the weather had shifted from a soft drizzle to an outright downpour. We encountered some soggy festival-goers in the hotel's open-air dining room, and they invited us to join them. We listened to their reactions to the festival as we all sat and watched the rain.

The enthusiasm that we had felt earlier at the festival had been dampened by the events of the past days—it was going to take a lot of hard work, not just optimism, to stem the tide of destruction lapping up on the *Selva Maya*'s shores. The mood had turned somber, and participants were quietly voicing doubts and cautions of three sorts.

A few felt that the mix of crafts presented at the festival was just fine but that those goods would require rapid development and marketing if they were to stave off deforestation. The promulgators of this worldview felt that researchers for nonprofit conservation groups did not have enough of the "business smarts" required to make this strategy work. Private entrepreneurs should be brought in to extend sales beyond tourists in Tikal and to reach worldwide export markets.

This strategy was precisely what worried the other two camps. As a Mexican woman, Graciela Guevara, put it, "I am afraid it's the beginning of a little Taiwan—cheap crafts products from Latin America that fail to satisfy any deep cultural needs. What is culturally functional about a T-shirt painted with the image of a *tigre*, to be sold to a tourist, compared to the meaning of the traditional *huipil* weavings in Mayan culture? What good is an ashtray sold as a curio in a national park or a basket that cannot be used to hold anything? If a person goes to buy a product *only* because it is 'going to save the rain forest' and not because it has intrinsic function, he will never buy a second one."

Marta Turok and Chip Morris would agree that the Mayan *huipiles* have more meaning than tourist T-shirts, for Marta and Chip had spent two decades assisting in the development of a "House of Weaving" among Tzontzil and Tzetzal Mayans in Chiapas, an enterprise that now supports nearly 800 indigenous women. However, while some mask carving and traditional embroidery persist, no comparable weaving legacy remains among the 1,300 native Itza speakers in the Peten. As Conservation International's Mercedes Esteves explained to me, "there is no surviving legacy of traditional arts and crafts in the Peten as there is in the highlands of Guatemala; that is exactly why we're attempting to promote new forms as part of ecodevelopment."

By "traditional," Mercedes meant that the remaining 1,300 Itza Maya in the area do not have anything as flamboyant in crafts production as the highland Mayan groups do. They are, however, fully involved in "ecodevelopment" in their own fourteen-square-mile Itza Biosphere Reserve, although that project too has been threatened recently by local corruption and clear-cutting.

Because of the difficulties such projects have faced, many classically trained conservationists are still not convinced that selling "mementos of tropical nature" have helped to save any rain forest. They are not enthusiastic about the concept of marketing *any* products from the Mayan Biosphere Reserve, for they remain skeptical that its resources can be protected and used simultaneously. Once you create wide new demand for tropical products, they argue, you run the risk that so-called sustainable forestry projects may inadvertently deplete their most susceptible resources.

Chip Morris, who has given this risk considerable thought, is not as sanguine about it as other crafts promoters might be: "Artisan production could definitely destroy the rain forest," he says. "That's why I've insisted that we study sustainable yields and harvesting pressures before we start cranking out a million baskets. But you know, there are no sustainable *products*, there are only sustainable *processes*. Harvesters of a palm called *xate*, for example, go through cycles of intensively cutting the palm's leaves, then letting them rest while new fronds emerge. What we are trying to do is smooth out the bumps in this cycle so that people have a steadier income, but without letting such harvesting lead to extinction."

These conservationists remain open to the possibility that crafts might endanger plants just as easily as other forest uses do. Since the basic reproductive capacity and resilience to harvesting pressures have been studied for very few tropical plants, these critics would err on the side of assuming that any harvesting is unsustainable until proved otherwise. They are encouraged when they see organizations such as Cultural Survival, Conservation International, and Aid to Artisans more formally monitor projects so that no tropical rain-forest product can be marketed in the United States as "sustainable" or "ecological" until some independent documentation is provided that will support this claim. In fact, Pro-Peten is now several years into evaluating whether the harvest of any of the new forest products being proposed for the region could irrevocably deplete these resources, and it has already removed *mora* and *puntero* woods and dyes from their potpourris, fearing that pressures on these tree resources are already too high. Pro-Peten has also moved its suppliers toward gathering the bulk of its potpourri ingredients from flower, seed, and leaf litter on the forest floor.

Such critiques and adjustments are not new to anyone who has been involved for long in attempting to conserve cultural and biological diversity. Yet innovators such as Marta Turok, Chip Morris, Jason Clay of Rights to Resources, and Mark Plotkin of the Ethnobiology and Conservation Team have been willing to try sidestepping the pitfalls and traps associated with the nontimber approach. Why? Because they believe that more-conventional conservation measures have failed to curb environmental deterioration in the Third World. Even when nature reserves have been set up, clandestine woodcutting and hunting have often continued to deplete the biological diversity in the reserves because local people have been given few other economic options.

"I have offered those same criticisms many times myself," Chip Morris admits, "but I would like to think our projects have positively responded to them." Pro-Peten claims it will restrict its development to products derived from only more common, resilient plants. Its staff, when questioned about the presumed contradiction between conservation and utilization, adamantly returns to their ultimate goal: "If we don't give these people real economic alternatives to large-scale logging, then we are bound to lose the forests here."

Conventional timber harvesting—whether clear-cutting or high-grading—is simply not suitable for the Peten. In 1970, 90 percent of the Peten was still forested; as a result of commercial logging, less than half of the original forest cover remains. Ultimately, local culture will have just as hard a time surviving in a cut-over rain forest as do endangered plants and animals. But until other means of making a living come to the *Selva Maya*, the poorest of the Peteñeros are caught between a rock and a chain saw. If no one else will employ them, the contraband timber merchants will. Just as with the logging interests bankrolling the "Wise Use" movement in the United States, these timber merchants benefit from having their workers believe that conservationists are out to take their jobs away from them.

Conservationists must demonstrate that ecologically based management and innovative development of a diversity of nontimber resources will create more jobs in the forest than they will destroy. Otherwise, their adversaries who grubstake the chain-saw *contrabandistas* in Guatemala are bound to get their way. No matter how rosy the benefits of forest protection on paper, there will still be many a poor wildcat woodcutter dead set on blocking the conservationist's pathway—unless, of course, the flowering that has begun in Flores soon bears fruit.

Restorying the Sonorous Landscape

*That desert—its firmness, resilience, and fierceness, its whispered
chants and tempestuous dance...shaped us as geography always
shapes its inhabitants. The desert persists in me, both
inspiring and compelling me to sing about her and her
people, their roots and blooms and thorns.*
PATRICIA MORA, "The Border: A Glare of Truth"

Out of nowhere, it seemed, came the deafening noise of airplane
engines. It overwhelmed everything: the rasp of cactus wrens, the
drone of cicadas, and the tales being shared among Seri Indians who
sat together in the sand. The blaring motors forced them to stop their
stories and songs. They glanced up from the beach on the Sea of Cortez
and saw an airplane landing. On that June day in 1993, the "sound
of summer heat"—a humming the Seri or Comcaac had heard in their
homeland for centuries—was supplanted by another, more contemporary noise.

While the engines still roared, the governor of the state of Sonora
descended from the aircraft and shook hands with Seri leaders. Then
he announced what everybody already knew: the Solidarity Program
had at last brought electricity to this, the only tribe of traditional
hunters and gatherers remaining within the entire Mexican republic.

With a cut of a ribbon and a flick of a switch, lights, televisions,
and *liquadora* blenders all spun into action. The governor quickly

waved good-bye, boarded the plane, and left. The noise of the motors swallowed up the crashing of the waves, the crying of the animals, the very sound of desert summer itself.

That's when the bartering began. Two handwoven baskets for one satellite dish, one wooden dolphin figurine for a floor fan. Within weeks, the Seri were swapping limberbush baskets, ironwood carvings, miniature balsa rafts, beads, dolls, and bull-roarers for dozens of electric radios, swamp coolers, televisions, videocassette recorders, and more satellite dishes.

Alfonso Torres laughed as he told us how he traded two *sapeem* baskets made by women in his family for the first *parabolica* dish to be set up in the village. "It was easy," he grinned. "Some Americans we had known for a while brought us the dish and even set it up. The women had been working on these baskets for a couple months, knowing that we might get the *parabolica* in exchange for them. Since then, these women spend their time making baskets while watching the *fotonovela* soap operas. The boys love the *box* and the *futbol*. You know, we get programs from Mexico City, Hermosillo, Los Angeles, everywhere."

Then he added, "We have just learned that the people from Los Angeles can take their clothes off on TV after midnight. What do you call it, *la pornografía?*... Unfortunately, we have so many people who must sleep in the room where we keep the television that it is hard to have it on after midnight. I have seen the Americans without clothes only once, when the rest of the family was away seeing relatives in Desemboque."

Weeks later, when I mounted a plastic Frisbee atop our temporary ocotillo-frame hut in the middle of the village, the Seri kids doubled over, squealing with laughter, "See, the gringos have a *parabolica* for their home too!"

One night, after the shows from Los Angeles had been turned off in the surrounding households, I listened for the sounds that have filled the air for centuries at the place the Seri call *Cailaapa*. The sound of kindling being snapped and stoked into a campfire. Dogs barking at shadows passing over them. The *hai heno moca*, a wind that blows from northern lands to the sea. The surf crashing on the cobble beach north of us, louder than that on the sandy beach closer to our hut.

I heard Chapo, the fifty-eight-year-old shaman, shaking a rattle and singing a whale song in a low voice. I heard Miguel Barnet tell of a dream he had in 1941, a dream of a singing cave, one in which a hot wind howls through a door; it was a dream that he drew with the very first crayons he had ever held. I heard a child crying out in his sleep, followed by the comforting pats and coos of his mother as he fell back asleep.

I heard all of this, interrupted by one last radio playing "I Can't Get No Satisfaction," a heavy-metal cover of the Rolling Stones in Spanish translation.

It was late at night when Ernesto Molina wandered into our camp. He was eager to hear what we had learned about the war in Chiapas, a war between the Mexican army and the Zapatista guerrillas. He recalled the times in Seri history when his forefathers skirmished with the same Mexican army, in the 1850s, 1890s, in 1904, and finally, in the 1920s.

His grandfather had told him details of these battles, details that haunt him to this day. He recounted the time when Seri men had left camp to scare up some food, leaving the women behind in a cave on Isla Tiburón. While the men were gone, the army found where the women and children were hiding. The troops shot all of them down, then heaped up the bodies in four huge piles. When the Seri men returned, the soldiers were gone. There amid the piles, one child was alive, crying, pawing at his mother's breast. Ernesto gulped. "When the child saw his father, he asked why his mother wouldn't wake up to talk to him and to feed him."

Ernesto carries hundreds of such stories in his head. "I don't have a television, don't need one," he said. Pointing to all the antennae on the houses around him, he shrugged; their noise seemed inescapable. I asked if he still hears enough of the older, more familiar sounds at night. He shook his head sadly, saying that he not only fears the changes that television is bringing but he fears waking up to another sound as well: "I worry that one day I will wake up to the sound of machine guns here, as they are hearing today in Chiapas."

The next morning, a Gila woodpecker woke me up. It was drilling at the metal fan turret atop one of the Seris' concrete-block houses. The wind flapped the tarps covering our ocotillo hut. I crawled out of my sleeping bag, snapped up the buttons of my pants and shirt, pulled on my boots, and wandered out beyond the village edge. I turned inland, and after a few minutes, I found myself deep in an ancient cactus forest of towering saguaro, cardón, and organ pipe. It was there that I stopped to listen to the sounds that have been here as long as this place has been desert.

It was early enough that Bendire's thrashers were still moving from shrub to shrub, repeating a *chuck, chuck, chuck* before letting loose with a melodic warble. They stayed low, as did the gnatcatchers, who buzzed along, flicking their tails up and down. Coveys of Gambel's quail scurried through the washes, mulling and grunting until one of them got scared. Then they all broke into flight, wingbeats booming. The cactus wrens would stop rasping whenever they heard this racket. And the mockingbirds would stop imitating the cactus wrens, dropping down from their perches and staying silent until all signs of danger had passed. Gila woodpeckers glided away from me, annoyed, settling on a giant *cardón* a hundred yards away. More gnatcatchers followed them. The uptilted white butts of antelope jackrabbits crashed through the burrobushes and elephant trees as they ran for deeper, darker cover.

Atop every large tree, phainopeplas *whurped* and fluttered. Flycatchers sallied out, *prrt*ing, then sallied back again. Towhees flitted through, peeking from behind every branch. Such notes announce the Sonoran Desert to my ears, the same way the giant saguaro cactus defines it for my eyes. Sonorous melodies. Like the volatile smell of creosote bush, they tell me that I have come home, home to a chorus of trilling birds, rattlers, cicadas, and coyotes. The desert choir.

Farther, I heard ravens and grackles cackle and whistle as they scavenged along the beach. They lured me to the water's edge, where I heard the whoosh of ospreys and long-billed curlews taking flight and the splash of a flock of Mexican wood ducks rising up out of the surf.

I was not *anywhere* in the desert. I was in a unique spot, where an extra-salty sea washes up onto the driest of sands. Maps call this stretch of water between Sonora and Isla Tiburón the Canal de Infiernillo; the Seri call it *Xepe Coosot*, "the little ocean." (I suspect the Canal de Infiernillo would have made a much better name for an all-night TV station broadcasting out of Los Angeles.)

A couple of years ago, I had to go halfway around the world, to another desert, to learn that natural and manmade music can form a tenuous harmony. I spent a blustery night with two Aussie mates in the Red Center of their continent. Marlene and Dennis Chinner drove us out in their four-wheel drive from Alice Springs onto the gravelly bed of the Hugh River. We heaped up branches of river red gums to make a huge bonfire, then sat in our swags, drinking and listening to the sound of the desert riparian forest reverberating in the night. It was a deep bass drone, one you felt in your chest, as if your body cavity had become an amplifier for some insect chant. There were thousands of cicadas there, but there was also something larger, more ancient, that thrummed in the dark. It was the desert forest, resonating, like the heartbeat of the entire, fire-charged arid continent.

Two nights later, during a native-foods feast of "bush tuckers" baked in the coals of a second gumwood campfire, another friend brought out his didgeridoo, a six-foot-long wind instrument, made from the trunks of trees hollowed out by termites in Arnhem Land. I've heard the aboriginal word *didjeridu* imitates the circular pattern of tongue movements that musicians use when playing the instrument as they shape the wind they blow into the trunk. It comes out the other end of the trunk sounding like the forest itself: deep, haunting syllables reverberating through the shadows, calling up creatures who had been hiding in the hollows, urging them to hoot and holler in the lonesome night.

After tens of thousands of years of Aborigines falling asleep to the sonic landscapes of desert eucalyptus forests, it was no surprise that their spirit had found its way into their music. That didgeridoo played a tune similar to one I had heard on the Hugh River, a tune of red gills and ghost gums and galahs, of nightjars and dry winds.

I was back in my own desert, wandering in the hills above a small village when the sun began to slip behind the mountains. It had rained hard recently, and the *charco* reservoir had filled to the brim, enticing egrets and kingfishers and plovers to stay in the heart of the desert longer than usual.

I walked with a friend down from a lava ridge above the *charco*. Just before sunset, a double rainbow arched over the entire scene. But that was not what riveted our attention. As darkness began to gain on us, something was moving around our feet. Was the ground itself vibrating, like grain shaking in an automatic sifter?

Then we heard them, tens of thousands of them—recently metamorphosed toads, bleating and bumping into one another. Dozens per square yard, they covered the banks of the reservoir, the lava ridge, and the trail back into the village. As darkness thickened, we also heard the rising chorus of their parents—Couch's spadefoot toads sounding like an endless herd of sheep coming in for roundup.

Below the ridge, dozens of headlights were streaming toward a ceremonial grounds. A line of ashes had been drawn around a huge arena, with a *ramada* or bower erected, facing east, at its western edge. A fire was built, a recently hunted javelina was hung in a gunnysack from a forked tree trunk, and a wild bunch of musicians and dancers assembled. Five men knelt in a line behind the fire, placed notched wooden sticks on the ground, and began to rub raspers across them, singing at the same time. The rasping had a timbre identical to the croaking of the toads, and the deep, gruff voices of the singers added to the effect. I could not understand the words, but I heard the gratitude in those voices: gratitude that the rains had arrived, that the crops had come up, that the birds had returned, and that the javelina had fattened up in time to become the sacramental meal for the community assembled to sing the songs. The abundance of the summer had been assured once again. The songs lasted all night. Lightning flashed all around. Now I knew that human, amphibian, and insect music accompanied each other not only in the deserts of Australia but in my American desert home as well.

Every year, the first time I hear vermilion flycatchers in the leafed-out foliage of cottonwoods and willows, I know that spring has come again to the Sonoran Desert. I hear a *tut-tut, tiddly-zing*, then watch a gorgeous crimson bird sally out from a catkin-laden branch to catch its insect prey. It hovers a moment like a butterfly, swallows, then sashays back again to the safety of the canopy.

Such sights and sounds cannot be found everywhere across the desert floor—they occur in the ribbonlike riparian corridors of cottonwoods, willows, and sycamores that grow along stretches where water trickles to the surface of the meandering floodplains. If the win-

ter has been cold enough to burn off other trees' leaves or if it has been
dry enough to leave the ocotillos barren and gray, spring restores life
to them through the chorus of orioles, warblers, tanagers, hummingbirds, and flycatchers.

In eastern Sonora, the first flush of foliage on cottonwoods and willows has an added significance. For a farmer in the villages of Cucurpe,
Mazocahui, and Moctezuma, it means that the new cuttings for his
hedgerows have taken root. He plants the cuttings on the exposed
edges of his *milpa*, edges recently cut by El Niño downpours. The tor-
rential floods of late autumn can churn up his cornfields and shift the
courses of meandering rivers. If he has no erosion control in place,
such floods can leave a farmer a mess so awful that he will have to deal
with it for years to come.

A few years before, however, this farmer had planted another hedge
along the edge of his field, a few feet in from the gravelly riverbank.
He had pruned the five-foot-long branches of cottonwoods nearby,
trimmed their branchlets off with quick chops from his machete, and
stuck them in the gravelly ground to root. Between these instant
saplings, he wove a layer of smaller branches to make a brush fence.
The next time a flood came, this *cerco tejido*—or woven fence—acted
like a sieve, breaking the force of any waters that surged this high,
letting the river-carried sediment filter out into his field.

"The trees and woven branches accept the floodwater and make it
tame," the farmer told Thomas Sheridan and me when we visited him
in his fields. He called the gentled flows *agua manza*, and because his
trees had tamed the flood, he ended up gaining rather than losing soil
from his fields. The trees of his living fence, all fertilized and irrigated, grew tall enough to lure vermilion flycatchers the next spring.

I have walked with elderly Sonorans out among the curving lines
of cottonwoods edging their fields, where each hedge recalls a storm,
a flood, an erosive event, a healing of scars, and a planting of more
protective trees. One farmer I know can rattle off the years of great
floods that have come within his lifetime, as well as those that came
during his father's time tending the land: 1887, 1890, 1905, 1914,
1915, 1926, 1940, 1961, 1977, and 1983. Farmers in other villages
nearby sing much the same litany.

They can point to trees they helped plant after each inundation.

They can read the growth on the floodplain as a living record of land-mark floods and the patterns of recovery that followed. Those trees are like the notched calendar sticks of the indigenous chroniclers of the desert's history, who use each notch to serve as a mnemonic prompt to a memorable episode in their community: a bumper crop, a searing drought, a roiling, rampaging tragedy.

Learning to read aloud the stories told by those rows of trees is what makes Sonoran farmboys literate. Learning to plant and tend trees that bring warbling birds is another cultural skill. It says that each can be a participant in the running of the desert river, can dance with its meanders, and sing with its birds. A gallery forest in the heart of the desert is no silent partner—it quakes and creaks to a larger music, a symphony so complex it has even incorporated some minor tunes of humans.

Ecologist Daniel Botkin has written that this naturally improvised symphony "is by its very essence discordant, created from the simul-taneous movements of many tones...flowing along many scales.... [It is] a symphony at some times harsh and at some times pleasing."

I, for one, cannot easily imagine how I could ever sit back and just listen to that symphony indefinitely; sooner or later, the unconscious tapping of my feet would make me a player, a part of the orchestra. So in adding my voice to those around me, I have chosen to be a choir-boy in the desert chorus, and not to pretend that I am only an onlooker.

By making that choice, I have joined the ranks of those who dance to the tune called *ecological restoration*. That band works and plays at reintroducing endangered plants and animals in habitats where they have disappeared. It seeks to restore the vibrancy of those habitats. It is as much an art as a science, for it allows us to improvise, to listen to the land, to intuit where the harmonics of a natural community are going, as well as where they have been. We sing over the wounds left on this earth and attempt to heal them. We recycle the oldest songs and stories, passing them on to the next generation.

We are learning of the need to restore not only the physical aspects of the habitats but also the cultural commitment to protect, to heal, to let the wildness of living communities continue to evolve. Like the Seri hunter-gatherer or the Sonoran farmer, we must be encouraged to listen, live, and work like natives, and to pass our work along.

To restore any place, we must also begin to re-story it, to make it the lesson of our legends, festivals, and seasonal rites. Story is the way we encode deep-seated values within our culture. Ritual is the way we enact them. We must ritually plant the cottonwood and willow poles in winter in order to share the sounds of the vermilion flycatcher during the rites of spring. By replenishing the land with our stories, we let the wild voices around us guide the restoration work we do. The stories will outlast us. When such voices are firmly rooted, the floods of modern technological change—of border-blasting radios and all-night pornography shows—won't ever have a chance to dislodge them from this earth.

Notes

Prologue: Cultures of Habitat

The epigraph comes from Michael Ondaatje's *The English Patient* (New York: Knopf, 1992).

In addition to the 1994–1995 maps in *The Atlantic Monthly*, see the article by A. P. Dobson, J. P. Rodriguez, W. M. Roberts, and D. S. Wilcove, "Geographic Distribution of Endangered Species in the United States," *Science* 275 (24 Jan. 1997): 550–53.

The discussion of characteristics of indigenous peoples persisting in their homeland draws on the work of Ned Spicer and his students. See Edward H. Spicer, "Enduring Peoples: A Human Type," in *The Yaqui: A Cultural History* (Tucson: University of Arizona Press, 1980), and a volume edited by George Pierre Castile and Gilbert Kushner, *Persistent Peoples: Cultural Enclaves in Perspective* (Tucson: University of Arizona Press, 1981).

Raymond F. Dasmann's *Wildlife Biology* (New York: Wiley, 1964) may have been the first book in English to introduce the concept of "ecosystem peoples," here rephrased as "cultures of habitat."

Wes Jackson's *Becoming Native to This Place* (Washington, D.C.: Counterpoint, 1996) is a must-read. Regarding genetic and metabolic adaptations of human populations to their respective regional environments, see Randolph M. Nesse and George C. Williams, *Why We Get Sick: The New Science of Darwinian Medicine* (New York: Vintage, 1994).

With regard to the issue of cultural stewardship of wildlands, William C. Cronon's controversial essay "The Trouble with Wilderness" is discussed several times in this book. Its most accessible printing is in *Uncommon Ground: Toward Reinventing Nature*, edited by Cronon (New York: Norton, 1995).

Finding Ourselves in the Far Outside

This essay was first presented as an opening lecture to Art of the Wild conference participants in the summer writing program at the University of California, Davis. It has been included in two anthologies, one edited by Kurt Brown, *Writing It Down for James: Writers on Life and Craft* (Boston: Beacon Press, 1995), and the other edited by David Burks, *The Place of the Wild* (Washington, D.C.: Island Press, 1995).

The epigraph comes from Mary Midgley's *Beast and Man* (Ithaca: Cornell University Press, 1978).

Scientists have noticed that most other primates exhibit a lack of attention to other animals. See Dorothy L. Cheney and Robert M. Seyfarth's *How Monkeys See the World* (Princeton: Princeton University Press, 1992).

John Daniel's *The Trail Home* (New York: Pantheon Books, 1991) and the quotations from Robinson Jeffers's sole speech at Harvard University, excerpted in the *American Poetry Review* in 1975, are both remarkable antidotes to anthropocentrism.

Hugh Brody, a fine novelist and ethnographer, made his comments about the periphery and the center at the Island Institute's summer workshop in Sitka, Alaska, in 1991. See his short story collection, *Means of Escape* (Vancouver, Canada: Douglas & McIntyre, 1991).

Poet-linguist Ofelia Zepeda speaks of the O'odham pull to the Sea of Cortez in *Ocean Power* (Tucson: University of Arizona Press, 1995).

Lynn Margulis and Dorian Sagan remind us of how many other organisms inhabit our body in their chapter, "God, Gaia, and Biophilia," pp. 345–64, in *The Biophilia Hypothesis*, edited by Stephen L. Kellert and Edward O. Wilson (Washington, D.C.: Island Press, 1993).

Edward O. Wilson has offered the view that scientists crave the same kind of societal recognition of their explorations today as did hunter-storytellers around the campfire thousands of years ago; see his dialogue with Barry Lopez on "Ecology and the Human Imagination," edited by Edward Leuders for *Writing Natural History* (Salt Lake City: University of Utah Press, 1989).

E. O. Wilson's humbling comments on how little we know about the vast majority of species remaining on this planet come from *The Diversity of Life* (Cambridge: Harvard/Belknap Press, 1992).

Joyce Carol Oates's absurd essay "Against Nature" is included in *The Nature Reader*, a collection edited by Daniel Halpern and Dan Frank (Hopewell, N.J.: Ecco, 1996).

I do not know where the aphorisms from Paul Ehrlich and William Carlos Williams were first printed; I just wish I had thought of them first.

Pledging Allegiance to All Sorts of Diversity

Earlier versions of this essay have appeared in the *Arid Lands Newsletter* (1995) and *Conservation Biology* (1995).

The epigraph is from David Abrams, "Returning to Our Animal Senses," *Wild Earth* 7 (Spring 1997): 7–11.

Among the various polls and surveys cited are those by the firms Beldon & Russonello, Inc., and R/S/M, collected in *Human Values and Nature's Future: American Attitudes on Biological Diversity* (Washington, D.C.: Beldon & Russonello Research and Communications, 1996). The 1994 Harris Poll on science literacy cited was commissioned by the American Museum of Natural History and discussed in a press release by that museum.

Kent H. Redford's definitions of biodiversity are highlighted in "Science and the Nature Conservancy," *Nature Conservancy Magazine* (Jan.–Feb. 1994): 15. D. M. S. J. Bowman's opinion editorial, "So What Is Biodiversity?," helped launch *The Biodiversity Letters* 1 (1995): 1. The analysis of the world's extant and moribund languages has been accomplished by David Harmon of the George Wright Society in a remarkable paper, "The Status of the World's Languages as Reported in Ethnologue," presented at the Symposium on Language Loss and Public Policy, Albuquerque, New Mexico, 1995.

There is much to ruminate over in Willett Kempton and James Boster's book, *Environmental Values in American Culture* (New York: Academic Press, 1995).

Vic Cherikoff coauthored a fine overview of bush tuckers with Jennifer Isaacs, *The Bush Food Handbook* (Blamain, New South Wales: Ti Tree Press, 1991). Among Marta Turok's many publications is *Como Acercarse a la Artesania* (Mexico City: Editorial Plaza y Janes, 1988). David Cavagnaro's books include his collaboration with Frans Lanting, *Feathers* (Portland: Graphic Arts Center Publishing, 1982). Adolfo Burgos's and Amalia Astorga's work is featured in an article by Janice Rosenberg and Gary Paul Nabhan, "Where Ancient Stories Guide Children Home," *Natural History* 106 (Oct. 1997), in press.

Missing the Boat

The epigraph is from a "gray report" on southwestern Ecuador written by Alwyn Gentry and other Rapid Assessment Project Team members in 1992, quoted in Ronald Sullivan, "Theodore Parker, Alwyn Gentry, Biologists, Die in Airplane Crash," *New York Times*, 17 Aug. 1993, C-1, C-15–16.

Charles Darwin's *Journal of Researches into the Natural History and Geology of Countries Visited during the Voyage of the Beagle* was first printed in London in 1839.

For their honesty in addressing the difficulties of indigenous participation in protected areas, I am indebted to all contributors in the collection edited by Kent H. Redford and Jane A. Mansour, *Traditional Peoples and Biodiversity Conservation in Large Tropical Landscapes* (Arlington: America Verde Publications/The Nature Conservancy, 1996). This includes Redford himself, Jorge Trujillo Leon, Natalia Wray, Jason Clay, and Jorge Alvarado.

Much of the biographical data on Al Gentry included here comes from a special edition, "Alwyn Howard Gentry, 1945–1993: A Tribute," *Annals of the Missouri Botanical Garden* 83 (1996): 433–60; and from Susan Cohen's "The Collectors," *Washington Post Magazine*, 9 Jan. 1994, 8–28.

The magnum opus of Alwyn H. Gentry came out the year he died: *A Field Guide to the Families and Genera of Woody Plants of Northwest South America* (Washington, D.C.: Conservation International, 1993).

Lynn Cherry, *The Great Kapok Tree* (New York: Harcourt, Brace/Gulliver Green Book, 1990).

Sierra Madre Upshot

The epigraph is from Derek Denniston, *High Priorities: Conserving Mountain Ecosystems and Cultures* (Washington, D.C.: Worldwatch Institute, 1995).

I have drawn heavily on Aldo Leopold's "Song of the Gavilan," in *A Sand County Almanac* (New York: Oxford 1949). I have drawn heavily on this essay, as well as Leopold's explorations of *guacamayas*, which first appeared as "The Thick-Billed Parrot in Chihuahua," *Condor* 39 (Jan.–Feb. 1937): 9–10. See also the collection of Aldo Leopold's journal excerpts edited by his son Luna B. Leopold, *Round River* (New York: Oxford University Press, 1953).

I am particularly indebted to the intellectual assessments of Leopold's work, especially of his time in the Rio Gavilan, accomplished by J. Baird Callicott and Curt Meine. See in particular Curt Meine, *Aldo Leopold: His Life and Work* (Madison: University of Wisconsin Press, 1988), and J. Baird Callicott, editor, *Companion to "A Sand County Almanac"* (Madison: University of Wisconsin Press, 1987).

The first explorations of the Sierra Madre by an ethnobiologist are recorded in Carl Lumholtz, *Unknown Mexico* (New York: Scribner's, 1902).

For an overview of biodiversity in the Sierra Madre, see the chapter by Richard Felger, Gary Paul Nabhan, and Robert A. Bye Jr. entitled "Apachian/Madrean Region of Southwestern North America, Mexico, and U.S.A.," pp. 172–80 in the third volume edited by S. D. Davis, and others, *Centres of Plant Diversity: A Guide and Strategy for Their Conservation* (Cambridge, U.K.: World Wide Fund for Nature, 1997).

To understand the plant richness at a single site, see Richard Spellenburg, Toutcha Lebgue, and Rafael Corral-Diaz, "A Specimen-Based, Annotated Checklist of the Vascular Plants of Parque Nacional 'Cascada de Basaseachi' and Adjacent Areas, Chihuahua, Mexico," *Listados Floristicos de Mexico* 13 (Mexico City: UNAM Instituto de Biologia, 1996).

With regard to crop diversity, see Barney T. Burns, Mahina Drees, Gary Paul Nabhan, and Suzanne Nelson, "Native Crop Diversity, Agrohabitat Heterogeneity, and Cultural Survival in the Tropical Deciduous Forest of the Sierra Madre," in the volume being edited by Robert Robichaux, *The Tropical Deciduous Forest of Northern Mexico* (Tucson: University of Arizona Press, in press).

Charles DiPeso's eight-volume masterpiece is entitled *Casas Grandes: A Fallen Trade Center of the Gran Chichimeca* (Dragoon, Az.: Amerind Foundation Publications 9, 1974). Paul Minnis has followed up on DiPeso's work with nearly a decade of his own efforts around Casas Grandes; see Paul Minnis, "The Casas Grandes Polity in the International Four Corners," pp. 269–306, in S. Upham and others, editors, *The Sociopolitical Structure of Prehistoric Southwestern Societies* (Boulder: Westview Press, 1989).

Derek Denniston, *High Priorities: Conserving Mountain Ecosystems and Cultures*, a global overview of montane ecology.

Children in Touch, Creatures in Story

This essay originally appeared in my book coauthored with Stephen Trimble, *The Geography of Childhood* (Boston: Beacon Press, 1993).

The epigraph is from Robert Michael Pyle's *The Thunder Tree* (New York: Houghton-Mifflin, 1993).

Leslie Marmon Silko's fine essay "Landscape, History, and the Pueblo Imagination" is included in several books—most recently, Daniel Halpern and Dan Frank's *The Nature Reader* (Hopewell, N.J.: Ecco, 1997).

I have had the opportunity to assist two fine graduate students with field studies of intergenerational retention of traditional ecological knowledge among the indigenous peoples of the binational Southwest. See Gary Paul Nabhan and Sara St. Antoine, "The Loss of Floral and Faunal Story: The Extinction of Experience," in Stephen R. Kellert and E. O. Wilson, editors, *The Biophilia Hypothesis* (Washington, D.C.: Island Press, 1993); and Janice Rosenberg and Gary Paul Nabhan, "Where Ancient Stories Guide Children Home," *Natural History* 106 (Oct. 1997), in press.

Jerry Mander interviewed Lennie, Smith and other Native Americans about media impacts on Native American children's perceptions for his book *In the Absence of the Sacred* (San Francisco: Sierra Club Books, 1991).

The quote from Italo Calvino comes from his novel *Mr. Palomar* (New York: Harcourt, Brace, 1983).

Richard and Nora Marks Dauenhauer's essay, "Native Language Survival," appears in *The Left Bank* 2 (1992): 115–22. Johnny Moses is quoted in Brenda Peterson's essay, "Animals as Brothers and Sisters," in Thomas J. Lyon's anthology, *On Nature's Terms* (College Station: Texas A&M Press, 1992).

Making Places Close to Home Where the Soul Can Fly

A section of this essay first appeared as the "Prospect" guest editorial, "Why Playgrounds Need to Go Wild," in *Landscape Architecture* (Oct. 1994): 176.

The epigraph is from Piers Vitebsky's "Dialogues with the Dead," *Natural History* 106 (March 1997): 36–38.

The dilemma of industrialized versus naturalized children's play spaces is discussed by Mary Ann Kirkby in "Nature as Refuge," *Children's Environments Quarterly* 6 (1989): 7–12; and by Brian Sutton-Smith, "School Playground as Festival," *Children's Environments Quarterly* 7 (1990): 3–7.

Carl Jung's concept of archetypes reached its widest audience ever during Bill Moyers's television interviews with Joseph Campbell, entitled *The Power of Myth* (New York: PBS, 1986). See also Joseph Campbell's *Myths to Live By* (New York: Viking, 1973).

Balaji Mundkur traced snake lore among various cultures in *The Cult of the Serpent* (New York: State University of New York Press, 1983). E. O. Wilson built on this base in "Biophilia and the Conservation Ethic," pp. 31–41, in S. R. Kellert and E. O Wilson, editors, *The Biophilia Hypothesis* (Washington, D.C.: Island Press, 1993).

Roben Stikeman works for the Evergreen Foundation in Canada. Her comments included here are from her presentation at the 1995 Gardening for Youth Conference in California.

Craig Tufts, *Schoolyard Habitats Planning Guide* (Vienna, Va.: National Wildlife Federation, 1996), and Craig Tufts, *The National Wildlife Federation's Guide to Gardening for Wildlife* (Emmaus, Pa.: Rodale Press, 1995). Special thanks to retired teacher Nancy Foote for an extended telephone interview.

Growing Up Othered

The epigraph is from Naomi Shihab Nye's *Never in a Hurry* (Columbia: University of South Carolina Press, 1996).

For Arab-American history, see Gregory Orfalea's *Before the Flames: A Quest for the History of Arab Americans* (Austin: University of Texas Press, 1988); Joseph Geha's *Through and Through* (St. Paul: Graywolf, 1990); Naomi Shihab Nye's *Sitti's Secrets* (New York: Simon and Shuster, 1994); and Diana Abu-Jaber's *Arabian Jazz* (Harvest Book/Harcourt, Brace, 1993).

Behind the Zipper

This essay originally appeared as "The Rapture of Discovering (How Wrong We Can Be)," in *The Trumpeter: Journal of Ecosophy* 12 (Spring 1995): 59–61. This journal was edited by David Rothenberg; it later metamorphosed into *Terra Nova*. Apologies to Gretchen Goetzman and a Gila monster.

The epigraph is from Ray Troll (illustrator) and Brad Matsen's *Planet Ocean* (Berkeley: Ten Speed Press, 1994).

Finding the Wild Thread

This essay has appeared in several forms, first as my John Burroughs Medal acceptance speech excerpted in *Wake Robin* (Spring 1985); then in *Petroglyph* and the *Land Report*; another version diverged into the "Going Truant" chapter for my collaboration with Stephen Trimble, *The Geography of Childhood* (Boston: Beacon Press, 1994).

The epigraph is from James Boster, included in his article with J. C. Johnson, "Form and Function: A Comparison of Expert and Novice Judgments of Similarity Among Fish," *American Anthropologist* 89 (1989): 866–81.

Our evolutionary destiny that preadapts us to be naturalists is discussed in Paul Shepard's *The Tender Carnivore and the Sacred Game* (New York: Scribner's, 1978).

I grew up in an area of the Indiana Dunes well covered by literary naturalists; before entering college, I had become familiar with Edwin Way Teale's *Dune Boy* (New York: Dodd, Mead & company, 1943); and Donald Culross Peattie's *Flora of the Indiana Dunes* (Chicago: Field Museum of Natural History, 1930).

Hummingbirds and Human Aggression

This essay was first published in *The Georgia Review* 51 (Summer 1992): 213–32, and later excerpted in the collection by Carolyn Servid, *From the Island's Edge: A Sitka Reader* (St. Paul: Graywolf Press, 1995).

The epigraph is from Eduardo Galeano, *Memory of Fire: Genesis* (New York: Pantheon, 1985).

For a full description of the cultural history of Tinajas Altas, see Gary Paul Nabhan and Jacquie Kahn, *Oral Histories of Tinajas Altas* (Phoenix: Gerarthy and Miller, 1997).

Sir Arnold Wilson's classic *The Persian Gulf* is now out of print (London: George Allen and Unwin, 1928).

Two remarkable studies of hummingbird sociality are William A. Calder III's "Site-Fidelity, Longevity, and Population Dynamics of Broad-Tailed Hummingbirds: A Ten-Year Study," *Oecologia* 56 (1983): 359–64, and

David L. Lyon, James Crandall, and Mark McCone's "A Test of the Adaptiveness of Interspecific Territoriality in the Blue-Throated Hummingbird," *The Auk* (July 1977): 448–59.

Kermit, Teddy Roosevelt's son, wrote several field accounts for magazines while still in his twenties. They were collected into *Happy Hunting-Grounds* (New York: Scribner's, 1920). Raphael Pumpelly covered much of the same territory in his travelogue *Across America and Asia* (New York: Leypoldt and Holt, 1870). Pumpelly's memoir, *My Reminiscences* (New York: Henry Holt, 1918), contains some of the same adventures but in a form closer to his original field notes.

Tom Childs Jr.'s most memorable quotes have been compiled by historian Wilton Hoy in *Organ Pipe Historical Research* (Lukeville, Az.: Organ Pipe Cactus National Monument, 1970).

Papago or O'odham views toward warfare are discussed in Ruth Underhill's *Social Organization of the Papago Indians* (New York: Columbia University Press, 1986), and in Clifford B. Kroeber and Bernard L. Fontana's *Massacre on the Gila* (Tucson: University of Arizona Press, 1986).

Two preliminary reports on ecological damage resulting from the Persian Gulf war are John Cox, "Waging War Against the Earth," *Environmental Action* (March/April 1991), pp. 21–22; and André Carothers, "After the Storm: The Deluge," *Greenpeace* magazine (Oct.–Nov.–Dec. 1991): 17.

The roots of anger and aggression are discussed by Carol Tavris in *Anger: The Misunderstood Emotion* (New York: Simon and Schuster, 1982), and in E. O. Wilson's *On Human Nature* (Cambridge: Harvard University Press, 1978).

Special thanks to David Lyon, William Calder, Amadeo Rea, and Tony Burgess for discussing the biological and moral aspects of this topic with me.

Searching for Lost Places

The epigraph is from Keith H. Basso's Western States Book Award-winning collection *Wisdom Sits in Places* (Albuquerque: University of New Mexico Press, 1996).

My place-name work with Bill Broyles and Jacquie Kahn will soon be appearing in the *Journal of the Southwest*.

Cultural Parallax

An earlier version of this essay was published in a collective response to post-modern deconstruction by conservation biologists and the environmental literati, compiled by Michael E. Soulé and Gary Lease, *Reinventing Nature?* (Washington, D.C.: Island Press, 1995).

The epigraph comes from Robert Hass's "A Note on 'Iowa City, Early April,'" included in *Sun Under Wood* (Hopewell, N.J.: Ecco, 1996).

There is no finer ethnomusicology in the Southwest than the book by Larry Evers and Felipe Molina, *Yaqui Deer Songs: Maso Bwikam* (Tucson: Sun Tracks and University of Arizona Press, 1987). It received the Chicago Folklore Prize.

The wilderness debate framework is best summarized by Arturo Gomez-Pompa and Andrea Kaus, "Taming the Wilderness Myth," *BioScience* 42 (1992): 271–79, and by Kat Anderson and Gary Paul Nabhan, "Gardeners in Eden," *Wilderness* (Fall 1991): 27–31.

Marcus Colchester's view that the wilderness concept should be abolished came from the Workshop on Indigenous Peoples and Parks, sponsored by the Pew Scholars on Conservation and Environment, at their New Hampshire retreat, fall 1995. The Cronon quote is from his essay, "The Trouble with Wilderness," previously cited.

See Thomas C. Blackburn and Kat Anderson, *Before the Wilderness: Environmental Management by Native Californians* (Menlo Park, Calif.: Ballena Press, 1993).

Leslie Marmon Silko's "Landscape, History, and the Pueblo Imagination" is in the collection edited by Daniel Halpern and Dan Frank, *The Nature Reader* (Hopewell, N.J.: Ecco, 1997).

Kent H. Redford's controversial essay, "The Ecologically Noble Savage," was first published in *Orion* 9 (1985): 24–29.

Jared Diamond discounts indigenous people as conservation practitioners in *The Third Chimpanzee* (New York: HarperCollins, 1992). Unfortunately, his interpretation of Chaco Canyon's prehistoric use of timber is distorted, as is his view of indigenous systems of folk classification and conservation practice. To counter these imbalances, I have drawn heavily on the following sources:

Amadeo M. Rea, "Resource Utilization and Food Taboos of Sonoran Desert Peoples," *Journal of Ethnobiology* 2 (1981): 69–83.

William M. Denevan, "The Pristine Myth: The Landscape of the Americas in 1492," *Annals of the Association of American Geographers* 82 (1992): 369–85.

William Cronon, *Changes in the Land* (New York: Hill and Wang, 1983).

Daniel Botkin, *Discordant Harmonies* (Oxford: Oxford University Press, 1990).

Suzanne Fish, Paul R. Fish, Charles Miksicek, and John Madsen, "Prehistoric Agave Cultivation in Southern Arizona," *Desert Plants* 7 (1985): 107–12.

Jack Turner, *The Abstract Wild* (Tucson: University of Arizona Press, 1996).

Ofelia Zepeda, "Where the Wilderness Begins," *AISLE* (1997): 85–107.

Mary Midgley, *Beasts and Man* (Ithaca: Cornell University Press, 1978).

When the Spring of Animal Dreams Runs Dry

The epigraph is from Peter Steinhart's "Dreaming Elands," *Audubon* (1982), also reprinted in the collection edited by Robert Finch and John Elder, *The Norton Book of Nature Writing* (New York: Norton, 1990).

I have drawn on Bill Broyles's "Wildlife Water Developments in Southwestern Arizona," *Journal of the Arizona-Nevada Academy of Science* 30 (1997): 30–42.

For an overview of the cultural importance of the bighorn, see the book in which this chapter originally appeared: Gary Paul Nabhan, ed., *Counting Sheep: Twenty Ways of Seeing Desert Bighorn* (Tucson: University of Arizona Press, 1993). An extensive bibliography of cited literature from this chapter and related work is presented there. I am particularly indebted to Exequiel Escurra, Amadeo Rea, Gordon Fritz, Julian Hayden, and Christine Szuter for sharing published and unpublished work with me during the shaping of this essay.

Killer, Fire, and the Aboriginal Way

The epigraph is from Stephen J. Pyne's *Burning Bush: A Fire History of Australia* (New York: Henry Holt, 1991). A classic Australian article on Aborigines and fire is Rhys Jones's "Fire-Stick Farming," *Australian Natural History* 16 (1968–1970): 224–28.

Richard Kimber's essay, "Beginnings of Farming? Some Man-Plant-Animal Relationships in Central Australia," first appeared in *Mankind* 10, no.3 (1976): 142–50.

With regard to hare-wallabies, see B. L. Bolton and Peter K. Latz, "The Western Hare Wallaby, *Langorchestes hirsutus* (Gould) (Marcopodidae), in the Tanami Desert," *Australian Wildlife Research* 5 (1978): 285–93. Also, see the many technical reports written by Ken Johnson, Don Langford, and others, summarized by Langford in "The Battle to Save the Mala," *Nature Territory* 3 (April-July 1993): 29. The same issue includes "Interview: Peter Latz," 39–43. Thanks also to Johnson, Langford, and Kimber for interviews.

Diabetes, Diet, and Native American Foraging Traditions

Earlier versions of this essay appeared in the *Journal of Gastronomy* 5, no. 2 (Autumn 1989), reprinted in Robert Clark's edited collection, *Our Sustainable Table* (San Francisco: North Point Press, 1990). I have since realized that the O'odham metabolic preference is for wild foods rich in soluble fiber, tannins, and insulins, not for native crops per se.

The epigraph is from Nina L. Etkin's introduction to her edited volume, *Eating on the Wild Side* (Tucson: University of Arizona Press, 1994).

The Chono interview is in Ruth Underhill's *Autobiography of a Papago Woman* (Menasha, Wisc.: American Anthropological Association, 1936). The first interviews of Candelaria Orosco and Miguel Velasco ever published were included with other O'odham oral histories in Fillman Bell, Keith Anderson, and Yvonne G. Stewart, *The Quitobaquito Cemetery and Its History* (Tucson: Western Archaeological Center, National Park Service, 1980). I have since recorded Candelaria Orosco several more times; she is now well over one hundred years of age.

Recent analyses of the value of wild foods in controlling blood-sugar and insulin levels challenge the National Institute of Health's view that this disease should be treated genetically, instead of as a cultural, nutritional dilemma. See Janette C. Brand, B. Janelle Snow, Gary P. Nabhan, and A. Stewart Truswell, "Plasma Glucose and Insulin Response to Traditional Pima Indian Meals," *American Journal of Clinical Nutrition* (1989). See also A. C. Frati-Munari, B. E. Gordillo, P. Alamiro, and C. R. Ariza, "Hypoglycemic Effect of Opuntia Streptacantha Lemaire in NIDDM," *Diabetes Care* 11 (1988): 63–66, and Charles W. Weber, Radziah B. Arrifin, Gary P. Nabhan, Ahmed Idouraine, and Edwin A. Kohlhepp, "Composition

of Sonoran Desert Foods Used by Tohono O'odham and Pima Indians,"
Journal of Ecology of Food and Nutrition 26 (Summer 1996).

I assisted National Institutes of Health researchers in reconstructing a historic Piman diet for the study by B. A. Swinburn, V. L. Boyce, R. N.
Bergman, B. V. Howard, and C. Bogardus, "Deterioration in Carbohy-
drate Metabolism and Lipoprotein Changes Induced by a Modern, High
Fat Diet in Pima Indians and Caucasians," *Journal of Clinical Endocrinol-
ogy and Metabolism* 73 (1): 156–64.

Janette Brand and I have compiled but have not completed editing an anthology, *Parallel Evolution of Australian Aborigines and Native Americans? Diet,
Lifestyle, and Diabetes,* from an international workshop held at Kims
Toowon Bay, New South Wales, Australia, 10–13 May 1993. Copies are
available to read at the Native Seeds/SEARCH library, Tucson.

I end with a quote from Melvin R. Gilmore, "Uses of Plants by Indians of
the Missouri River Region," *Bureau of American Ethnology Annual Reports*
33 (1919): 43–154.

Let Us Now Praise Native Crops

The epigraph is from Nelson Foster's preface to his collection edited with
Linda Cordell, *Chiles to Chocolate* (Tucson: University of Arizona Press,
1994). This chapter appeared in that book and, later, in *Native Peoples*
magazine. It builds on the scholarship of environmental historian Alfred
W. Crosby Jr. In particular, see Crosby's *The Columbian Exchange: Biological and Cultural Consequences of 1492* (Westport, Conn.: Greenwood Press,
1942) and *Ecological Imperialism: the Biological Expansion of Europe
900–1900* (Cambridge: Cambridge University Press, 1986).

I have also drawn on the fine scholarship of many dedicated archaeobotanists.
For example, our history of New World beans would be wanting were it
not for Lawrence and Lucille N. Kaplan, "Phaseolus in Archaeology,"
edited by Paul Gepts in *Genetic Resources of Phaseolus Beans* (Dordrecht,
the Netherlands: Kluwer Academic Publishers, 1988). The works of Vor-
sila Bohrer, Charles Miksicek, Robert Bye Jr., Garrison Wilkes, Karen
Adams, Molly Streuver Toll, and Suzanne Fish are likewise essential to
understanding the history of native crops north of Mexico. To understand
these crops as they have persisted in Mexico, there is no finer introduction than that of Teresa Castello Yturbide, Michel Zabe, and Ignacio Peña
Lujan's *Presencia de la Comida Prehispanica* (Mexico City: Fomento Cul-
turál Banamex, 1987).

Regarding the impacts of the Green Revolution, see Carl O. Sauer quoted in Angus Wright's "Innocents Abroad: American Agricultural Research in Mexico," in Wes Jackson, Wendell Berry, and Bruce Coleman, editors, *Meeting the Expectations of the Land* (San Francisco: North Point Press, 1984).

Doug Unger's fine novel *Leaving the Land* also tells a true history of agriculture in America (New York: Harper and Row, 1974).

Harvest Time

This chapter originally appeared in my book, *Enduring Seeds* (San Francisco: North Point Press, 1989), which includes a full bibliography, and was later included in Russell Martin's collection, *New Riders of the Purple Sage* (New York: Pantheon, 1993).

The epigraph is from Thomas Jefferson's diaries; see also Wendell Berry's memoir of traveling with me to visit Hopi and O'odham farmers, "Three Ways of Farming in the Southwest," *The Gift of Good Land* (San Francisco: North Point Press, 1981).

Melvin R. Gilmore, "Uses of Plants by the Indians of the Missouri River Region," *Bureau of American Ethnology Annual Reports* 33 (1919): 43–154.

George F. Will and George H. Hyde, *Corn Among the Indians of the Upper Missouri* (St. Louis: William Harvey Miner, 1917).

George F. Will, "Indian Harvesting," *North Dakota and South Dakota Horticulture* 20, no. 9 (1947): 131.

Gilbert Livingstone Wilson, *Buffalo Bird Woman's Garden: Agriculture of the Hidatsa Indians* (St. Paul: Minnesota Historical Society, 1987).

Roy W. Meyer, *The Village Indians of the Upper Missouri: The Mandans, Hidatsas, and Arikaras* (Lincoln: University of Nebraska Press, 1977).

I also recommend the *Seed Savers Exhange Harvest Edition*, published from Decorah, Iowa, which has run numerous articles on the Native American seeds from the Upper Missouri, including my own perspective, "Regional Seedstocks and Oscar Will's Vegetables: Learning from Agricultural History," *Seed Savers Exchange Harvest Edition* 8 (1986): 178–80.

Tequila Hangovers and the Mescal Monoculture Blues

The epigraph is from Howard Scott Gentry, "The Man-Agave Symbiosis," *Saguaroland Bulletin* (Phoenix: Desert Botanical Garden, 1975).

The best technical overview of the production of tequila is Ana Guadalupe Valenzuela Zapata's *El Agave Tequilero: Su Cultivo e Industrialización* (Zapopan, Jalisco: Monsanto, 1994). See also her article "La Agroindustria del Agave Tequilero, *Agave Tequilana* Weber," *Boletín de la Sociedad Botanica de México* 57 (1995): 15–26.

The social history of tequila production is capably told by Rogelio Luna-Zamora, *La Historia de Tequila, de Sus Regiones, y Sus Hombres* (Mexico City: Consejo Nacional para la Cultura y las Artes, 1991).

Agave diversity is best elucidated in Howard Scott Gentry's *Agaves of Continental North America* (Tucson: University of Arizona Press, 1982) and in Miguel I. S. Franco's "Conservación *In Situ* y *Ex Situ* de las Agavaceas y Nolinaceas Méxicanas," *Boletín de la Sociedad Botanica de Mexico* 57 (1995): 27–36.

The recent tequila epidemic has been discussed in M. Daniel Rosen's "Monsanto in Mexico's Agave Fields," *Monsanto Magazine* 2 (1995): 20–23.

Hornworm's Home Ground

This article appeared in a special issue of *Wings* 20, no. 1 (Spring 1997): 16–21, dedicated to pollination. It draws on fieldwork by Felger, Ford, Fowler, Kester, Nabhan, Raguso, Rea, Romero, Rosenberg, Turner, and others.

The epigraph is from David Abram's *The Spell of the Sensuous* (New York: Pantheon Books, 1996).

See also Verne Grant and Karen Grant, "Behavior of Hawkmoths on Flowers of *Datura metaloides*," *Botanical Gazette* 144, no. 2 (1963): 280–84. The datura hunting song was originally translated in Frank Russell, *The Pima Indians* (Tucson: University of Arizona Press, 1984).

The Seri examples come from my own fieldwork, that of Janice Rosenberg, and the published ethnobotany by Richard S. Felger and Mark Beck Moser, *People of the Desert and Sea* (Tucson: University of Arizona Press, 1985). For a discussion of intergenerational loss in knowledge, see Rosenberg's thesis, *Documenting and Revitalizing Traditional Ecological Knowledge* (Tucson: University of Arizona Department of Latin American Studies, 1997).

The Parable of the Poppy and the Bee

The epigraph is a stanza from Kim Stafford's poem "Oregon Reunion of the Rare," in the John Risseaux chapbook *Spirit Land* (Tempe: Arizona State University School of Fine Arts, 1996).

This essay begins with my remembrances of a field trip with Stephen Buchmann that is also covered in "Steve Remembers" in our coauthored book, *The Forgotten Pollinators* (Washington, D.C.: Island Press, 1996). Terry Griswold first described the poppy-loving bee in his technical article, "New Species of Perdita (Pygoperdita) Timberlake of the *P. californica* Species Group (Hymenoptera: Andrenidae)," *Pan-Pacific Entomologist* 69 (1993):183–89.

The flower-loving fly of the Delhi Sand Dunes in California was featured in Verne G. Kopytoff's article, "A Fly Changes California Builder's Plans," *New York Times*, 1 June 1997, 30, and in Kenneth Kingsley's "Behavior of the Delhi Sands Flower-Loving Fly (Diptera: Mydidae), A Little-Known Endangered Species," *Annals of the American Entomological Society of America* 89 (1996): 883-91.

The Pollinator and the Predator

This essay first appeared in *Wild Earth* 6 (Fall 1996): 24–26, and was later excerpted in *The Whole Earth Review* (1997).

The epigraph is from Mark Deyrup's essay, "Learning the Language of Life," in *Wings* 20 (Spring 1997): 12–15.

The contrast between pollinators and predators builds on a classic ecological parable by Paul Colinvaux, *Why Big Fierce Animals Are Rare* (Princeton: Princeton University Press, 1978).

Gary Paul Nabhan and Stephen L. Buchmann, "Services Provided by Pollinators," in Gretchen C. Daily, ed., *Nature's Services* (Washington, D.C.: Island Press, 1997).

It amazes me that pollination did not even receive a full page of discussion among the 1,120 pages edited by V. H. Heywood for the *Global Biodiversity Assessment* (New York: United Nations Environmental Programme/Cambridge University Press, 1995).

Janet N. Abramovitz covers pollination economics nicely in her chapter, "Valuing Nature's Services," 95–114, in *State of the World 1997* (Washington, D.C.: Worldwatch Institute, 1997).

For a discussion of Native Americans' homages to predators, see Richard K. Nelson, *Make Prayers to the Raven* (Chicago: University of Chicago Press, 1983).

Sergio Medellin-Morales and M. M. Cruz-Bojorquez have described Mayan beekeeping and ceremonies in *Xunan-Kab: Una Experiencia Étnoecologica y de Transferencia de Technología Tradiccional en una Comunidad Maya de Yucatán* (Riverside: Proyecto Sostenibilidad Maya, University of California, 1992).

Why Chiles Are Hot

Another version of this essay appeared as "Findings: Why Chiles Are Hot," *Natural History* 106, no. 5 (1 June 1997): 24–27. It draws on data collected with Josh Tewksbury, Don Norman, Humberto Suzan, Jim Donovan, and John Tuxill. See also J. Tewksbury and G. P. Nabhan, "In Situ Conservation of Wild Chiles and Their Ecological Associates: Maintaining Interaction Diversity in Protected Areas," *Conservation Biology*, submitted. The epigraph is from an unknown source.

See also Marco Antonio Vásquez-Dávila's recent paper on proto-cooperation between Mayan farmers and birds in chile dispersal in "El Amash El Pistoqué: Un Ejemplo de la Ethnoecología de los Chontales de Tabasco, México," *Ethnoecologia* 3 (1997): 59–69.

For an overview of chile diversity, see the report written by numerous (anonymous) scientists associated with the International Board of Plant Genetic Resources, *The Genetic Resources of Capsicum* (Rome: IBPGR Secretariat/FAO, 1983).

Where Creatures and Cultures Know No Boundaries

This essay appeared in the summer 1997 special issue of *Orion* magazine, 16 (1997): 15–17.

The epigraph is from William Kittredge's essay, "Doing the Good Work Together: The Politics of Storytelling," from *Who Owns the West?* (San Francisco: Mercury House, 1996).

U.S. Interior Secretary Babbitt and Mexican Environment Secretary Carabias signed "the letter of intent for joint work on protected areas on the United States-Mexico border" in Mexico City on May 5, 1997.

Showdown in the Rain Forest

The epigraph comes from a statement by the Bio-Itza Commitee, San Jose, Peten, Guatemala, issued 7 Feb. 1997 over the Internet, translated by Luisa Maffi, University of California, Berkeley.

Many of the details in this essay were fact-checked against a series of articles that came out on 5, 6, 7, and 15 Dec. 1992, in the following Guatemalan newspapers: *Prensa Libre*, *Siglo Veintiuno*, and *La Hora*. My debt to the courageous Guatemalan journalists who covered this story on the front line can never be repaid.

With regard to sustainable harvesting, see Mark Plotkin and Lisa Famolare, editors, *Sustainable Harvest and Marketing of Rain-Forest Products* (Washington, D.C: Island Press, 1991).

The pact between rebels and the Guatemalan president signed 29 Dec. 1996, ended Latin America's longest and bloodiest civil war, according to Juanita Darling, "Signing of Accord Ends Thirty-Five-Year Civil War in Guatemala," *Los Angeles Times*, 30 Dec. 1996, A-1.

Epilogue: Restorying the Sonorous Land

This essay was inspired by the work of Steven Feld, *Sound and Sentiment* (Philadelphia: University of Pennsylvania Press, 1982) and by that of Feld's colleague Jack Loeffler, both experts in "aural ecology."

The epigraph is from Pat Mora's essay, "The Border: A Glare of Truth," *Nepantla* (Albuquerque: University of New Mexico Press, 1993).

Seri material culture and oral literature have been recorded in several special issues of *The Kiva*; see, for example, Juan Mata's basket song in Edward Moser's essay "Seri Basketry," *The Kiva* 38 (1973): 105–140.

Regarding the Sonoran desert fencerows, see Gary Paul Nabhan and Thomas Sheridan, "Living Fencerows of the Rio San Miguel, Sonora: Traditional Technology for Floodplain Management," *Human Ecology* 5 (1977): 97–111, and Thomas Sheridan's excellent political ecology of a Sonoran village, *Where the Dove Calls* (Tucson: University of Arizona Prss, 1988).

Daniel Botkin's natural symphony metaphor is in *Discordant Harmonies* (Oxford: Oxford University Press, 1990).